DISCOVERY, DEVELOPMENT AND DELIVERY OF NEW DRUGS

DISCOVERY, DEVELOPMENT AND DELIVERY OF NEW DRUGS

By
Karl H. Beyer, Jr., M.D., Ph.D., D.Sc.
Department of Pharmacology
The Milton S. Hershey Medical Center
Pennsylvania State University
Hershey, Pennsylvania

SP MEDICAL & SCIENTIFIC BOOKS
a division of Spectrum Publications, Inc.
New York • London

SPECTRUM PUBLICATIONS, INC.
175-20 Wexford Terrace, Jamaica, New York 11432

Library of Congress Cataloging in Publication Data

Beyer, Karl H.
  Discovery, development and delivery of new drugs
  (Monographs in pharmacology and physiology; v. 3)
  Includes index and bibliographies.

  1. Drugs. 2. Pharmaceutical research. 3. Drugs—Marketing.
I. Title. (DNLM: 1. Drugs. 2. Pharmacology. QV55 B573)
RM 300.B48   615'.1'072   77-28628
ISBN 0 89335-052-4

Dedication

To the rest of the team.
The men and women with whom
I worked for thirty years,
and to all those who have made this
the golden age of therapy.

Contents

Preface

The University of Wisconsin biomedical program during the exciting years of the 1920's and 1930's was a powerful incentive to lasting productiveness. The faculty was distinguished and the students were keen. Charles Bardeen (1871–1935), a great anatomist, was Dean of the Medical School and set the pace. It was Walter Meek (1878–1963), a leading physiologist, Arthur Loevenhart (1878–1929), distinguished pharmacologist, and William Middleton (1870–1975), the keen internist, who really stimulated the students.

Into this exciting atmosphere came Karl Beyer, with sharp intelligence and much calm good humor. He quickly made his way; a Master of Philosophy in 1937, his Ph.D. in Medical Physiology in 1940, and, finally, the M.D. degree in 1943. Karl Beyer had been one of several strong broadly trained students who came from Western Kentucky State College within his time to work at Wisconsin. Over the 7 years as a student at Wisconsin his research productivity was counted in some eighteen publications, no mean accomplishment considering the breadth of his research interests. On graduating from medical school, he became associated with the well-known drug company of Sharp and Dohme.

Doctor Beyer has pleasantly told about his "career or two" in the opening chapter of *Annual Review of Pharmacology and Toxicology* Vol. 17, (1977). In this, he makes abundantly clear how his careers were shaped by the inspiration of his early teachers, and later by his associates. And he says much about "serendipity." His "serendipity" was largely, I think in his own keen creativity: in his ability to see relationships between concepts not hitherto thought to be related. From this creativity came a succession of new and useful drugs, one of which, Diuril, attained worldwide fame and brought tremendous growth to the Company to which Doctor Beyer devoted 30 years of intense effort.

Doctor Beyer tells in detail the "Discovery of the thiazides: where biology and chemistry meet" (*Perspectives in Biology and Medicine,* 20: 410–420, 1977). Characteristically, he gives full credit to his chemical and pharmacological associates for the brilliant teamwork which he so well organized and directed. Modestly, he acknowledges the ideas coming to him from a wide variety of sources.

For the successful development of the thiazides for treating hypertension and for getting rid of excess sodium ions, with their attendant ills of water retention, the 1975 Albert Lasker Special Award was given to Karl Beyer and his associates, James Sprague, John Baer, and Frederick Novello. A scientific symposium commemorating the event was held at the New York Hospital–Cornell Medical Center. At this, Doctor Beyer said that the development of the thiazides "can be traced not merely to individuals, but to the effective partnership of chemistry and biology, brought together on a rational basis in ideal circumstances."

In writing of his work, Doctor Beyer "attests the reality of what we have fancied to call 'designed discovery' – a process whereby clinical need and understanding, biological concepts and analogies, and chemical ingenuity and perseverance, brought together in a stimulating environment, can yield a specific result that has been empirically conceived."

Now, in this book, Doctor Beyer goes on to elaborate his thesis in detail. He discusses creativity and spontaneous discovery, he talks about luck and serendipity, and he describes designed discovery, as well as other ways to discovery. Then he goes on to tell about tailoring new drugs, with the pharmacological testing necessary for assessment of possible effectiveness and essential safety. He deals with chemical and pharmaceutical development, and then proceeds to discuss clinical trial both from the standpoint of structure and function. His practicality is shown in his account of patents, trademarks, and copyrights. He is wisely cautious in discussing the regulation of new drug evaluation. He concludes with the practical details of drug delivery.

Thus, this book is a rationally designed effort to tell clearly and well those details that are important in the discovery, development, and delivery of new drugs. That it is eminently successful in its undertaking is apparent on a quick survey of its contents. It is just another example of how well Karl Beyer does things. Now that he is getting into a belated teaching career, he is certain to be successful again, and fortunate indeed are those students who will be inspired by him. They will go on to careers similar to his, and, thus, his great contribution will continue.

Chauncey Leake

Comment

When George E. Farrar gave me his comments on the prefinal draft of this book, he suggested the names of several persons who might be asked to write a preface. They represented a cross section of distinguished men: scientists and physicians whom I have known. Among them were men better known for the prizes their works have attracted, or by their world renowned leadership, or by their delightful writings about the birds and bees, so to speak. And there was Chauncey D. Leake's name too, an outstanding friend to both of us for many, many years. At first, I could not decide. A book like this costs a great deal of effort and one is inclined to have it promoted well, even by the choice of who should be asked to write the Preface. Ultimately, my choice had nothing to do with promotion or marketing the book, or who was the greatest or most distinguished. Scientists deal in comparatives; to me the superlative is rarely an appropriate adjective.

Chauncey Leake is a remarkable man. His past at the Medical School of the University of Wisconsin was legend when I arrived there as a student in 1936. It was many years later that our paths finally crossed. Since then our ways as pharmacologists have kept us close together, but our paths have crossed and crossed again as his inclination to adapt ideology to reality has been less than my need to do so. Which is to say that Dr. Leake may view many aspects of this book, especially the latter part dealing with development and delivery as he thinks they should be rather than as I think they are. Nevertheless, there is no question about his remarkable insight into and beyond what is written herein.

He is no mean philosopher. His accumulation of the history of medicine began well before his own substantial contributions to knowledge and to therapy. For many years his delight has been the teaching of ethics, logic, and esthetics to fledgling scientists and physicians. His mark on those who have studied long with him is unmistakable, and they count themselves the more privileged for that association.

If just a "touch" of the ethic be admitted to what may seem at times too-hard realities in the chapters to follow, I would quote a translation from "The Way of Life According to Lao Tsu" (seventh Century B.C.) which appears in Dr. Leake's "What are We Living For?" *Practical Philosophy I. The Ethics* pp. 44, 45. PJD Publications Ltd., Westbury, N.Y. (1973).

> People at their best, like water,
> Serve as they go along:
> Like water they seek their own level,
> The Common level of Life,
> Love living close to the earth,
> Living clear down in their hearts,
> Love kinship with their neighbors,
>
> The pick of words that tell the truth,
> The even tenor of a well-run state,
> The fair profit of able dealing,
> The right timing of useful deeds,
> And for blocking no one's way,
> No one blames them.

Dr. Leake died January 10, 1978, within a few hours of having collapsed while at leisure among friends. Except for his last few months of loneliness, most of his vigorous 81 years seem indeed to have been symbiotic with that of Elizabeth who he credited with so much of what he was — an unusual, a fine individual.   K. H. B.

DISCOVERY, DEVELOPMENT AND DELIVERY OF NEW DRUGS

Introduction

To know things well, one must know them in detail, and as this is infinite, our knowledge is necessarily superficial.

—LaRochefoucauld (1613–1680)

This is a book about research, about the discovery, development, and delivery of new drugs. It is intended to teach concept and practice, the many ways of going about discovery and bringing new therapeutic breakthroughs to patients. In the sense that examples are employed to illustrate ways of going about discovery, the making, and marketing of a drug, the text is historical but it is not a history of modern drug research. Such examples of discovery inevitably encompass the ways of scientists and something about their environment. On the other hand, it is not an exposition or a defense of the importance of the university, the independent or the governmental research institute, or the pharmaceutical research laboratories. Where each of these has offered a proper environment for research, scientists at work therein have been productive.

The book is written for a broad coverage of people who might be or should be interested in what it takes to make an interesting new discovery a useful new drug. It is not likely to appear in the waiting rooms of many doctors, but the text can be generally understood by the educated patient or person. To be sure, there are technical details, particularly in Chapters 6, 7, and 8, that are needed to round out each of the three case histories of discovery dealt with, but even in these chapters the general reader will find much of interest. I had in mind that the first seven chapters might be interesting to the young person who wants to be a doctor or a medical scientist. As training progresses, interest in the rest of the book seems inevitable. The author has employed the outline of the book and then the text in draft form in teaching a course for graduate students in Pharmacology at Hershey, but anyone who has finished the first year of medical school or who is well along in a school of pharmacy or of nursing should have no trouble with the subject matter. The medicinal chemist is likely to find much to learn or to applaud herein, depending on how far along he is in his career.

This book has been written from the viewpoint of the biologist, one reasonably familiar with the scope of the subject matter by way of interest and experience. Although there are many references to the works of others to illustrate specific points, the author has made use of research leading to new drugs in which he played some role, more or less. This has been done to keep the teaching material as factual and relevant to the point being made as possible. It is difficult to reconstruct the events of research precisely, even that in which one played an active role, and next to impossible to get the facts straight secondhand. For this reason, again, factual material with which the author has had some personal contact is used in the Discovery section, even though the familiarity be only through personal friendship with the participants.

Chapter 1, on Creativity, was the most difficult to write and quite a challenge. It was written straight out of 30 years as a scientist responsible for the productivity of fellow scientists. It has been written and rewritten over a period of 3 years without the benefit on the distraction of the philosopher's keen or the personnel man's encantations, hence, the risk that it be only sincere and neither very original nor well done. If you like it, fine; if not, read on a bit before you decide to put the book aside. The next two chapters are short and more easily written and read. I have read longer, duller things about what is entitled here Spontaneous Discovery. The chapter about Luck and Serendipity was rather fun to write, though I despair that scientists should have come to use such an otherwise happy word as serendipity.

Designed Discovery, Chapter 4, deals with the ways of discovery best known to the author and those to whom the book is dedicated. Chapter 5 is in effect the acknowledgment that the way to discovery can be absurdly simple or vague and complex.

Depending on why one is reading the book, the next three chapters, 6 through 8, on Tailoring a New Drug, are worth a great deal of study, or may be skipped. They are a series of case histories of discovery out of the author's past. They are of increasing complexity from the standpoint of concept and involvement of manpower. They should be recommended reading for some and required reading for others because of the strengths and weaknesses represented therein as examples of designed discovery.

The next two chapters, 9 and 10, relate to the assessment of the scope of activity of a new compound in the laboratory and the safety assessment of that compound prior to clinical trial. These are substantial chapters about the research from which *The Preclinical,* the document that the clinical investigator is given as background information for his clinical research, is derived.

What it takes by way of effort, materials, and planning to take the synthesis of a new compound from milligram to megagram quantities and from the test tube to factory production is little-known outside of the chemical industry. Likewise, the innocence with which one is apt to refer to a tablet as a pill belies the complexities that can befall the development of almost any dosage form of a new compound. Chapters 11 and 12 are intended to give a more realistic insight into these critical aspects of new drug development, chemical and pharmaceutical development.

Chapters 13 through 15 have to do with making a useful new drug out of an interesting new compound. Beginning with the transition of information from the laboratory to the clinic, the clinical pharmacologist determines how the patient (his bodily processes) treats the compound. In turn, the clinical investigator assesses the utility and safety of the new drug in the management of disease — a long, tedious, and expensive process.

Seldom does one see a reasonably short discussion of patents, trademarks, and copyrights, such as appears in Chapter 16. Perhaps, if more people realized the importance even our founding fathers attached to the rights of writers, inventors and discoverers by setting these forth in our *Constitution,* they might wish to know more about this subject. Almost any consideration of The Regulation of New Drug Assessment and Use is likely to be considered a misrepresentation on an adversary basis, regardless of one's point of view. Regulatory agencies have and in turn generate their share of problems and the Food and Drug Administration (FDA) in this country is no exception. Chapter 17 is intended to deal with the regulations that guide the interaction of the FDA and industry rather than their practices.

Chapters 18 and 19 are about marketing, though it is introduced in the title as Delivery. The input from marketing can influence research programs, can determine whether or not the process and plant are adequate to fulfill the demands for the new drug, and can determine whether the full potential of the drug is realized by physician familiarity with the product and its proper use. Although some interactions between research and marketing are treated lightly in the text, the importance of a cordial interaction between these divisions of a company is not likely to be overestimated.*

Finally, we come to the acknowledgment that while one may write such a book as this, many have helped to make it worth whatever credit it may deserve. When the course upon which this book is based was first given to my students, distinguished men, each expert in his field, gave with me the ten 2-hour lectures, beginning with Dr. H. Houston Merritt who shared the designed discovery of Dilantin. Dr. Edward J. Cragoe, Jr., presented his own concept of tailoring a new drug. He shared credit for the chemistry from which ethacrynic acid and amiloride were derived. Dr. James Gillin discussed chemical and pharmaceutical development. Mr. Robert L. Banse and Mr. John L. Huck gave the lectures on patents and regulatory affairs and on marketing, respectively. Each has read the corresponding chapters as I have written them. In addition, Drs. Harold M. Peck and Robert E. Zwickey have read Chapter 10. Dr. Kenneth R. Heimlich reviewed Chapter 12 and Dr. Max Tishler reviewed Chapters 11 and 12. Dr. Gilbert M. Bayne and Dr. Robert J. Bower criticized Chapters 13 through 15. Dr. John E. Baer, friend and close associate in research, reviewed the first nine chapters as did Dr. Allan D. Bass. The greatest burden of review fell to long-time friends, Dr. Elliot S. Vesell and Dr. George E. Farrar, Jr., who reviewed the whole manuscript from their points of view. I can only hope that such just criticism as may befall the book and its author are no greater than the praise I would address to all these and still others who have been so helpful.

COLLATERAL LITERATURE

deKruif, P. (1926): *Microbe Hunters* Harcourt, Brace & Co., Inc., New York.
Slosson, E. E. (1919): *Creative Chemistry: Descriptive of Recent Achievements in the Chemical Industries* Garden City Publishing Co., Inc., Garden City, New York.

*The first time these introductory remarks were drafted was when the writing of this book was initiated. They were written then, not with the expectation that they would survive, but, out of curiosity as to how I might view this undertaking before and after the manuscript was completed. Mostly, these words were about why I thought it might be a worthwhile undertaking – the reason being that at the time I read and enjoyed Edwin E. Slosson's *Creative Chemistry* (1919) and Paul deKruif's *Microbe Hunters* (1926), some 46 years ago, I would have devoured a book such as this is intended to be. Like the good chemist I wanted to be, I signed my copy of the chemistry text and dated it. It was a Christmas present I had asked for and received from my parents in 1931 and so was the *Microbe Hunters*. The flyleaf of the latter book carries the more recent inscription, "For Karl H. Beyer – hoping to not let you down" Paul deKruif, 9/11/58. Paul deKruif's comment refers to the importance I attach to such books for vocational guidance. A lot had happened for the advancement of medicine in those intervening 27 years from 1931 to 1958. The advancement of therapy in those few years was more profound than in any other period in the history of medicine. Hopefully, it was just the beginning – there is so much yet to be done.

SECTION I
DISCOVERY

1.
Creativity

GENERAL CONSIDERATIONS

To discover a drug, a useful drug, is an uncommon occurrence. In the first place, most investigators who make a career of the biomedical sciences are not primarily interested in discovering a new drug. The reason is simple enough. They have been taught how to do research toward the accumulation of knowledge, which is a worthy mission in its own right. How to discover a new drug simply is not taught purposefully as a part of one's training. Few have the opportunity or the spontaneous interest to seek such knowledge for themselves. This is as true of Pharmacologists as any other class of biomedical scientists [Microbiologists, Biochemists]. Even Pharmacologists are more inclined to study how drugs affect or are affected by the body than to discover new drugs useful for the advancement of therapy.

On the other hand, it is my feeling that in this day of idealism among young people entering medical sciences (doctors, pharmacists, nurses, paramedics) more of them would be interested in the advancement of therapy if they were exposed to what it takes, by way of preparation, for such adventure.

Discovery does carry the element of adventure, of bringing to light something which has not been available. Discovery does imply that what is sought exists actually or conceptually (the gas laws or a cure for cancer), materially or theoretically (a "new" constellation or an immunochemical cure for a specific neoplasm). Obviously, it cannot distinguish between the actual (or material) and the conceptual (or theoretical) except by some measure of being or accomplishment. Faith that the conceptual can be reconciled with the actual by achievement (by the successful exploration of theory) tends to distinguish the scientist who must make this reconciliation by experimentation from the public who must pay for it, or from the philosopher − poet who might make little distinction between theoretical and material, or from the executive who is dependent on the successful conversion of today's theory to tomorrow's therapy by the scientist.

For example, a practical nonimmunosuppresant cancer cure as safe and effective as some of the antibiotics for bacterial infections may actually exist among the thousands and thousands of organic compounds that have been made. It may be some yet-to-be synthesized chemical, one not yet created. To say that such a cancer cure may actually exist is to recognize the singularity of biological characteristics of a compound just as we recognize that agent by such distinguishing physical characteristics as melting point, solubility, adsorption properties, etc. That even close chemical congeners may differ substantially in their pharmacodynamic characteristics is a well-established fact. This principle forms the basis for successfully examining thousands of compounds for many purposes.

In the total processes leading to discovery, *creativity* may be the first or ultimate determinant of success. The investigator may need to start with one or more concepts, one or more new ideas as to what compound may be effective when tested as a cancer cure (what to do). He may decide from his experience and the literature that a new procedure is needed if he is to recognize the merits of the compound for which he is searching (how to do it). What is needed to get on with the work may be a new concept of how or where the agent should work if it is to be effective. In a larger sense, if there is to be any real assurance of success, these concepts need to have been developed and reduced to an operational level, usually in the laboratory, before one gets on with a discovery. If one is to proceed with the designed discovery (the deliberate, purposeful discovery) of a new drug, he or she may have to create at least part of the basis for discovery. So, let's start with creativity. Let's start at the beginning.

THE ELEMENTS OF CREATIVITY

What is creativity? What are the elements of creativity? Is creativity some sort of divine virtue or an acquired trait? Can creativity be taught? How do you develop it or improve this quality in a scientist? When creativity was in vogue, these questions were the subject of many articles in the professional journals. Creativity was to the scientist who read *Chemical and Engineering News* what beauty was to the woman who read *Vogue* magazine. Creativity was a favorite subject for symposia at meetings of research directors before the more recent preoccupation with methods of management took its place. Now, we have more management and less creativity. In this day of pant suits, beauty evidently is less important than whether both female and male pronouns appear concurrently in a text such as this.

There are two elements of creativity that, really, we should be able to take for granted as present in the capable scientist. They are two of the three basic attributes of creativity. They are (1) a capacity for hard *work* and (2) *intelligence*. They go together, or they should. Neither virtue suffices to qualify a person for an ordinary job as a scientist. Certainly, a well-intentioned, hard-working individual is not the one to whom we go for creativity, if these are his only strong points. Intelligence definitely is an important factor in the equation for creativity.

There is still a third factor in the equation for creativity. This is *discernment,* the quality of being able to grasp and comprehend what is obscure. Discernment may be no more important than work or intelligence, but without it many an ambitious, hard working, intelligent scientist has ultimately been a disappointment to himself and his management or peers.

AN EQUATION FOR CREATIVITY

From these three elements, work (W), intelligence (I) and discernment (D), an interesting equation for Creativity (C) can be constructed as follows:

$$C = \left[\left(\frac{W}{D_1} \right) \times \left(\frac{I}{D_2} \right) \right] = 1$$

Let us consider this more philosophic than algebraic equation in greater detail. It does not matter in the expression of this equation whether (W/D) or (I/D) comes first; creativity is the product not the sum of the two.

ANALYSIS OF THE CREATIVITY EQUATION

From the standpoint of creativity, work is whatever needs be done conceptually or physically to fulfill the ideational aspect of the equation. Work may be the effort required to accumulate a background of ideas, techniques, experience, data collection and collation, study, and the putting together of all this in a form useful for discovery. As one watches scientists work, it becomes apparent that how much work they do usually is not as important as what they do. This should be obvious to all, but the harder one works the less apparent it seems to become.

The effective use of work requires discernment. In one form, this has been introduced into the equation for creativity as W/D_1. To simplify the equation, when discernment, D_1, is perfect or maximally effective then the work that needs be done is minimized and the value W/D_1 approaches 1.0. D_1 belongs in the denominator, it is reductionistic. When discernment is greatest, work is reduced to the most relevant level though it still may be considerable. Where discernment approaches zero, the absolute value for W/D_1 becomes infinitely large.

In the equation for creativity, this relationship of work to discernment is expressed as a single value (W/D_1) with the aid of the parenthesis. This single value may be given the term *exploration* (E). Thus $(W/D_1) = E$. Exploration is directed work, work governed, determined, modulated by discernment and by the ability to judge appropriately, even wisely. Exploration is the more technical aspect of the equation. Expressed differently, if the exploration is successful and $E = 1.0$ then $W/D_1 = 1.0$ and the amount of useful work is equivalent to the discernment with which it is approached. If $D_1 \simeq 0$, then $E \cong 0$), or no amount of work will solve the problem.

For example, in the history of the discovery of Insulin (Chapter 20), a great deal of work had gone into trying to extract the active hypoglycemic principle from the pancreas by numerous workers but without success $[(W/D_1) \cong 0]$. Banting discerned, from that work, that what needed to be done was to protect whatever active ingredient was in the pancreas from destruction (oxidation) in the process of extraction. This Banting and Best did by very direct means, and in a relatively short while they obtained an active pancreatic extract capable of controlling the hypoglycemia of pancreatechtomized dogs and diabetic patients $[W/D_1) \cong 1]$.

WHAT ABOUT THE ROLE OF LUCK

It should be evident that terms such as "luck" and "serendipity" do not belong in this portion of the discussion. They relate to discovery but their relevance to creativity is remote, at best.

FURTHER ANALYSIS OF CREATIVITY

Intelligence (I) definitely is an important factor in the equation for creativity. Intelligence in this context is basic to the acquisition of knowledge, which is the stock-in-trade of the capable scientist. The greater the scope and depth of knowledge relevant to the field of endeavor the greater the resources one has with which to work. Intelligence also incorporates *the ability to use knowledge.* This latter element of intelligence is approximated by the term *Imagination,* the ability to recall information in a new context or new form. Everyone is familiar with the "bright," well-educated person who seems to have more ideas, even more imagination, than anyone among his peers and who seems bound to have a great idea or make a great discovery some day. This, frequently hyperkinetic, individual too often does not live up to his own or his associates' expectations. Why? The most probable explanation is an inadequate ability or unwillingness to exercise the reductionistic factor of discernment (D_2); reductionistic in the analytical sense of rejecting the less (not just the least) relevant of alternative propositions.

The expression (I/D_2) could be considered an Ideational factor (M) or disciplined imagination. Thus, if discernment (D_2) is sufficient to reduce the imaginative use of knowledge to its most relevant level, then $(I/D_2) \cong 1$, and there may be a rational basis for creativity. One of the simplest examples where the exploratory factor (W/D_1) was not limiting, technically, and where the ideational factor was precise and simple $[I/D_2 \cong 1]$ was David Lehrs' solution to the tremendous problem with sulfonamide chemotherapy — crystalluria, which could cause damage to and even block the patient's urinary track (Chapter 4). By combining three different, but more or less equisoluble sulfa drugs in the same tablet, the total therapeutic sulfa dose could be administered with negligible risk of renal damage by crystalluria.

Only in the most general way can weighted values be placed on each component of the equation. Even the members of a successful research team might do this differently for their own accomplishment. There may be only one or numerous elements of the ideational aspect of the equation that must be solved, where discernment (D_2) (what to do) must be adequate for (I/D_2) to approach 1. This is true for the exploratory factor as well, where D_1 (how to do it) must be adequate for (W/D_1) to equal 1.

Perhaps it is in the unanticipated value of discernment or the difference in value two investigators place on D_1 or D_2 that makes the creativity of one appear lucky or serendipitous and the effort of another appear to be unlucky. For example, if one investigator has many ideas, and fails to distinguish the most likely of them, he may dissipate his resources fruitlessly. In another instance, a scientist may discern both an appropriate approach to a problem and the problem itself in a proper perspective different from current teaching. His or her pursuit of the problem might well be successful. Creative, to be sure, but it may appear to be serendipitous to less discerning contemporaries in the field of research who place different values on the information at hand.

There is one more aspect of the equation for creativity that deserves comment, for it has an inapparent significance. Discernment (D) appears in both factors. This may well account for why the bright individual with lots of ideas but little discernment never seems to be creative or to come forth with a discovery, which requires creativity as an essentiality. An error in judgment with respect to *either what to do* or *how to do it* is likely to result in failure (no creativity).* Since creativity is the capacity to bring something new into being, it is best expressed as the product of proper ideation and appropriate exploration.

THE PERSONAL NATURE OF CREATIVITY: A SUMMING UP

Now that we have considered creativity and the elements of creativity in terms of work, intelligence, and discernment, from which we derived the exploratory (technical) and the ideational (intellectual) aspects of the term, let's turn to some of the questions on page 8 with which to conclude this chapter. Perhaps an acceptable answer to the personal nature of creativity, like personality, is that of a mingling of "divine virtues" and acquired traits. Such a view would not distinguish the scientist from the artist. It would admit that creativity could be sought and taught. It would demand an intellectual discipline that could be cultivated but seldom is — an indifference to the distinction between what is or is believed to be, between the theoretical and that which is conceptual but remotely so. Since such a characterization of the individual takes us to the peak of the curve that represents a Gaussian distribution of men, as by ability, it is not remarkable that original ideas come to few or that the capacity for original thought and its expression seems extraordinary.

COLLATERAL LITERATURE

Kneller, G. F. (1965) *The Art and Science of Creativity,* Holt, Rinehart and Winston, Inc., New York.

---

*Discernment has been introduced into the equation as D_1 and D_2. Whereas the actual mental process might not distinguish between D_1 and D_2, the values that might be placed on the discernment of most people as to what to do (D_2) and how to do it (D_1) do clearly differ, in any specific situation, and for good reason.

2.
Spontaneous
Discovery

Until man had created bodies of knowledge for his use, indeed sciences such as bacteriology, virology, organic chemistry, and what we know about the physiological correlates of disease (or how the aberrations of function, which we call disease, take place), he was dependent first on spontaneous discovery and then on serendipity for advancement of his well being.

WHAT IS MEANT BY THE TERM SPONTANEOUS DISCOVERY

What do we mean by spontaneous discovery? Perhaps it would help to think of spontaneous discovery much as one would think of spontaneous combustion where the circumstances of nature so evolved as to give rise to forces ultimately recognized as heat (fire) or light (revelation, discovery). These circumstances did not require any more knowledge of medicine on the part of one person than another. On the other hand, there had to be a discoverer for a discovery to be made. This is to say, someone, such as a tribal priest, an elder tribesman or an older woman, perhaps a midwife, had a purpose in trying some concoction in or on an ailing believer. In such cases evidence of efficacy was obviously sought. This was more important to discovery than that the benefit must have been largely subjective much of the time. Without evidence of efficacy being sought, without there being an assessment of utility, the chances are there would have been no discovery. Very likely, in any instance the discovery of efficacy, say of quinine, must have been missed many more times than made, considering the fundamental nature of the clinical assessment of its benefit.

THE ROLE OF TIME AND CONCURRENCE

It seems likely that time and concurrence, regarding efficacy, were more important to discovery than was divine guidance. The insistence of someone using a concoction of the bark of the cinchona tree to treat malaria may have been passed along to his successors for so many generations that the origin of the custom was as obscure as the source of other remedies of less certain utility. Actually, this "blind" method of treatment with or without the patient's informed consent, may have been as disastrous on occasion as helpful. One can imagine that it would not have taken an Indian medicine man many experiences with the administration of curare, had it been active when swallowed, to appreciate that this stuff might be put to some better lethal, rather than medicinal, use, as on the tips of arrows.

It is easy enough to understand that once a brew was established to be effective in some cases many uses would be claimed for it. The basis for good differential diagnosis is as recent as Virchow's descriptive pathology developed toward the end of the last century (R. Virchow, 1821–1902). (Definitive methods for clinical investigation are still in the formative stages today.) The distinction between many respiratory diseases could not have been made long ago, hence, ephedrine was used by the Chinese for many situations. Likewise, when reserpine was introduced from the ancient Indian pharmacopia to clinical research in this country and Europe the list of situations for which it had been considered to be effective was enough to discredit the rauwolfia alkaloids. More recently, they had been subjected to excellent research in India. This led to the use of rauwolfia as a tranquilizing agent and for hypertension.

GEOGRAPHIC DISTRIBUTION OF DRUGS
FOR COMMON AILMENTS

Prior to the useful development of chemistry and the biomedical sciences, each civilization, each culture, each geographical area tended to meet the common ailments of man wherever he be with whatever was at hand. For example, several sources of cardiac glycosides seem to have been available. The drug for heart failure most of us are apt to be familiar with, historically, is digitalis. Apparently, this principle from the Foxglove was used in folk medicine in England for centuries before Withering (1785). On the other hand, it was Withering's remarkable *discernment* as to when and how it should be used that assured us of the tremendous importance of digitalis as a drug. Ovabain from strophanthus grown in Central Europe, remains a useful cardiotonic drug. Less well known in this country is Urinin, a cardiotonic drug derived from squill grown in the Mediterranean area. The venom of a number of oriental toads resembles the action of digitalis or squill.

All of which is to say that the ailments common to man and the need to care for and cure them provided a purpose and structure for the spontaneous discovery of the therapeutic value of the natural products at hand. Some of these discoveries, like quinine, evolved indigenously to their area of special need. The discoveries of other compounds, such as the cardiac glycosides and their functional analogs, were as broadly distributed by pharmacodynamic utility as was the problem of heart failure, which has plagued all of mankind without regard for where he has lived. These discoveries evolved by the process of selection over a period of many generations of healers and sick people, neither of whom had any real insight into what the potions actually were doing beneficially; medicine had not sufficiently developed to support these insights. On the other hand, it has only been with the past generation of scientists that the rauwolfia alkaloids or D-tubocurarine and curarimimetic drugs have found their useful place in so-called Western medicine.

NATIONAL CULTURES AND LOCAL REMEDIES

In closing these few comments on the origins of some of our basic therapies, I do not intend to give the impression that only the great drugs discovered spontaneously have been handed down to us century by century. This isn't so. Each national culture rooted in antiquity has its own armamentarium of remedies. Some of these are still distributed nationally or locally but are not recognized elsewhere. This myriad of ancient local remedies is an important reason why there is no European Pharmacopeia or uniformity among the national regulatory agencies that deal with the licensing of drugs.

SUMMARY

Many of our most useful drugs, drugs we still do not understand, had their origins in antiquity well before the development of useful bodies of knowledge, the sciences. With time there developed a social structure wherein the responsibility, the interest, and the need to care for the sick came to rest on a few people in each generation. Obviously, there were no medical journals, no *Index Medicus,* or *Chemical Abstracts* and so the assessment of usefulness of local remedies was passed along by "preceptorship," from person to person by word of mouth. Some remedies, good and bad, must have been forgotten and some must have been rediscovered many times ultimately to persist today. This was the circumstance of spontaneous discovery, gone as the dependent basis for progress but still familiar within our medical mores. Whether it is past, the place of spontaneous discovery in the advancement of modern medicine is not likely to be of more than historic significance to one planning a career in drug research.

COLLATERAL LITERATURE

Fulton, J. F. (1930): *Selected Readings in the History of Physiology,* Charles C. Thomas, Springfield, Illinois.

Garrison, F. H. (1929): *An Introduction to the History of Medicine,* 4th ed. W. B. Saunders Co., Phila., Pa.

Holmstedt, B., and Liljestrand, G. (1963): *Readings in Pharmacology,* The Macmillan Co., New York.

Major, R. H. (1939): *Classic Descriptions of Disease,* Charles C. Thomas, Springfield, Illinois.

Withering, W. (1785): *An Account of the Foxglove and its Medical Properties,* Miles Swinney Pub., Birmingham, England.

3.
Luck and Serendipity

The one connecting link between *the ways* discovery has been made, whether it be spontaneous, serendipitous, or designed is circumstance. The circumstance of spontaneous discovery, when there was no science, was considered in the previous chapter.

GENERAL CONSIDERATIONS

Serendipity had to await eons for the gradual development of whole bodies of knowledge and methodology before it could play a role in discovery. Whole bodies of knowledge, such as organic chemistry, microbiology, physiology, and their derived disciplines, such as biochemistry and pathology, and sufficient instrumentation must have reached a stage of development that permitted the inquiring mind to induce change. To the alchemist concerned with the interconversion of metals, a cure for diseases, and the prolongation of life, chance or luck must have been the basis for progress. The background of knowledge, which by this time was recorded in some measure, was too fanciful to be very helpful for understanding much less anticipating what this progenitor of the scientist was doing. Curiosity and trial were his greatest resources — trial and an occasional result recognized for its significance. One of the most profound statements I know derived from these early days is: "Science progresses by successive approximations to the truth."

As the "approximations to the truth" we call knowledge became more secure and as their numbers and continuity increased, the basis for understanding improved. As the instrumentation and methodology improved, so did the rate and sureness of man's progress. Ultimately, the scientist could ask a question of his science, such as the nature of the synthesis of an intended compound (for example, urea — the first-synthesized organic compound prepared by Friedrich Woehler in 1828). In time, the scientist could inquire about the effect of an agent on the function of some biological structure, with the reasonable assurance that the answer might be recognized. The answer may not have been what was anticipated, but to the prepared mind the answer was recognizable. Even its significance might have been appreciated. This was *Serendipity*. It was the beginning of *designed discovery,* but it was not designed discovery because its product was not sought. The discovery was unanticipated in purpose and substance. Serendipity is more advanced than luck as a basis for discovery. It is a more disciplined concept of discovery, without the full randomness that luck implies.

DERIVATION OF THE WORD SERENDIPITY

The dictionary defines serendipity as "the gift of finding valuable or agreeable things not sought for." Clear enough, but the source of the word would seem to be as important to its usage as the definition. Where and how a word was used at its inception should have a great deal to do with the appropriateness of its usage now. This lilting happy word, serendipity, derives from a fairy tale, *The Three Princes of Serendip.*

It was coined by Horace Walpole who wrote in a letter of January 28, 1754 about a French version of a fairy tale published in 1721 and entitled "Voyage des trois princes de Serendip." There evidently are several versions of the tale, an earlier one having been published in Italian in 1557. The story is laid in the fifth century A.D. in the time of Anuradhapura in Ceylon. Parenthetically, this lovely island off the end of India is claimed by legend to have been the place to which Adam and Eve journeyed. It was their home when they had to leave the Garden of Eden. Sri Lanka is the much more lovely and appropriate name for this beautiful island today.

A delightful version of this tale by Elizabeth Jamison Hodges (1964) relates to three princes: Balakrama, Vijayo, and Rajahsingha, all full of wisdom and great learning, lived in a land far off at the end of the earth. At their maturity, their father, King Jaiya, sent them forth to other lands to further their education and to seek a secret formula (*Death to Dragons*) that would rid the seas around their homeland of great beasts, denizens of the deep that destroyed ships, hence making travel to and from the mainland precarious. In the course of their search for the formula each prince fell upon unexpected and remarkable adventure that required kingly courage, knowledge, kindness, and humanity and in return for which he received rare treasures. Needless to say, their real mission was accomplished ultimately and the dragons were destroyed. "Thus, the three princes of Serendip all became rulers." Balakrama, the oldest son, was propositioned by many monarchs each of whom wanted to arrange a marriage with one of his daughters. But, as might be expected, *he* fell in love with a peasant's beautiful daughter as he was nearing home. He ended up with the fair Podihamine and his own father's kingdom, which is not bad – no serendipity there as fairy tales go. Anyway, "the three princes of Serendip all became rulers, each so filled with virtue, wisdom, and science that, governing well, he was much beloved" – which ought to be a lesson to us scientists.

THE DIFFERENCE BETWEEN LUCK AND SERENDIPITY

Clearly, by anyone's choice of words, serendipity differs from luck. Luck may be defined as a force or a resultant of forces derived from the effect of chance events or circumstances that bring good fortune or adversity. Luck is a useful word, much more boardly applicable than serendipity because of the random or unguided nature of both circumstance and effect. Sometimes, there is woven into its fabric an identification with a person, or circumstance, as though the "force" were something more than natural, something less than supernatural. This aspect that some people are luckier than others is about as close as luck and serendipity seem to approach a commonality of usage.

THE GREEN THUMB SYNDROME

Both serendipity and luck differ from a third expression by which scientists recognize differences in productivity among themselves on some basis other than their ability. In the gardener's terms, this difference in ability is recognized in earth-bound verbiage as the *green thumb.* Thus, it would seem that for no particular reason, no immediately evident reason, some people have a penchant for making things grow or go better than do their associates; they have a green thumb. Obviously, having a green thumb is different from being lucky. It carries the connotation of a consistently favorable outcome of enterprise, whereas luck implies an inconsistency of outcome both in frequency and kind. (Any farmer would rather be known as having a green thumb than just being lucky, especially to his banker.)

The person with the green thumb differs from the serendipitous individual qualitatively. The green thumb relates to a gift of doing the ordinary or usual thing unusually well, whereas serendipity is the gift of finding valuable things not sought after.

These three terms, the green thumb syndrome, serendipity, and luck carry quite different values in the minds of some scientists. Most scientists recognize the green thumb scientist as being different somehow; not necessarily better but different in that somehow things done by this individual usually seem to turn out very well. Serendipity is the euphemism sometimes used to explain the unanticipated discovery by the thinking scientist. Serendipity has come to carry the connotation, among scientists, of happenstance more than the quality of a gift or trait. It isn't the same as luck, though. Most scientists would consider luck as something unanticipated that could happen to him or her, too.*

The green thumb distinction does relate to a level of unusual discernment for approaching and doing what needs to be done most sensibly, most directly, or most thoroughly. It is not the equivalent of creativity. It relates to doing, not discovering.

LUCK AND CREATIVITY

I have been interested in the reaction of individual scientists to the formula for creativity (Chapter 1) when introduced into a general conversation, as at lunch. Usually, they have thought so little about the subject of creativity in an organized way that its formulation in terms of the basic attributes of exploration and ideation seems more or less acceptable. But where, they ask, does luck fit into the equation? Luck is certianly part of being creative, my friend would insist. Usually, the challenger is intelligent, hard working, top flight, responsible, but not particularly distinguished by his accomplishment. To him, the latter characteristic is a matter of luck, and so it may be. Creativity and accomplishment are different. Accomplishment is not necessarily dependent on creativity, but it helps.

Was it luck that brought Earle Loew and his associates to the discovery of the antihistamine, Benadryl (diphenhydramine), which they described in 1945? The state of the literature at that time related histamine to allergy only controversially. The French investigators Fourneau, Bóvet, and Halpern, had shown that it was possible to inhibit the effects of histamine, but their earlier

---

*It has been pointed out to me that the history of feeding liver in the management of anemia might be used to illustrate these three terms. Accordingly, the excellent observations reported in 1925 by G. H. Whipple and F. S. Robscheit-Robbins that feeding raw liver to dogs was beneficial for the regeneration of blood cells in anemia was perhaps serendipitous. R. G. Minot's application of this observation to the successful management of pernicious anemia patients by the feeding of raw liver (1927) exemplified the green thumb principle. The participation of Minot's associate, W. P. Murphy, a resident physician at the time, might have been more of the nature of luck.

compounds were not sufficiently potent or specific. Loew was fortunate in the series of compounds George Revieshel made available to him and from which diphenhydramine was derived. But he was no more lucky in having made the discovery of the first useful antihistamine in this country than the rest of us were unlucky for not having made it. His was the discernment to know what to do, what to believe, and how to go about the discovery of that new and useful drug. It could be argued that Loew was lucky to have had the Revieshel benzhydryl ethers to compare with the Fourneau compounds. On the other hand, it is clear from his publications that his insight into the problem was sound and that his methodology was adequate to have picked up antihistaminic activity in any of the many series of compounds in which it is present.

Luck should not be introduced into the creativity equation; it can be and frequently is a part of the circumstance of success. For instance, in our search for a saluretic agent, the chemists on the team were of two groups. One group made sulfhydryl binding agents for the inhibition of a dehydrogenase that might be involved in the reabsorption of sodium by the kidney. The second group made sulfamoyl carbonic anhydrase inhibitors for the same ultimate purpose of inhibiting sodium reabsorption. The efforts of the second group of chemists came to fruition first — in the benzothiadizine compounds. The first of these compounds was chlorothiazide. Not long after the discovery of the thiazides, the phenoxyacetic acid lead was brought to fruition by the other team of chemists. This latter group of compounds eventually gave us much more potent saluretic agents and resulted in the marketing of Edecrin (ethacrynic acid). Luck was not an element of discovery, but chance certainly influenced the structure of the initial compounds in the historical development of that important field of research.

SERENDIPITY AS AN ALTERNATIVE TO CREATIVITY

Biomedical scientists are not so apt to insist on serendipity being introduced into the formula for creativity. They are inclined to consider serendipity a more likely alternate to creativity in the process of discovery. Their image of serendipity is that of the happy scientist working on some esoteric project of interest (but with no particular direction or goal) who stumbles over a stone in the path which on closer scrutiny turns into an acre of diamonds, medically speaking, of course. Superficially, this image of serendipity might seem identified with the earlier discoveries of antibiotics, such as penicillin, streptomycin, and aureomycin, discovered by Fleming (1929), Waksman (1947), and by Duggar (1948), respectively; but the facts belie this impression. The reason for this misconception was that these antibiotics were so important to mankind, for the medical rescue of the seriously ill soldier, for the patient doomed otherwise to die of tuberculosis, or the broad spectrum management of bacterial infections in modern medicine that they were sought by the public in the 1940's as miracle drugs. The situation at that time could not be exaggerated by one's recollections. These were among the miracle drugs that came about first under the forced draft of war and then the general approbation of medical research that the public manifested at that time, unstintingly, individually and through their national legislature.

SERENDIPITY VERSUS DESIGNED DISCOVERY

It probably would occur to no one, though, to identify these three men, Fleming, Waksman, and Duggar, at the time of their discoveries with the *Three Princes of Serendip*. These three were past their maturity at the time their epoc-making findings reached the patient. Alexander Fleming's career was that of a clinical bacteriologist. Whereas he described the accidental observation of the antibacterial action of penicillin in 1929 and appreciated its significance, Chain and Florey in 1940, and with Abraham in 1941, did the work at Oxford that motivated its development as a chemotherapeutic antibiotic. Selman A. Waksman, a well-known soil microbiologist at Rutgers University, first described Streptomyces griseus in 1915 when he was a graduate student. Over the intervening years leading up to 1939, both René Dubos and Waksman developed the concept that soil microorganisms produced chemicals that prevented pathogenic bacteria from accumulating in the ground. At that time, Waksman determined to find such an antibiotic. He and his associates isolated streptomycin from this actinomycete in 1943 and found it to be active against *Mycobacterium tuberculosis.* Benjamin Duggar had been at the Lederle Laboratories some 3 years or so when he and his associates discovered aureomycin in 1947. Later, they discovered tetracycline. He had been invited to Lederle Laboratories when mandatory retirement caught up with him at age 70 at the University of Wisconsin. At Wisconsin, he had been a well-regarded scientist and teacher on the faculty of the College of Agriculture most of his life. He was hired by Lederle to help his former students discover a new antibiotic among the thousands of soil samples that were being collected. The trail blazing work by Waksman, Fleming, Florey, and Chain earned for them the Nobel Prize. Duggar shared with them the gratitude of the world by introducing the broad spectrum antibiotics.

William Withering's discovery of the use of an extract of the Foxglove might be considered serendipitous though its origin seems to have been an example of spontaneous discovery. Legend (recorded to be sure) has it that this digitalis extract was called to his attention as a secret family recipe by an old woman of Shropshire who had used it to treat the dropsy effectively. The recipe was said to contain some twenty herbs and to produce its effect by inducing vomiting and by purging. From this concoction, he discerned the active ingredient and learned both how to prepare and use extracts thereof. It was in 1785 that he published his *Account of the Foxglove and Some of Its Medical Uses.*

In Withering's day, there were other sophisticated medical investigators whose work has been forgotten. He seems to have believed the drug to act primarily on the kidney rather than the heart. He was an intelligent successful physician and there is nothing to indicate that his work on digitalis was other than purposeful. Was he *lucky*? I suppose so, but the tale doesn't tell us how many other physicians around Birmingham, England, knew of the "secret recipe" or what they did about it. Was this *designed discovery*? No, he did not set out to discover a cure for dropsy, he assessed one. So far as we know, his interests were too broad to identify him with cardiovascular medicine. He does seem to have had the gift of recognizing a remarkable finding and of being able to describe the product and its great utility within the precision of knowledge available to him. This would seem to be *serendipity*.

In the Synopsis of this book (Chapter 20), the discovery of the anticoagulant activity of heparin (1916) in extracts of tissues prepared for the study of their thromboplastin activity in blood coagulation by Howell and his associates is recited as being serendipitous. The more recent history of the development of chlorpromazine from the antihistaminic activity of the earlier phenothiazines, the "lytic cocktail," and the concept of "artificial hybernation" by Laborit for the induction of anesthesia in France (1952–53) and its use in the United States first as an antiemetic agent and the ultimate discovery of its tranquilizer properties is too complex a story to introduce here. This discovery of the tranquilizer activity of chlorpromazine and the concomitant exploration of rawolfia (from the *Rawolfia serpentina* known from ancient time by the natives of India) for tranquilizing effects brings serendipity within our day, dramatically. These drugs introduced a revolution in the management of the psychiatric patient. Serendipity is likely to remain an important factor in the discovery of new therapy, especially where the fundamental aspects of disease are poorly understood.

Actually, it is most difficult to get the "true" story of any discovery, even from those who have participated in the event. My first encounter with this human frailty came during student days when the unfortunate split-up of a team over who contributed what to an important discovery became well known. Any biomedical discovery can be told from many points of view and in ways that may serve different, well-intentioned purposes. This is a little like the story of the way the four blind men described an elephant as each felt only a leg, the trunk, the tail, or an ear of the polymorphic creature.

Closing this chapter on luck and serendipity as though they do not exist in research would be unrealistic. On the other hand, luck in biomedical research relates to circumstance, not to creativity. The scientist with the so-called "green thumb" is that person whose discernment is so consistently good that what he undertakes frequently turns out well. He may or may not be creative. In Chapter 5 how to search beyond the limits of knowledge will be discussed. Such work may give rise to serendipitous findings, that is, observations or results one had not, but could have, anticipated if the newly created knowledge had been available at the outset of the research.

COLLATERAL LITERATURE

Abraham, E. P., Chain, E., Fletcher, C. M., Gardner, A. D., Heatley, N. G., Jennings, M. A., and Florey, H. W. (1941): Further observations on penicillin, *Lancet 2:* 177–178.

Bovet, D., and Staub, A. (1937): Action protectrice des éthers phenoliques au cours de l'intoxication histaminique, *C. Ro. Soc. Biol. 124:* 547–549.

Chain, E., Florey, H. W., Gardner, A. D., Heatley, N. G., Jennings, M. A., Orr-Ewing, J., and Sanders, A. G. (1940): Penicillin as a chemotherapeutic agent, *Lancet 2:* 226–228.

Duggar, B. M. (1948): Aureomycin, a product of the continuing search for new antibiotics, *Ann. New York Acad. Sci. 51:* 177–181.

Fleming, A. (1929): On antibacterial action of cultures of penicillium with special reference to their use in isolation of B. influenzae, *Brit. J. Exper. Path. 10:* 226–236.

Fleming, A. (1946): Antiseptics, old and new. [Mayo Foundation Lecture], *Proc. Staff Mtg., Mayo Clinic 21:* 65–75.

Hodges, E. J. (1964): *The Three Princes of Serendip,* Atheneum, New York.

Loew, E. R., Kaiser, M. E., and Moore, V. (1945): Synthetic benzhydryl alkamine ethers effective in preventing experimental asthma in guinea pigs exposed to atomized histamine, *J. Pharmacol. Exper. Therap. 83:* 120–129.

Loew, E. R., MacMillan, R., and Kaiser, M. E. (1946): The antihistamine properties of Benadryl, β-dimethylaminoethylbenzhydryl ether hydrochloride, *J. Pharmacol. Exper. Therap. 86:* 229–238.

Minot, G. R., and Murphy, W. P. (1927): A diet rich in liver in the treatment of pernicious anemia, *J.A.M.A. 89:* 759–766.

Schatz, A., Bugie, E., and Waksman, S. A. (1944): Streptomycin, a substance exhibiting antibiotic activity against Gram-positive and Gram-negative bacteria, *Proc. Soc. Exp. Biol. Med. 55:* 66–69.

Schatz, A., and Waksman, S. A. (1944): Effect of streptomycin and other antibiotic substances upon mycobacterium tuberculosis and related organism, *Proc. Soc. Exp. Biol. Med. 57:* 244–248.

Waksman, S. A. (1947): Antibiotics and tuberculosis, a microbiological approach, *J.A.M.A. 135:* 478–484.

Whipple, G. H., and Robscheit-Robbins, F. S. (1925): Blood regeneration in severe anemia. II. Favorable influence of liver, heart and skeletal muscle in diet, *Am. J. Physiol. 72:* 395–407.

Withering, W. (1785): *An Account of the Foxglove and its Medical Properties,* Miles Swinney Pub., Birmingham, England.

4.
Designed Discovery

Everyone has had the experience of marveling at the maple seedling that has sprung up in a crack in the sidewalk, or the tiny flower growing in the dust accumulated on the windowsill of an old dilapidated building, or the new-found tomato plant prospering unaccountably in some unlikely spot in one's garden. Drugs accounted for by spontaneous discovery that eventuated in folk medicine must have been so persistent. Wherever the background of science became adequate to permit one to ask a question of a research procedure and then recognize an unanticipated but useful answer, then serendipity found its place. How well serendipity characterizes very much of modern advances in therapy is hard to assess with certainty. (The less one knows or thinks about the circumstance of biomedical research in the past few decades, the easier it is to ascribe important discovery to serendipity.) Now we come to another type of discovery, the existence of which seems underestimated. This is *designed discovery:* the deliberate, the purposeful discovery.

DESIGNED DISCOVERY – SEVEN FEATURES

Designed discovery is the exciting way of discovery today and tomorrow. However, elegant examples of this approach go back as far as scientists have systematically sought to modify the function of cells, organs, or systems of organs with the aid of chemical compounds. Perhaps the first generally recognized example of designed discovery of useful drugs is the work of Ehrlich and his chemist associate Bertheim who synthesized and tested a number of compounds before Ehrlich and his Japanese associate, Hata, decided in 1910 that what they called arsphenamine (Salvarsan) or "606" was their most effective compound against experimentally induced syphillis in rabbits. Although 606 has been set forth historically as signifying the enormity of their effort, *the really important aspect of their work was that they succeeded in their undertaking. They set out to make a discovery and they did.* Even today this outcome of a research project is less common than it should be; many scientists rationalize their pet biomedical project not on what they expect to accomplish but on the possibility that something worthwhile might come of it, serendipitously.

First Feature: Ideas and Leads

A research project from which a designed discovery is derived has to start off with a purpose and an idea or a lead. Ideas and leads only differ in that a greater selectivity or discernment may have gone into the lead. The lead may be someone else's idea that seems plausible, or it may be a chemical compound that seems worth exploring. It may turn out that the idea of an expert knowlegdeable in the field was better than a more remotely derived lead, but not necessarily so. For example, the phthisiotherpist expert in the treatment of tuberculosis is less likely to know how to go about the discovery of new therapy for this condition than the bacteriologist who can manipulate the tuberculosis organism, the mycobacterium, meaningfully.

Second Feature: What Makes an Idea Worthwhile?

An idea for a research project, for designed discovery, is only as useful, one might say only as good, as the scientist to whom it occurs or to whom it is transmitted. This should be pretty obvious. A good idea is no better than a poor one in the hands of someone who does not know how to use it. To this point, we have identified two aspects of success in designed discovery: (1) the idea or lead must be good or sound; and (2) it must occur to or be accepted by the biomedical scientist who has the background and capability to use it. Otherwise, the best chemical support in the world is for naught.

How do you identify the scientist who is to be entrusted with the good idea or the right lead? This is not a rhetorical question; there are numerous examples of success that may serve for our guidance. Whether or not Fleming's role in the pencillin story was to be considered serendipitous, it is clear from his 1929 publication that he reconized the likely utility of the mold containing penicillin. A number of investigators in England and elsewhere studied its growth and characteristics before Florey and Chain confirmed once again Fleming's findings and isolated the amorphous product reported in 1940. With Abraham, they reported in 1941 that penicillin seemed to be safe. It was effective in protecting mice against induced infections and the results were favorable in a limited clinical experience. Taking an old observation as a lead, they explored it, recognized the potential of this difficult microbiologically synthesized product and expounded its virtues to the world. Florey was the physician, the pathologist, who recognized the clinical significance of the discovery. Chain was the remarkable chemist of the two. Both were brilliant men, capable of vision, work, and leadership – each in his own way quite capable of handling a good idea in his field of interest. Good ideas are most apt to reach fruition in the hands of men and women who not only appreciate the significance but who have the capability and motivation to see the work through.

Third Feature: Keep the Idea Simple

One very simple idea that any of us who worked on sulfonamides should have thought of was a discovery that solved in a practical way a problem common to sulfonamide chemotherapy – crystalluria. This was the precipitation of the sulfa drug in the urinary tract as evidenced by the presence of crystals in freshly voided urine. It was difficult to circumvent this hazard in the critically ill patient by sustaining a considerable urinary output following the administration of fluids. These drugs were more soluble in an alkaline urine, but giving the patient large amounts of sodium bicarbonate only added to his burden. By 1947, it was well established that all the sulfonamides employed for the management of systemic infectious diseases worked the same way therapeutically, and the pharmacodynamic characteristics of several were not so dissimilar. Thus, when David Lehr showed that the solubility of each of these sulfonamides in water was essentially independent of the other, he set the stage for the triple sulfonamide formulations that were effective and relatively safe. They reduced dramatically the risk of renal damage due to crystalluria. The combination of sulfadiazine, sulfamerazine and sulfamethazine (all sulfapyrimidines) is such a triple sulfonamide combination. Dr. Lehr's use of a good idea, an old principle in chemistry applied to an appropriate problem in therapeutics, might be considered a simple but important example of the way to designed discovery.

This example of Lehr's good idea has a basic quality that merits its place in this discussion – *simplicity*. Usually good ideas for research can be expressed, as well as conceived, simply, at least to people knowledgeable in that field; i.e., *keep the good idea simple*. An easily remembered, appropriate acronym is *KISS*; keep it simple.

The two most important drugs for the treatment of epilepsy, for the management or prevention of grand mal seizures, provide us with more or less classic distinctions between serendipity and designed discovery. In 1912, a

German physician by the name of Hauptmann happened to have been assigned his living quarters in the hospital immediately over a ward of epileptic patients for whom he was responsible. Nightly, both he and the patients were disturbed by their fits. Finally, as the story goes, he decided to try on them a new hypnotic with the hope that they, and thereby he, might sleep better. Actually, the new German barbiturate, phenobarbital (Luminal), did quiet the epileptic patients. As a matter of fact, they not only slept better at night, they had fewer fits during the day, as well. Whether or not Hauptmann's own added rest had anything to do with his acuity, he did appreciate the significance of this serendipity. He was the first to describe the usefulness of phenobarbital for the management of epilepsy. It remains one of the two most important drugs for this purpose, in spite of the sedation it produces. According to his own account, this discovery of the anti-epileptic effect of phenobarbital was sheer serendipity.

The discovery of the anti-epileptic feature of diphenylhydantoin (Dilantin) described in 1938 by H. Houston Merritt and Tracy J. Putnam has many of the basic features of modern drug research, of designed discovery as we have come to think of the process.

Fourth Feature: The Environment of Discovery

Although Merritt and Putnam are credited with this discovery, Merritt has stressed the importance of the setting, the circumstance and the outstanding capability of their associates in Neurology at Harvard at that time. In other words, he stressed *the environment of discovery*. In effect, he accounted for this success as a team effort undertaken for the specific purpose of discovering better therapy for the epileptic patients who constitute about one percent of the population of this country — well over a million patients.

Fifth Feature: Physiological Correlates of Disease

These men knew the physiological correlates of the clinical disease in its various forms, within the knowledge of neurophysiology that was applicable and adequate. (By physiological correlates, we mean the actual physiological processes which when altered excessively give rise to the signs and symptoms of the patient's abnormal situation, his disease.) Listed here as a fifth feature of designed discovery, *the better the physiological correlates of disease are understood and expressed in the laboratory procedures the more likely is the success of the venture.* Putnam was interested in electroshock convulsive therapy, which he adapted to induce electroshock seizures in cats. The electroshock seizure induced in cats was envisaged as a laboratory approximation of the grand mal seizure in the patient.

Even the choice of animal species or strains can be important to discovery. Over the course of many years the neurologist has come to prefer cats for his research. Just as dogs are the choice of the renal physiologist, the immunologist has preferred guinea pigs, and the nutritionist has built the literature of his findings on the rat. Selection of a particular animal species for study probably has its greatest virtue in that it introduces a certain continuum to a body of knowledge that contributes to its substance. Choice of animals is not necessarily a factor basic to the success of such a project, although for many reasons I would argue its importance. Diphenylhydantoin could have been discovered by its ability to block electroshock seizures in rats, if these investigators had been as familiar with rats as they were with cats.

Sixth Feature: The Need to Control Experiments

There is a sixth requirement among the elements of designed discovery, in which familiarity with the animal employed is important; *the need to control the experiment. The experiment must be capable of being quantified.* Putnam and his associates learned to quantify the threshold for electroshock seizures in the cats, no mean accomplishment and one critical to success. For the quantification to be meaningful, there needs to be the assurance that the experiment is satisfactory, technically. An expedient that I adopted over the course of years in evaluating individual experiments in renal research on unanesthetized trained dogs is a series of three questions that should be asked of the results, the data. The answers to the questions can be summarized under the abbreviation, E.S.T. The questions are: (a) Does the compound appear to be *effective* (E)? (b) Is the experiment *technically satisfactory* (S)? (c) Could the effect have been influenced by *any toxicity* (T) of the compound? Unless the latter two questions can be answered satisfactorily, what may appear to be a real effect of a compound may be misleading qualitatively and/or quantitatively.

Seventh Feature: Adequacy of Assessment

The seventh feature is a generalization important to the therapeutic realization of the designed discovery of a new compound. *The better the preclinical assessment of safety and efficacy and the better its initial clinical exploration the surer is the transposition of laboratory results of the new agent to man.* This is what Chapters 9 through 15 are all about.

Although Merritt and Putnam did not have the advantage of medicinal chemists as part of their team at the outset, they were confronted with the same important question that the chemist would have asked of them: "Where do we start?" What compounds should we look at first? (The way this question

(I)
PHENOBARBITAL

(II)
DIPHENYLHYDANTOIN

has been answered has determined the outcome of important intended designed discoveries and the fate of companies.) The best leads, the best drugs at the time, were potassium bromide (which was not much of a lead) and phenobarbital (which makes the patient sleepy). Phenobarbital was active in blocking electroshock-induced convulsions in the test systems of Merritt and Putnam. The barbiturates and their analogs represented an almost infinite number of possible compounds for studying the relationship of chemical structure to biological activity. They wrote to several pharmaceutical research laboratories for samples of barbiturates and related compounds, preferably those that were poor sedatives. Hundreds of such compounds had been made as each company sought to market its own barbiturate sedative, such as Abbott Laboratories' pentobarbital (Nembutal) and the Ely Lilly Co.'s, secobarbital (Seconal), two of the more popular drugs of this class.

Of the first eight compounds sent to them from the Parke Davis Laboratories one was diphenylhydantoin, which was first synthesized in 1908. The hydantoins were analogs of the barbiturates, as may be seen from the structures of phenobarbital and diphenylhydantoin (I, II), but they were not sufficiently sedative to be useful for that purpose. As in this case, it is frequent that the most useful compound is discovered early in such a study. Diphenylhydantoin blocked electroshock-induced convulsions in cats. The agent was safe and effective in their careful trials on epileptic patients, particularly those who had grand mal seizures. This compound came to be known as Dilantin.

Inevitably, hundreds of compounds were tested in the cat. Some were more active than diphenylhydantoin. 5-Isopropoxymethyl-5-phenylhydantoin was very effective in the cat. Several of these active compounds were checked for safety in laboratory animals at the Parke Davis Laboratories and then were administered to patients. Mostly, they were not well-tolerated by the patients. The transposition of laboratory findings in animals to the clinical situation in patients has always been an uncertain process about which more will be presented in Chapter 10 on Safety Assessment.

SUMMARY

Designed discovery has been defined as the deliberate, the purposeful, discovery. Its features as discussed in this chapter are the following:

(1) It starts with a good idea or lead.
(2) The idea has to occur to or be transmitted to someone who can use it.
(3) The idea should be conceived and expressed simply.
(4) The environment for research can be critical for good work, for discovery.
(5) The adequacy of the laboratory representation of the clinical correlates of the disease is critical.
(6) To be useful the laboratory experiments should be capable of meaningful quantification.
(7) The more adequate the appraisal the surer the transposition of laboratory results on the new agent to man.

COLLATERAL LITERATURE

Abraham, E. P., Chain, E., Fletcher, C. M., Gardner, A. D., Heatley, N. G., Jennings, M. A., and Florey, H. W. (1941): Further observations on penicillin, *Lancet 2:* 177–199.

Beyer, K. H. (1977): Discovery of the thiazides: Where biology and chemistry meet, *Persp. Biol. Med. 20:* 410–420.

Chain, E., Florey, H. W., Gardner, A. D., Heatley, N. G., Jennings, M. A., Orr-Ewing, J., and Sanders, A. G. (1940): Penicillin as a chemotherapeutic agent, *Lancet 2:* 226–228.

Ehrlich, P. (1910): Pro and contra salvarsan, *Wien. med. Wochschr. 61:* 14–19.

Ehrlich, P., and Bertheim, A. (1910): Diaminodioxyarsenobenzene. A remedy for syphilis produced under the name "606" or Salvarsan, U. S. Patent 986, 148, Mar. 7.

Hauptmann, A. (1912): Luminal bei Epilepsie, *München med. Wochschr. 59:* 1907.

Lehr, D. (1945): Clinical toxicity of sulfonamides. Inhibition of drug precipitation in the urinary tract by the use of sulfonamide mixtures. I. Sulfathiazole-Sulfadiazine mixture, *Proc. Soc. Exper. Biol. 58:* 11–14.

Merritt, H. H., Putnam, T. J., and Schwab, D. M. (1937): A new series of anticonvulsant drugs tested by experiments in animals, *Trans. Am. Neurol. Assoc. 63:* 123–128.

Merritt, H. H., and Putnam, T. J. (1938): Sodium diphenylhydantoinate in the treatment of convulsive disorders. *J.A.M.A. 111:* 1068–1072.

5.
Other Ways
to Discovery

"To be astonished at anything is the first movement of the mind towards discovery."
L. Pasteur [1822–1895]

The discovery of many useful drugs in the past quarter century or so did not come about by design, not in the sense set forth in the chapter on designed discovery. Individually, the examples cited in this chapter carry the elements of spontaneous discovery, luck, and serendipity as a dominating feature. As one thinks back over the circumstances that attended the discovery of these useful drugs, they seem to fall naturally into two categories. The first of these "other ways to discovery" has to do primarily with the individual (and his support). The second is a pharmacometric approach that only works very well under the supervision of the exceptional individual (or individuals).

Basic to each discovery was the alert investigator with the prepared mind. These discoveries "happened" to men knowledgeable and experienced in their respective work. As I have shown them, these "discoverers" have been willing to think beyond the facts. They have been willing to speculate or to rationalize from a background of facts and to experience a point of view and a course of action that go beyond the limits of knowledge, beyond the limits of what is accepted as factual.

THE BIOLOGISTS' APPROACH

In the first instance, the discovery derives from the way the physician, the biochemist, the physiologist, or the pharmacologist uses the elements of creativity, such as discernment, to circumvent the limits of knowledge. The most

35

(I)
CORTISONE

(II)
α-METHYLDOPA

dramatic example that comes to mind was the request by Phillip S. Hench, famed rheumatologist at the Mayo Clinic, for the "last gram" of cortisone that Lewis H. Sarett had synthesized (I). To that point, no particularly good use had been found for the steroid, the total synthesis (by Sarett) of which was an important contribution to chemistry in its own right. The basis for the request was the clinical impressions that some women were relieved of their rheumatoid arthritis during pregnancy and that arthritis tended to improve during illness with hepatitis and jaundice. Hench reasoned, or surmised, that under these conditions an increased production of hydrocortisone by the cortex of the patients' adrenal glands might be responsible for the relief from arthritis they experienced. Cortisone from Merck might help his patients. It did. He had made a discovery worthy of the Nobel Prize that he shared with his associate, E. C. Kendall, who was eminent among steroid chemists.

In a less spectacular but highly important situation, there were several papers in the literature on the inhibition of dopa decarboxylase by α-methyldopa [L-3-(3, 4-dihydroxyphenyl)-2-methyl-alanine] (II) when Sidney Udenfriend and Alfred Sjoerdsma, working at theNational Institutes of Health, requested a sample of that inhibitor for laboratory studies. They wanted to see whether it interfered with catecholamine synthesis sufficiently to lower the blood pressure of hypertensive patients. A number of α-methylamino acids, including methyldopa, had been made by Karl Pfister and his chemists who supplied the compound to Udenfriend. It was hypotensive in the patients at the National Institutes of Health. Methyldopa (Aldomet) has become one of the best accepted drugs for the management of hypertension.

In the area of mental health not a great deal is known about the physiological correlates of clinical disease. However, the recent introduction of L-Dopa [3-(3, 4-dihydroxyphenyl)-L-alanine] (III) for the management of Parkinson's disease is based on the fact that dopamine is the adrenergic amine responsible for the chemical transmission of nerve impulses between the caudate nucleus and the substantia nigra of the midbrain. This region is the so-called midbrain or extrapyramidal system because of its intermediate role in the development of the human brain. As this region of the brain ages, the local synthesis of dopamine seems to become inadequate to sustain the smooth flow of impulses to, especially, the postural voluntary muscles. This autonomic imbalance of dopaminergic and the opposing cholinergic nerve impulses results in the gross tremor and rigidity that are so trying for the advanced Parkinsonian patient.

The condition was best managed for years by an extract of belladonna alkaloids, of which the anticholinergic agent, atropine, was the principle active ingredient. When it was realized that both anticholinergic and antihistaminic agents had some beneficial effects, by bringing into better balance the opposing or balancing adrenergic and cholinergic nerve impulses, benztropine mesylate (Cogentin) was synthesized (IV) to provide both these attributes. The effect was to create a more favorable balance between the inadequate dopaminergic control of voluntary muscles and the relatively overriding or dominant cholinergic influence. Even so, it seemed reasonable that this imbalance might be managed better by adequate replacement of a dopamine deficit, if actually or functionally this was the case.

Providing dopamine *per se* orally or parenterally was not the answer because it did not cross the blood brain barrier. It could not get where it was

(III)
[3- (3, 4-Dihydroxyphenyl)-L-alanine]
(L-Dopa)

(IV)
COGENTIN

needed. On the other hand, L-Dopa (the amino acid from which dopamine was derived metabolically) given orally or otherwise was absorbed and did penetrate the brain. It was decarboxylated (metabolized) enzymatically to dopamine where it was needed in the brain. In most cases of Parkinsonism, the use of L-Dopa to control the tremors has supplanted substantially the use of previous anticholinergic agents because of the more favorable clinical response. Much of the credit for establishing the utility of L-Dopa (levodopa) in Parkinson's Disease in this country goes to G. C. Cotzias, M. D. Yahr, and the Research Division of Hoffmann–LaRoche (USA), the predominant source of this drug during its clinical study.

There is one more aspect of the L-Dopa story that is reminiscent of the probenecid designed discovery (Chapter 7). In this instance, much of the levodopa that is absorbed following oral administration is subject to decarboxylation by the dopa decarboxylase of other tissues, such as the liver, as well as by the midbrain. This systemic decarboxylation not only wastes the amino acid, but, also, the dopamine thus formed behaves as a pressor or adrenergic amine to create its own set of side effects that are sufficiently bothersome to preclude or limit the use of L-Dopa in some patients.

To negate the systemic build up of dopamine from L-Dopa outside the brain, a dopa decarboxylase inhibitor was sought that would be absorbed following oral administration but which would not cross the blood brain barrier. Such a compound would minimize the threat of systemic dopamine side effects while increasing the availability of L-Dopa for accumulation and decarboxylation where dopamine was needed. Such a compound, L-α-hydrazino-α-methyl-β-(3, 4-dihydroxyphenyl) propanoic acid (Carbidopa, V) was discovered and ultimately was coadministered orally with L-Dopa to Parkinsonian patients by the collaborative effort of a team of scientists and physicians at Merck. The practical therapeutic ratio of levodopa dosage to that of Carbidopa was 1:10.

The net result of the combined therapy (Sinemet) was to reduce the needed dose of L-Dopa and to minimize the systemic side effects that would have been attributable to dopamine, while seeming to introduce no untoward effects of its own.

(V)
L-α-Hydrazino-α-methyl-β-(3,4-dihydroxyphenyl) propanoic acid
(CARBIDOPA)

THE BIOCHEMISTS' APPROACH

The following is an example where a personal knowledge of comparative biochemistry and persistence sufficient to match conviction paid off. David Green, then a Director of Animal Science Research at Merck, reasoned that a certain sulfonamide, noted to be active against some form of the malaria parasite, should be studied in chickens infected with coccidiosis. Coccidiosis was a common scourge of the broiler and egg industries. I suppose I knew at one time why Dave was so certain of his belief, but the thing that is remembered more clearly is the lack of conviction his idea engendered in his associates, other than Max Tishler, Director of Development Chemistry at that time, who saw to it that the compound was made available and was evaluated for this purpose. The compound was effective in preventing infection. Sulfaquinoxaline (VI), the compound Green fancied, was the first of a series of coccidiostats without which the poultry industry could not exist economically today.

(VI)

SULFAQUINOXALINE

Thirty years ago, biochemists adapted the microbiologists' tools and methods to bring nutritional research, including vitamins B_{12} and folic acid, to its culmination. At that time (the 1940's), the derivatization of natural products and the synthesis of analogs thereof seemed certain to sustain the antimetabolite concept of new drug discovery. Except for some cancer chemotherapy, compounds so modeled were frequently too profound in their actions to be regarded as generally safe. On the other hand, cooperative effort of biochemists and microbiologists for the development of fermentation chemistry has been fundamental to both the discovery of interesting useful antibiotics, such as the tetracyclines and the penicillin congeners, and the production of other semisynthetic agents, including steroids.

THE CHEMISTS' APPROACH

Organic chemists as well as biochemists, biologists, and clinicians become personally involved in discovery — very much so. Time was when there was little, if any biomedical research of consequence in the pharmaceutical industries. The chemists mostly made the compounds and inadvertently or otherwise tried them on themselves or in some simple, usually *in vitro,* tests.

Beginning with a simple example, if I have my facts straight, a Sharp and Dohme chemist by the name of Frank Crosley had the task many years ago of making hexylresorcinol (VII), which the company was having studied as an anthelmintic agent. When one saw Frank he seemed always to have a pipe in his mouth. One day he decided to see what the stuff (hexylresorcinol) tasted like. He noted the local anesthetic effect of the compound on his tongue and passed along his observation. Formulated into a candy lozenge, this local anesthetic activity of hexylresorcinol figured conspicuously in the product history of that company years ago and is still prominently displayed in just about every drug store as Sucrets.

More seriously, it was the chemist, Albert Hofmann, who inadvertently discovered the hallucinogenic effect of D-lysergic acid diethylamide (LSD-25) by contact with the agent while working with lysergic acid derivatives (VIII). This was in the laboratories of Sandoz, a Swiss pharmaceutical company that had a heritage of this type of excellent chemistry. Discoveries of the nature recited in these two examples are more luck than serendipity and are off the mainstream of therapeutic advancements in spite of their importance.

Medicinal chemists are organic chemists who make their contribution to the discovery of new drugs by the synthesis of novel compounds that have therapeutic activity. Like chemists in other industries, they have their own way of interpreting what is novel. To them, any compound that has not been made previously is novel, and if it is discovered to have a utility that was unanticipated it may be patentable — a product patent may be obtainable. A

(VII)
4-HEXYLRESORCINOL

(VIII)
D-Lysergic acid diethylamide
(LSD)

(IX)
CHLORTRIMETON

compound that has been made even many years before its utility was dis-covered may still be considered novel and patentable as a product if it has not been disclosed in the literature. More about this in Chapter 16 where patents are discussed.

There are two conceptual extremes within which the medicinal chemist works in his search for useful compounds. On the one hand, he may search among analogs of an exciting new drug or one well established for another novel, useful agent. This is a more likely though less distinguished approach to a patentable compound, which may provide a protected way to enter a market to which a company did not have access, previously. "Molecule manipulation" was the lay derogation for this way of introducing the "nth" dissimilar antihistamine, anticholinergic, diuretic, etc. There is always the possibility that a product so arrived at may be important in its own right. For example, Schering's chlorpheniramine maleate (Chlortrimeton) (IX) was so superior in efficacy without burdensome sedation for many patients that its acceptance came to overshadow that of antihistaminic drugs marketed prior to its availability to physicians.

At the other extreme is the creative or independent chemist who searches among the physical aspects of organic chemistry for unique compounds that express his professional interest and which by example, class, or category may be unknown to the biologists. This approach runs the risk of little to show for substantial effort. Both the investigator and his management must be prepared for this outcome. On the other hand, given suitable biological support, the outcome may be a unique contribution to therapy, such as the discovery of Librium.

Leo H. Sternbach planned "to seek a hitherto little-explored class of heterocyclic compounds and then to synthesize new members of such a group in the hope of finding derivatives possessing the desired properties," in this instance new types of tranquilizers. He started by putting functionalizing groups on benzheptoxdiazines with which he had worked some 20 years earlier as a postdoctoral research assistant at the University of Cracow in Poland. Whereas the ones with which he had worked and the initial derivatives he made in the Hoffman–La Roche Laboratories, U.S.A., were inert or unin-teresting biologically, a secondary amino analog seemed to be what his pharmacologist counterpart, Lowell O. Randall, was seeking. Actually, in the

(X)

LIBRIUM

course of the chemical reaction of the starting material with methylamine a ring enlargement occurred unexpectedly to yield a benzodiazepine derivative. The compound survived preclinical and clinical investigation to reach the physician as Librium (X). From related 1, 4-benzodiazepin-2-ones came Valium and still other useful drugs.

It is by no means unusual that the break through compound in a new therapeutic advance is of a new class in medicinal chemistry. Sometimes the compound is arrived at directly without anticipation of a specific utility, as for diphenhydramine, the antihistaminic activity of which was discovered serendipitously, so far as the chemist was concerned. This seems to have been the case for the chemistry from which Librium and Valium were derived, also. On the other hand, the chemistry fit the predetermined objective of a type of biological activity for which the pharmacologists were searching in each instance.

THE PHARMACOMETRIC UNIT

The second approach to discovery discussed in this chapter relies more on the availability of many chemical compounds and a number of biological assays that represent to one extent or another the functions of enzymes, cells or organs, or organ systems. The test systems may represent the physiological correlates of disease or key determinants thereof. The procedures may be very sophisticated or complex involving whole animals and considerable instrumentation, time, and compound. They may be very simple tests, such that hundreds of assays on very little chemical can be performed in, say, a week's time. Some such tests can be computerized and, indeed, need be if they are to be analyzed systematically and economically. In some instances, such assays are best done under the supervision of an expert in a particular field. On the other hand, a satisfactory way to handle a number of not-too-difficult procedures is by organizing a pharmacometric unit of technicians under the supervision of an alert, capable, broadly interested pharmacologist.

The reason for such a pharmacometric unit of useful tests is the dictum around a large pharmaceutical research laboratory that every compound is a

(XI)

2, 4-Diamino-azo-benzene sulfonamide
(PRONTOSIL)

(XII)

4-Aminophenylsulfonamide
(SULFANILAMIDE)

new and potentially useful agent when submitted to a biological test in which it has not been tried previously. Examples that support this attitude about the potential utility of any compound include diphenylhydantoin (Dilantin) submitted by the chemists of Parke Davis and Co. to Merritt and Putnam in 1936 and which had been made by them some 10 years previously for testing as an hypnotic. Its synthesis was first described in 1911. It was not until the agent was tested by the neurologists in their cat electroshock test that it

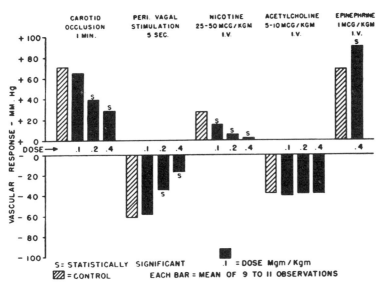

FIG. 1.   Effect of intravenous mecamylamine on various vascular autonomic responses in the vinbarbitalized dog. The response to carotid occlusion is in terms of an adjusted percent response, after the recommendations of Prochnick et al. (1950). This adjusted percent response may be read from the ordinate by considering mm Hg as percent change, as compared to controls. Note that only those responses requiring transmission of impulses through ganglia were significantly reduced by the drug; those effected through more peripheral mechanisms were not reduced. From Stone et al. (1956): J. Pharmacol. 117: 169–183.

$[(CH_3)_3N^+-(CH_2)_6-N^+-(CH_3)_3]2Br$

(XIII)
HEXAMETHONIUM BROMIDE

(XIV)
3-Methylaminoisocamphane hydrochloride
(MECAMYLAMINE)

seemed likely to be useful. Likewise, sulfanilamide, tested by the French scientists Trefouël, Nitti, and Bovet in 1935 as a metabolite of Domagk's prontosil, was first synthesized in 1908. The relationship between prontosil (XI) and its metabolite, sulfanilamide (XII) is evident from their structures.

The discovery of mecamylamine (Inversine) in a pharmacometric unit was certainly serendipitous. I recall being invited on the way to lunch one day to see a tracing or record from a cardiovascular experiment in Clement A. Stone's pharmacometric laboratory. Karl Pfister had submitted an isocamphane to that laboratory because the chemist thought it looked something like a cycloaliphatic amine. It might cause vasoconstriction and so raise blood pressure, for instance, in one of their tests. The compound had been made many years before when the chemists were synthesizing novel insoluble salts of penicillin. A merger of Merck with Sharp and Dohme had recently brought the two, chemist and pharmacologist, together. Dr. Stone's recording, such as is illustrated in Fig. 1, showed this secondary amine to be a ganglionic blocking agent, which was unprecedented. Heretofore, ganglionic blocking antihypertensive agents (such as hexamethonium; XIII) were mono- or di-quaternary ammonium compounds, erratically and poorly adsorbed when administered orally. The 3-methylaminoisocamphane, marketed in due time as mecamylamine (XIV) (Inversine), was a secondary amine and was very well absorbed when administered orally. Where physicians knew how to use ganglionic blocking antihypertensive agents, as in the British Commonwealth, the compound was well received. In the United States it mostly served to introduce the Merck Sharp and Dohme marketing area to the problems and practices of treating hypertension — which was worthwhile. It was their first product in that important field — before chlorothiazide (Diuril) and methyldopa (Aldomet).

So far as I know, I coined the term "pharmacometrics." The more usual concept of a screening program seemed hum drum and to be avoided as an unlikely source of fun and good fortune. In my experience, pharmacometric programs are most productive when kept small enough and sufficiently relevant to an eventual therapeutic end application to hold the attention and interest of the expert. Expanding the number of compounds tested from, say, six to sixty or six hundred per week by oversimplifying the tests and accepting a lesser relevance to clinical end application is to substitute largeness for greatness, in-so-far as productivity is measured.

BEYOND THE LIMITS OF KNOWLEDGE

To speak or write about working beyond the limits of knowledge is apt to evoke a disparity of reactions by the listeners or readers. Most of us have been trained to go to the literature for our "facts" based on how the investigators have interpreted their data. This always has been good practice and still is.

We are taught to believe that if we can understand a disease it should be easy enough to figure out, say, the molecular configuration of a definitive receptor mechanism somewhere along the line and to design a specific drug based on molecular orbital considerations or something. (The history of drug discovery does not bear this out.) And so we start out to understand the disease but never get around to doing much about therapy. There are vogues in interpreting what we believe to be "the facts." This can be misleading to the unwary. These failures to distinguish fact from fancy distort what we dimly recognize as the limits of knowledge. What we know — *what we think we know* — can be as much a limitation as an aid to progress.

To some extent, the intellectual shackles that bind us more and more as we probe deeply into a supposed cause and effect relationship become less bothersome the broader our knowledge, experience, and understanding of the ways of science and medicine — the greater our discernment between fact, important fact, and fancy.

Another reaction to the concept of working beyond the limits of knowledge reminds me of the way people must have felt when they thought the earth was flat. How can one dare to talk of working beyond the limits of knowledge, how hazardous, how fruitless, how misleading! What is there with which to work, beyond the limits of knowledge; as though there was just space or even a vacuum.

From a philosophical standpoint, one might argue that the body of knowledge is spherical; that to pursue one thought very far is to encounter another and so on until ultimately one is confronted with the original idea. This might account for why some problems are solved from different directions by different people, sometimes more or less concurrently. But, it is the nature of the void beyond the limits of knowledge that entertains us momentarily. It offers no resistance to either new knowledge or new therapy, though people do. The nice thing about discovering new therapy is that it invariably carries with it a moiety of new knowledge, a dual accomplishment.

SUMMARY

To my mind, it is a conceit for a scientist to insist that he can work productively from within the limits of (his) knowledge. I do not recall any really useful new drug that was discovered this way. Although it was not intended to be so, every discovery mentioned in this chapter contributed to knowledge. In some instances it would seem that clinical impression or the desire to explore a theory of dopaminergic neurohumoral transmission in the peripheral or central nervous system led to a useful new drug. This is not serendipity, but perhaps the first two examples of discovery by chemists (the local anesthetic effect of hexylresorcinol and the hallucinogenic effect of LSD) might be considered so. Perhaps the discovery of Librium and Valium might be considered designed discovery, but I would not argue that this was so. From what has been published about the chemistry leading to Librium and Valium, it seems that Sternbach decided to explore a series of compounds for biological activity. This led to chemicals that fitted the pharmacologist's, Randall's, interest; very much like the discovery of the antihistamine diphenhydramine by Loew at the Parke Davis Laboratories.

The example cited for how a pharmacometric unit works represents a faith that most every compound has a biological effect that only needs to be discovered. Chances are that a compound will not become a useful drug, but whether a biological effect is found depends on how broadly it is tested, the relevance of the laboratory test to the clinical situation, and the acuity of the biologist entrusted with that assessment.

Having discussed the many ways to discovery, we turn in the next chapter to the tailoring of a new drug — an exciting, exacting process.

COLLATERAL LITERATURE

Birkmayer, W., and Hornykiewicz, O. (1961): Der L-3, 4-dioxyphenylalanin (DOPA) effekt bei der Parkinson — Akinese, *Wien, Klin. Wochenschr. 73:* 787–788.

Cotzias, G. C., vonWoert, M. M., and Schiffer, L. M. (1967): Aromatic aminoacids and modification of Parkinsonism, *N.E.J.M. 276:* 374–379.

Polley, H. F., and Slocumb, C. H. (1976): Behind the scenes with cortisone and ACTH, *Mayo Clinic Proceedings 51:* 471–477.

Sternbach, L. H. (1972): The discovery of Librium, *Agents and Actions 2:* 193–196.

Stone, C. A., Torchiana, M. L., Navarro, A., and Beyer, K. H. (1956): Ganglionic blocking properties of 3-methylaminoisocamphane hydrochloride (mecamylamine): a secondary amine, *J. Pharmacol. Exper. Therap. 117:* 169–183.

Trefouël, J., Trefouël, Mme., Niti, F., and Bovet, D. (1935): Activite de p-aminophenylsulfamide sur les infections streptoccocciques de la souris et du lapin, *C. R. Soc. Biol. (Paris) 120:* 756–758.

Yahr, M. D., ed. (1973): Treatment of parkinsonism – the role of dopa decarboxylase inhibitors, *Adv. Neurol.*, New York, Raven Press, Vol. 2.

Yahr, M. D., Duvoisin, R. C., Hoehn, M. M., Schear, M. J., and Barrett, R. E. (1968): L-Dopa (L-3, 4-Dihydroxyphenylamine) – Its clinical effects in parkinsonism, *Trans. Amer. Neurol. Assoc. 93:* 56–63.

Hench, P. S., Kendall, E. C., Slocumb, C. H., and Polley, H. P. (1950): Effects of cortisone acetate and pituitary ACTH on rheumatoid arthritis, rheumatic fever and certain other conditions: a study in clinical physiology *Arch. Int. Med. 85:* 545–666.

Hench, P. S., Kendall, E. C., Slocumb, C. H., and Polley, H. F. (1949): The effect of a hormone of the adrenal cortex (17-hydroxy-11-dehydrocorticosterone; compound E) and of pituitary adrenocorticotropic hormone on rheumatoid arthritis, *Proc. Staff Mtg., Mayo Clin. 24:* 181–196.

6.
Tailoring a
New Drug

THE FOUR KEY ELEMENTS

Tailoring a new drug is the definitive work that goes into designed discovery, fitting the attributes of a compound to clinical needs. The project should start with (1) a specific, clearly defined objective, (2) a well conceived, relevant biological approach at the laboratory level to the critical physiological correlate(s) of the clinical situation, one that can be quantitated, (3) a good idea as to where to start the chemical effort, and (4) a good appreciation of what conditions need to have been met if a compound is to be judged suitable for development. In the sense we have used the expression, tailoring a new drug pertains to the procedures and decisions that go into the chemical and biological assessments for the selection of one or more compounds for development. It might be argued that everything that goes into finding a new drug and fitting it to the patient, including a final dosage form and package circular, is relevant to tailoring a new drug. This latter attitude is too general to be helpful.

Inevitably, every story about the discovery of a new drug is different in detail. On the other hand, there are basic aspects of the designed discovery of new drugs that are common to most. By analogy, managing one company is bound to be different from directing another. Even so, there are principles of decision making and of management that are applicable to running different companies in dissimilar industries. If one were to consider whether these factors mentioned in the previous paragraph were unique to drug discovery, he or she would realize that they are really specific applications of decision making. Every successful executive knows that the more precisely one can define an objective, the more accurately the approach thereto can be set forth. The more surely the realities imposed on an objective are appreciated, the better the basis for decision will be, and the better assurance that the decision will be correct. The designed discovery of new therapy is not so different.

First, let us consider some general comments, mostly about pitfalls in the search for new drugs, and three examples of increasing complexity to illustrate designed discovery and the tailoring of a new drug. The first example, metaraminol, is in this chapter. The others, probenecid and chlorothiazide, are presented in the next two chapters.

INTERACTION BETWEEN BIOLOGIST AND CHEMIST

Given good biological support and enthusiastic motivation, the medicinal chemist will try to give the biologist most anything he wants. More precisely, the chemist will try to make a compound that will do what the biologist says he wants it to do. If the biologist expresses his criteria for a specific purpose in terms that are too general, he is likely to get one or more compounds that are active but which may do enough other things about as well that would render the agent useless. It is likely to induce a multiplicity of effects, pharmacodynamic or toxic, that are so profound as to render the agent unsatisfactory – except, perhaps, as a life-saving or life-prolonging measure. Much of today's cancer chemotherapy falls into this category of limited utility.

If the investigator expresses *the principal criterion* as the *in vitro* inhibition of a "pure" or specific enzyme, the likelihood of the inhibitor proving therapeutically useful and safe for that reason alone is remote. This is regardless of the relevance of that enzyme to the modulation of a specific function the abberation of which constitutes disease. Today it still seems unpopular to insist that cells are a great deal more than bags of many important things. Coordinated function does require structure as well and it is the integrative actions of cells, many tissues and several organs with which we must deal carefully as we tailor a new drug. (So-called "models" of disease are less apt to intrigue the biochemically oriented investigator. They will be dealt with in Chapter 8.)

HOW NOT TO GO ABOUT TAILORING A NEW DRUG

The less sophisticated biochemically oriented biologist (or chemist) tends to find the following unlikely hypothetical approach to the search for new drugs irresistible. For example, our investigator has just learned of an enzyme (preferably a newly discovered one as yet poorly understood) that is reported to be involved fundamentally in a biological reaction associated with some important function like contraction, secretion, growth, etc. Ergo, a potent inhibitor of that enzymatic reaction may be just what is needed to treat some disease of which our uninitiated but enthusiastic friend has heard. All he needs to solve the problem is a simple *in vitro* assay that involves the indirect measurement of that enzymatic reaction in a cell-free medium. Compounds can be added, one or several at a time, to determine their inhibitory effect on the system. Simplicity and capability to assay large numbers of compounds make the proposal irresistible – almost rational. Thus, the search is on. The course of his enthusiasm for the project, up to the point that an equally "rational" idea takes its place, can be anticipated as follows.

After screening a few hundred or a thousand compounds as enzyme inhibitors in the simple test system, there are likely to be 8 to 10 structures in perhaps as many chemical series that inhibit the *in vitro* system at 10^{-3} molar concentration and at least a couple that are active at 10^{-5}. This can be counted on. The investigator is likely to rationalize that "obviously, those active at 10^{-5} molar concentration should be tried in patients, tomorrow. We can do the animal safety stuff later, if it works. This is for people, not dogs and cats, and the disease is important, isn't it?" The polite answer is "Let's see what else the compound you want to put in patients does, first."

Actually, the experienced medicinal chemist is apt to prevail quietly on a pharmacologist friend to slip such a compound into an animal or two to see what happens. This, too, can be misleading. Most times one of three things will happen when the chemical is given to animals – preferably systemically: (1) absolutely nothing, or (2) something devastating, or (3) it is unclear whether something happened. The results depend on whether the dose was selected on a body weight basis commensurate with the *in vitro* inhibitory concentration, or one big enough to do something, or on the appropriateness and adequacy of the examination. To carry the project further usally involves other scientists and a sharing of enthusiasm and priorities regarding time and responsibilities. Such a natural barrier is ordinarily, but not necessarily, too much for the poorly conceived impulse to surmount.

IMPORTANCE OF COLLATERAL OR
SUPPORTIVE RESEARCH

What is wrong with the research approach just dramatized? After all, the basic concepts of enzymology have stood us in good stead in our research. What is wrong is that such an approach to discovery as that described above is inadequate. In one sense it is too restrictive and in another it is too general. It is too restrictive in that the *in vitro* assay was the primary approach to the problem rather than supportive. Such methodology should not have to stand alone as a primary basis for selection of compounds for clinical trial. It needs to be supported by or, better still, supportive of other protocols that encompass more of the relevant physiological or clinical situation. The *in vitro* assay could not possibly anticipate other actions of effective compounds such as their absorption or elimination. The assay may be too general in that it would be unlikely to discriminate, except perhaps grossly, between toxic and non-toxic inhibitors. Unless such projects receive much collateral concurrent, rather than sequential, support from animal experimentation relevant to the clinical situation, their chance of success is poor.

Several examples will illustrate the importance of including collateral or supportive approaches in the tailoring process. For instance, metaraminol (Aramine) derived from a modest program in the late 1930's and early 1940's to develop a safer, more metabolically stable pressor amine for the management of shock, as during surgery. The three types of current research that were essential to the structure/activity studies leading to metaraminol (racemic form) were (1) the relationship of structure to cardiac irritability induced by pressor amines during cyclopropane, ether, or chloroform anesthesia, (2) the relationship of structure to pressor potency, duration, and reproducibility of action of such compounds and (3) the refractoriness of such agents to metabolic degradation as understood at that time. The metabolic studies alone were inadequate by themselves but were critical to the thought that led to the synthesis and study of this compound.

APPLICATION OF BASIC PRINCIPLES OF
ENZYMOLOGY TO PHYSIOLOGY

Probenecid is an example of the application of a well known principle in enzymology to the development of an adjunct to penicillin therapy. This principle of competitive inhibition of one enzyme substrate by another substrate (or compound) which may or may not be refractory to the action of that enzyme was important to the structure/activity work leading to probenecid (Benemid). However, the information that penicillin was secreted by the tubules of the kidney was also needed. Under appropriate conditions, discussed in Chapter 7, it could be shown that both probenecid, which had no effect on enzyme systems critical to cellular metabolism, would block penicillin or *p*-aminohippurate (PAH) uptake and secretion by the cells of the renal tubules, competitively and reversibly.

IMPORTANCE OF SITE OF ACTION

The concept of carbonic anhydrase inhibition was critical to the structure/activity research leading to chlorothiazide. However, where these compounds act in the nephron (the functional unit of the kidney) and their relative lipid solubility are more important to their saluretic (salt and water excreting) activity and dosage than is the order of carbonic anhydrase inhibitory activity, per se. Perhaps the following more detailed accounts of these three examples in this and the next two chapters will be helpful for an understanding of the initial aspects of the tailoring of a new drug.

METARAMINOL – CASE HISTORY

In the late 1930's and early 1940's those of us who worked with Walter J. Meek, Professor of Physiology at the University of Wisconsin Medical School, were interested in one aspect or another of sympathomimetic (adrenergic) amines. (See Fig. 1 for chemical structures of such compounds.) Also, the resident staff of Ralph Waters, Professor of Anesthesiology, spent a year or so of their training in the laboratory working with Meek and his graduate students. Mostly, the work that involved the anesthesiologists pertained to cardiac arrhythmias that occurred during general anesthesia. Adrenalin (epinephrine) and norepinephrine, the most potent blood pressure raising (pressor) agents, were also the worse offenders in inducing arrhythmias as is diagrammed in Fig. 1. These drugs were commonly employed to raise blood pressure of patients undergoing surgery under general anesthesia, such as cyclopropane.

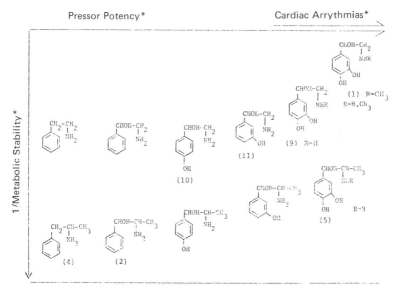

FIG. 1.   Metabolic stability, pressor potency, and proclivity to induce cardiac irregularities of certain β-phenylethylamine analogs. Numbers refer to compounds listed by name in Table I. (*Not to scale.)

TABLE I

Cardiac Arrhythmias Resulting from Injection of Blood Pressure Raising
Drugs in Doses Equal in Effectiveness to 0.01 mgm. of Adrenalin per
Kilogram during Surgical Cyclopropane Anesthesias[a]

Procedure	Dosage	Number of Animals	A-V Block	A-V Nodal Extrasystoles	Ventricular Extrasystoles	Nodal Rhythm Slow Ventricular Rhythm	Ventricular Tachycardia	Ventricular Fibrillation	Sino-Auricular Tachycardia
	mgm. per kgm.								
1. Adrenalin control	0.01	19	10	12	7	15	5	3	0	0
Adrenalin with cyclopropane	0.01	20	1	9	10	7	0	20	5	17
2. Ephedrine control	4.0	13	9	9	8	8	5	1	0	0
Ephedrine with cyclopropane	4.0	13	0	0	10	5	0	2	0	13
3. Propadrin control	3.0	11	10	5	5	4	5	0	0	1
Propadrin with cyclopropane	3.0	10	0	0	3	0	0	0	0	8
4. Benzedrine control	5.0	11	1	6	4	2	0	0	0	2
Benzedrine with cyclopropane	5.0	10	1	0	1	1	0	1	0	10
5. Cobefrin control	0.025-	11	6	6	5	7	4	1	0	0
Cobefrin with cyclopropane	0.05	10	0	2	4	6	1	10	1	3
6. Kephrine control	1.0	4	2	3	2	3	1	0	0	0
Kephrine with cyclopropane	0.50-0.75	4	0	0	4	2	0	4	0	4
7. Epinine control	0.10	6	2	1	2	4	0	0	0	0
Epinine with cyclopropane	0.10	7	0	0	6	5	0	7	1	5
8. Paredrine control	0.75-	8	1	5	2	6	0	0	0	0
Paredrine with cyclopropane	1.0	7	0	1	3	0	0	1	0	5
9. Arterenol control	0.01	6	2	5	2	5	4	0	0	0
Arterenol with cyclopropane	0.01	5	1	1	4	3	2	4	0	2
10. Synephrin control	3.0-	6	2	2	5	1	3	0	0	0
Synephrin with cyclopropane	5.0	4	0	0	3	1	0	0	0	4
11. Neosynephrin control	0.05	10	4	3	5	2	1	1	0	0
Neosynephrin with cyclopropane	0.05	10	0	0	1	0	0	0	0	0

[a]From Orth et al., *J. Pharmacol. 67:* 1-16, 1939.

The combination of cyclopropane with either of the catecholamines, epine-phrine or norepinephrine, was perhaps the greatest offender in general use. This was unfortunate since cyclopropane was the favored anesthetic at Wisconsin at the time, and these were the most potent pressor amines. These potent pressor agents were transient in their duration of action which required that they be administered continuously intravenously and monitored carefully when they were used to sustain blood pressure.

In the one example where Orth, Leigh, Mellish, and Stutzman could com-pare the *para* and *meta*-hydroxyphenyl-β-ethanolmethyl amines, the *meta* compound seemed less inclined to upset the normal rhythm of the heart (Table I, compounds 10 and 11, respectively). Only the compounds that possessed a methyl group adjacent to the carbon atom bearing the primary or secondary amine had a more useful duration of action (Table I, compounds, 2, 3, 4, and 8). However, such α-methyl-β-phenylethylamines (also called phenylisopropylamines) rapidly induced tachyphylaxis (decreasing pressor response) to their repeated intravenous administration, if they possessed no hydroxyl group on the benzene ring. At the other extreme, the catecholamines that bore an α-methylphenylethylamine side chain were among the most in-clined to induce cardiac irregularities (compare compounds 5 and 6 with 1, 7, and 9 of Table I).

My own interests in such compounds came to be in their pressor potency and their metabolic disposition (the way they were altered in the body and excreted). It seemed that this matter of how the drug was attacked by the body could be influenced to yield a more stable, potent compound that might not possess the proclivity of the catecholamines to induce cardiac arrhythmias. Important compounds, that will be discussed in the next several paragraphs, and their structure/activity relationships are set forth in Fig. 1.

A first step in this effort to discover a safe, stable potent compound was to confirm Herman Blaschko's then new observation that arylalkylamines, such as phenethylamine, were deaminated by the monoamine oxidase of liver and other tissues unless the compounds were protected from deamination by an alkyl group, such as methyl on the carbon bearing the amino group (Fig. 2). Such α-methyl-β-phenylethylamines (otherwise known as phenylisopropyla-mines) were stable metabolically and active orally, amphetamine being an example (Fig. 2). In neither the metabolic work nor the experiments on blood pressure in dogs did it seem to matter much whether one was dealing with a primary amine ($R-NH_2$) or a secondary methyl amino group ($R-NHCH_3$), but tertiary amines or longer chain alkylamino agents were less pressor. Com-parisons of effects on blood pressure showed that β-hydroxylation of the side chain enhanced activity and so these two features (α-methylation and β-hy-droxyisopropanolamine side chain, were retained for the new compound.

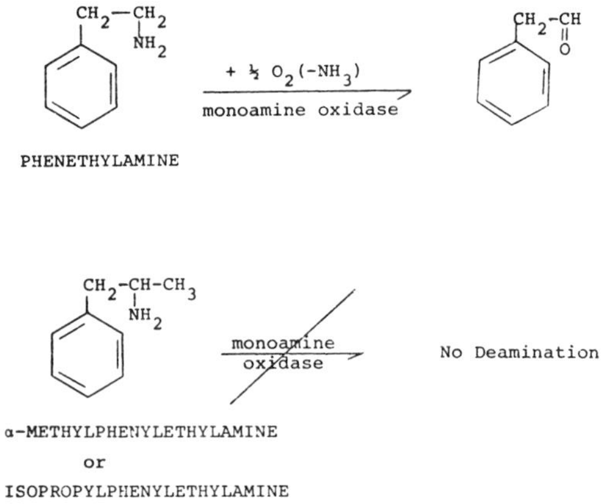

CH$_2$—CH$_2$
NH$_2$

$+ \frac{1}{2}$ O$_2$ (-NH$_3$)
—————————————→
monoamine oxidase

CH$_2$—CH
‖
O

PHENETHYLAMINE

CH$_2$-CH-CH$_3$
NH$_2$

monoamine
oxidase

No Deamination

α-METHYLPHENYLETHYLAMINE
or
ISOPROPYLPHENYLETHYLAMINE

FIG. 2.   Relationship of structure to the ability of monoamine oxidase to deaminate certain arylalkylamines.

As a second step the catechol nucleus, the 3, 4-dihydroxy substitution on the ring, was ruled out, conceptually. It was too unstable (Fig. 3). It underwent oxidation to an orthoquinone and beyond by the phenol oxidase and ascorbic acid/dehydroascorbic acid oxidation systems we had at the time. In addition, the catechol nucleus was conjugated enzymatically and excreted as the inactive sulfate. [Later it was shown by Axelrod (1966) that the catechol nucleus could also undergo methylation (Fig. 3). In turn, the methylated nucleus could undergo conjugation as a sulfate or glucuronide.]

The effect of positioning a single hydroxyl group in the ring on its activity and stability was examined. The *ortho*-hydroxy substitution in such compounds was not important to pressor potency, but the *meta* or *para* positioning of the phenolic group was. The organic chemistry literature recognized

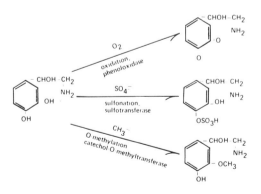

FIG. 3.

at that time that a *para*-hydroxy compound would be easily converted to the corresponding still more unstable catechol by introducing the adjacent *meta*-hydroxyl group oxidatively. In my experience, phenol oxidase converted the *para*-hydroxy analogs to the corresponding catechols rapidly, regardless of the nature of the side chain. The same chemical literature taught that it was difficult to introduce a second hydroxyl substitution into the ring in a position adjacent to a *meta*-phenolic group. From this precedent, the *meta*-hydroxy ring system should be the more stable. Actually, it was not oxidized by phenol oxidase in the one example available to me at the time. That compound (Neosynephrine or phenylephrine) was a potent pressor agent. Its short duration of action was interpreted as being due to the sensitivity of the β-phenylethanolamine side chain to deamination by monoamine oxidase.

From the sum of my studies on pressor potency and factors that contributed to the metabolic stability of potent compounds, β-(*meta*-hydroxyphenyl)-β-isopropanolamine (I) seemed to be the compound that I wanted. The synthesis

[β-(Meta-hydroxyphenyl-β-isopropanolamine]
(ARAMINE®; METARAMINOL)

of the racemic form of the compound was then found to have appeared in the foreign patent literature. Also, Walter Hartung had patented it in the United States in 1935. That it had been made was not remarkable. Hundreds of these compounds had been made since the classic paper of Barger and Dale in 1910, wherein they likened the action of some of these amines to stimulation of the sympathetic nerves. They called them *sympathomimetic amines.* The importance of this *meta*-hydroxy compound seemed to have gone unnoticed, understandably. I synthesized sufficient of the racemic compound to permit me to confirm the theoretical basis for its selection. After I joined Sharp and Dohme in 1943, my new associates, Edward Engelhardt and James Sprague resolved the isomers, the levo form of which is marketed as metaraminol (Aramine). In spite of the academic equivocation as to whether a pressor amine should be given to a patient in shock (that originated before the initiation of this work), metaraminol has continued to serve this purpose since it was made available some 30 years ago. This was my first experience in designed discovery; one idea, one compound, one drug.

There is a bit of serendipity to the story, though. When I reviewed the field of sympathomimetic amines in 1946 for Physiological Reviews, there was still a great deal of uncertainty about how such compounds acted. Two decades later, when we were intensely interested in the mode of action of the important antihypertensive agent, a-methyldopa (Aldomet), both compounds (metaraminol and a-methyldopa) came to assume importance in the development of the false transmitter theory of adrenergic drug action. Metaraminol has served its purpose well as a therepeutic agent and as it contributed to a better understanding of neurohumoral adrenergic nerve transmission. Possibly, this story contributes some understanding of designed discovery by its simplicity. That first step in tailoring a new drug consists basically of a critical (a definitive) analysis of what needs to be done and then the reconstruction or synthesis of the determinants of these needs as in the structure of a new drug.

SUMMARY

Oversimplified, there are two parts to every designed discovery, analysis of the problem then synthesis of its solution. This is not different, conceptually at least, from the process by which sound decisions are made regardless of whether they be research, or management, or just one's daily affairs. There are better examples of greater complexity that represent the tailoring of a new drug, such as the work leading to probenecid (Benemid) discussed in Chapter 7.

COLLATERAL LITERATURE

Axelrod, J. (1966): Methylation reactions in the formation and metabolism of catecholamines and other biogenic amines: the enzymatic conversion of norepinephrine (NE) to epinephrine E, *Pharmacol. Rev. 18:* 95–113.

Barger, G., and Dale, H. H. (1910): Chemical structure and sympathomimetic action of amines, *J. Physiol. 41:* 19–59.

Beyer, K. H. (1941): The enzymatic inactivation of substituted phenylpropyl-(sympathomimetic)-amines, *J. Pharmacol. 71:* 151–163.

Beyer, K. H. (1943): The relation of molecular configuration to the rate of deamination of sympathomimetic amines by aminase, *J. Pharmacol. 70:* 85–95.

Beyer, K. H. (1943): Relation of molecular configuration to inactivation of sympathomimetic amines in the presence of phenol oxidase, *J. Pharmacol. 77:* 247–257.

Beyer, K. H. (1946): Sympathomimetic amines: the relation of structure to their action and inactivation, *Physiol. Rev. 26:* 169–197.

Beyer, K. H., and Lee, W. V. (1942): The fate of certain sympathomimetic amines in the body, *J. Pharmacol. 74:* 155–162.

Orth, O. S., Leigh, M. D., Mellish, C. H. and Stutzman, J. W. (1939): Action of sympathomimetic amines in cyclopropane, ether and chloroform anesthesia, *J. Pharmacol. 67:* 1–16.

7.
Tailoring a Second New Drug

PHYSIOLOGICAL ECONOMY OF PENICILLIN

The pharmacological properties of penicillin made it seem as though Providence never intended this antibiotic for use by man. It seemed to be poorly absorbed when administered by mouth. It was unstable at acid pH, such as that found in the stomach. It was bound to plasma proteins, which limited the effective concentration in the body to the lesser amount that was free in plasma for diffusion into tissues. Every bit brought by the bloodstream to the kidney was excreted as the drug passed through that organ. Moreover, it was present in only trace amounts in the broth in which the earlier strains of *Penicillium notatum* were grown, even when the mold was cast on the surface of a culture medium. It was easier to recover the antibiotic, that which had escaped destruction, from the urine of patients for recycling to the next patient, so to speak, than to produce the agent. (Actually, it turned out that there were several natural penicillins that all had the same bad features, penicillin-G being the one that received the greatest attention.) On the other hand, penicillin was by all odds the safest and most effective chemotherapeutic agent known. It was man's will that the many perversities of its nature be overcome. They were overcome, from the development of a deep culture fermentation process for the culture of strains of Penicillium that produced the chemotherapeutic agent in abundance to the recent availability of semisynthetic penicillins more amenable to the physician's use (ampicillin, for example).

OTHER EFFORTS (DOSAGE FORMS) TO RETAIN PENICILLIN

When penicillin was so scarce, in the days of World War II and into the later 1940's, any means for retaining it in the body seemed important. The pharmaceutical chemists made poorly soluble salts such as procaine penicillin for injection so as to prolong its stay in the body, even at low tissue concentrations. To serve the same purpose, the potassium salt of penicillin was suspended in a horrendous mess of bees-wax and oil (mineral oil) to be injected with awe and enthusiasm into the buttocks of "my fair lady" or her pooch, depending on which was being presented to the doctor. It still hurts to think about such a pharmaceutical indignity.

This latter penicillin formulation was not our invention, but it taught me a great deal about the marketing of drugs as we tried to compete with such a conceptually simple overwhelmingly successful product. Our own physiologically sophisticated, microbiologically much more rational, and pharmaceutically unprecedented oral formulation of probenecid (Benemid) with penicillin-G was new, conceptually, hence, poorly understood and seldom used by the physician.

THE MUTUAL SUPPRESSION OF RENAL FUNCTION TESTS

It seemed to us that penicillin must be secreted by the tubules of the kidney to be so rapidly excreted. Homer Smith and his school of renal physiologists at New York University had shown renal tubular secretion to be the case for phenol red, iodopyracet (Diodrast) and the then new p-aminohippurate (PAH). The iodinated compounds were developed for the radioscopic visualization of the drug in the kidney or as renal function tests, phenol red (phenolsulfonphthaline, PSP), having been used for this latter purpose for years. Smith and his associates had reported that these renal function tests had to be used separately. If the clearance of two such compounds was measured concurrently, their values were less than when measured individually; the "apparent" renal function so measured was abnormally low. To measure renal function reliably, the compounds had to be given individually.

FACTORS THAT MOTIVATED RESEARCH
ON PENICILLIN EXCRETION

The following two problems available from the literature — the problem of rapid penicillin excretion and the problem of mutual suppression of renal function tests — served as a partial basis for our first experiment in designed discovery as a team. There were five other factors that served to motivate us at the outset of our work on penicillin excretion.

(1) The tremendous need for the physiological conservation of penicillin by the patient.

(2) The Sharp and Dohme pharmaceutical chemists occasionally filled ampules with *p*-aminohippurate (PAH) for Smith's development of function tests on renal blood flow and the functional capacity (Tm) of the renal tubules to secrete that hippuric acid analog. Thus, PAH was available to us.

(3) In 1943, we had established a capability to conduct modern renal clearance studies in trained dogs so that we could study the elimination of sulfonamides. (This was done following a brief visit, to learn this basic technique, to the laboratories of James A. Shannon and his remarkable team, then at the Goldwater Memorial Hospital, New York City.)

(4) The knowledge of and experience with sulfonamide chemistry possessed by James M. Sprague and his medicinal chemists on the team were unique.

(5) A concept of how to use these resources to conserve penicillin in the body.

CONCEPT OF COMPETITIVE INHIBITION APPLIED TO PENCILLIN EXCRETION

The initial objective of our research on penicillin excretion was simple but unique conceptually. It could be expressed in two simple questions. (1) Was penicillin secreted by the renal tubules? and (2) If penicillin was secreted by the renal tubules, could that secretion be inhibited by the concurrent administration of PAH? The unique part, so far as we knew, was introducing the concept of competitive inhibition of the action of a definitive enzyme in what might be a very complex transport system. In enzymology, the inhibition of succinoxidase action on succinate by malonate was a classic example of competitive reversible inhibition of an enzyme's action on one substrate by another compound. In my own analogous experience, α-methyl-β-phenylethylamine (β-phenylisopropylamine) was refractory to monoamine oxidase, but it could inhibit the deamination of β-phenylethylamine by that enzyme (Chapter 5, II). This was one way of looking at the opposite side of what Smith had seen as a problem in the clinical laboratory assessment of renal function — the organic acids could only be used one at a time as renal function tests because of their interference one with another.

To do the experiments that would answer these two questions regarding penicillin excretion a team, composed of biologists for the renal clearances in trained dogs and analysts for both the chemical and microbiological assays, was employed. The certainty with which these rather complex experiments could be controlled and interpreted by a well coordinated team made them seem simple and exciting. The psychology of team research can be that such studies extended around the clock in anesthetized dogs for 72 to 96 hours take on the nature of carefully monitored clinical situations where the modulation of electrolyte balance and the physiological well being of the (animal) patient become the excited concern of the whole laboratory. Sleep doesn't seem very important at such times. This is a proper atmosphere for discovery, such as was mentioned as a fourth factor (the environment of discovery) in Chapter 4.

The renal tubular secretion of penicillin was evident from the first clearance experiment performed on the compound. Like PAH, its rate of elimination approximated renal plasma flow, which is to say that the blood circulating

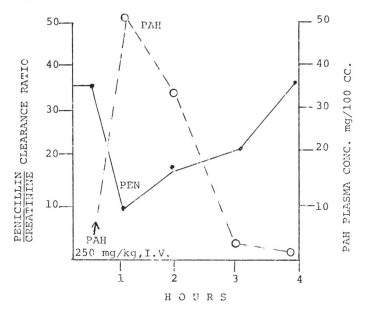

FIG. 1. Inhibition of penicillin (PEN) rate of excretion (penicillin/creatinine clearance ratio) as a reversible function of p-aminohippurate plasma concentration (PAH) in the dog. Penicillin-G was administered at a constant rate before and following PAH injection. PAH was administered intravenously at an initial rate sufficient to produce saturation of the renal tubular secretory mechanism and then at progressively slower rates to permit a gradual fall in its plasma level.

through the kidney was completely cleared of the antibiotic in a single passage.

The coadministration of PAH did inhibit the tubular secretion of penicillin (Fig. 1), the extent of the inhibition depending on the relative amounts of the two compounds presented to the tubules simultaneously for secretion. This inhibition of penicillin excretion, except for glomerular ultrafiltration, did give a three-and-one-half to fourfold increase in plasma antibiotic concentration in the dog. The same prompt elevation of penicillin plasma concentration by the coadministration of PAH and its immediate reversibility when the inhibitor was removed could also be demonstrated easily in patients.

Whereas PAH served the purpose of demonstrating the principle of competitive inhibition of a renal tubular transport mechanism, it was not anticipated to be a practical solution to the penicillin conservation problem. PAH was even less well absorbed than penicillin when administered orally. Moreover, it was as rapidly excreted as was penicillin and although it seemed perfectly safe and could be administered intravenously at any needed dosage together with penicillin, the daily dose of as much as 200 grams was unrealistic except as a life-saving measure. It was used for this dramatic purpose in a few patients to reaffirm that if the plasma concentration of penicillin could be gotten high enough and sustained for a manageable amount of time, the antibiotic could save the life of a patient who previously would have died of subacute bacterial endocarditis, a uniformly fatal disease until the advent of penicillin.

COMPETITIVE INHIBITION BY REFRACTORY SUBSTRATES

The principle in enzymology that formed the rationale for this work would admit the possibility of inhibiting the tubular secretion of penicillin by a compound which was not secreted *per se* by that transport mechanism. Exploration of this concept called for the addition of medicinal chemists to the team in the hope of synthesizing such an inhibitor.

When the question of where to start the chemical effort came up, modifying the PAH structure seemed reasonable. We had the biological background of our research on PAH and penicillin. Moreover, PAH seemed attractive to our chemists. As illustrated in Fig. 2, one could build on either end of *p*-aminobenzoic acid, its metabolic progenitor, with the hope of introducing oral absorption and a reduced rate of excretion of the inhibitor. Actually, it did not seem far-fetched that good oral absorption and slower excretion could be built into the same molecule.

Our first approximation of what we wanted was the compound carinamide (Staticin), which will be recognized by its structure (Fig. 2) as a sulfonamide.

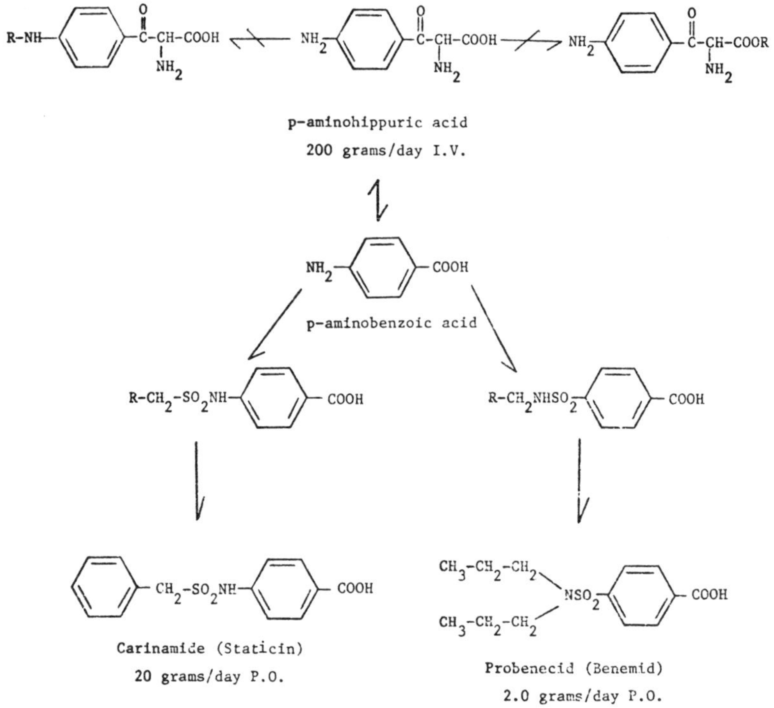

FIG. 2. Structure/activity relationships pertaining to the discovery of carinamide (Staticin) and probenecid (Benemid).

It did inhibit penicillin secretion. The clearance of the compound seemed at first to be equivalent to glomerular filtration rate which would require a daily dosage higher than one would want for man. In the "spit and polish" pre-clinical work on the agent we found that a large amount (about half) of the carinamide given to animals was actually conjugated in tissues and appeared as the glucuronide in both blood and urine. This metabolism of the drug had the effect of doubling the anticipated clinical dose to 20 grams a day; again much too high an oral dose to be practical though it was safe. This drug was studied clinically as carinamide (Staticin) without great enthusiasm or high hopes. It was not marketed. We continued our effort to find the right compound.

Two things came of it, though. To our embarrassment, there already was the name caronic acid in the literature for a different structure, so the name of our compound had to be changed to carinamide. That was easier in those days than now. Secondly, investigators at the University of Michigan (Wolfson *et al.*, 1948) had made the observation that PAH increased the excretion of uric acid by patients. It was a curiosity, salicylic acid would do the same thing, but they asked to see if carinamide would be uricosuric (would increase uric acid excretion). It did, but there seemed no point in carrying that further. Who would want to take 20 grams of any drug daily even for a few days? The patient who suffered from the pangs of gout might expect to take a useful uricosuric drug for the rest of his life, one that would lower his blood uric acid concentration to normal by increasing its excretion. We put aside the observation of an uricosuric effect of carinamide, expecting to find it in a more suitable compound, one with the same sort of activity and safety at a tenth the dose or less, preferably.

THE PHYSIOLOGICAL ECONOMY OF PROBENECID

It was conceivable that a compound could be found that (1) inhibited the tubular secretion of pencillin, (2) could not be secreted by those same cells lining the renal tubules, and (3) if ultrafiltered at the glomeruli, would undergo more or less complete reabsorption back into the bloodstream as the urine was exposed to still other cells of the renal tubules farther along the nephron. The daily oral dose of such a compound would be expected to be milligrams to a few grams, that is, if it was well absorbed and if it escaped destruction, metabolism, in the body. This set of attributes was our objective for the compound we wanted, expressed in rational physiological terms. The chemists added still another attribute they felt such a compound needed, in addition to sustaining what they had succeeded in building into the carinamide structure, which had amounted to (1) good oral efficacy, (2) a greater inherent activity, and (3) safety. This added property, that of (4) substantial back diffusion or reabsorption by the tubules, was to be gained by increasing the lipid solubility of the compound we sought.

The chemists decided it might be to their advantage to find out whether the substituted sulfamoyl portion of the molecule needed to be situated as in carinamide or whether it could be reversed. If it could be reversed, as in the comparison of the structures for carinamide and probenecid (Fig. 2), their job of influencing lipid solubility of the molecule would be more directly approachable; at least it would increase considerably what could be added on that end of the molecule. The switch from $R_2SO_2NHR_1$ to $R_2NHSO_2R_1$ (Fig. 1) worked, as they had hoped. Substitution of one or two straight or branched chains for R_2 in the second general formula gave good activity and control of lipid solubility. This was reflected beautifully in the physiological effects of the compounds, even to optimizing efficacy as compared to acute toxicity. Clearly, activity and toxicity were unrelated, as illustrated in Fig. 3.

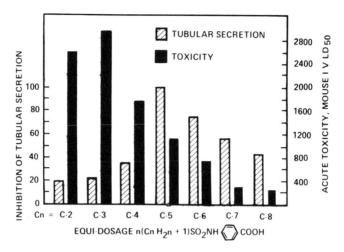

FIG. 3. Comparison of activity and toxicity of a series of related inhibitors of the mechanism for tubular secretion of phenol red and penicillin. Toxicity figures pertain to the acute LD_{50} values for the compounds administered i.v. to female Carworth CF-I mice. The lower the LD^{50}, the greater the i.v. toxicity of the compound. Data for the inhibition of tubular secretion pertain to the percentage inhibition of penicillin secretion by the renal tubules of the dog under the general conditions described by Beyer *et al.,* *Am. J. Physiol. 149:* 355, 1947.

The lack of a relationship between toxicity and activity of probenecid and its analogs was important to its use. Inhibitors of oxidative metabolism, such as cyanide, or the uncoupling of oxidative phosphorylation as by dinitrophenol are also capable of blocking the transport of PAH, etc. However, the use of inhibitors that have such far-reaching effects is unjustifiable because of their serious toxicity. Probenecid has no effect on these basic respiratory or energy transfer systems. The dipropyl compound in that series had everything we wanted including such nearly complete reabsorption that it was hardly possible to measure its clearance. Ordinarily, its rate of excretion was low. Moreover, it was uricosuric. All these features transposed to man, to the clinical situation precisely including the anticipated clinical daily dosage of 2 gm per day.

There were a few problems, though, with this designed discovery that hurt its market potential and our ego. First, we were too long in discovering the compound. By 1950, when probenecid was marketed, penicillin was plentiful, deep culture fermentation had been worked out. This made the antibiotic available and the cost of therapy accessible. In and of itself, the greater availabiliy of penicillin probably was not the cause of the indifferent acceptance of Remanden, the oral formulation of penicillin-G, and probenecid that was marketed. The concept of how probenecid worked was too advanced for the time. To *inhibit* a particular renal function beneficially went beyond the general knowledge of the kidney at that time.

Whereas the chemists on the team were chagrined when they found they had overlooked caronic acid in their search of the literature that led to the name caronamide which had to be changed to carinamide, the pharmacologists goofed when they assumed that probenecid was refractory to secretion by the renal tubules. Had the compound been refractory to secretion it could not have more perfectly fulfilled the practical prerequisites for this new drug, but it was later shown that the drug actually was secreted. Compared to its less lipid soluble analogs, probenecid was hardly present normally in the urine of dogs to which effective dosages of the drug were administered. Our oversight was in not checking the known effect of urinary pH, an alkaline urine, on the renal back diffusion of many compounds such as sulfonamides. Mudge and Weiner pointed out later that, under conditions wherein the back diffusion of probenecid was inhibited by making the urine alkaline, its rate of clearance could be increased to exceed glomerular filtration rate. This we promptly confirmed, to our embarrassment, but the experience taught us a lesson worth passing along in this context of designed discovery. That is, it is quite possible to design an experiment based on one concept that will admit an adequate fulfillment of the physiological correlates of a clinical problem in an unanticipated way. Actually, the unanticipated mechanism might not be known. In another context we discussed how to work beyond the limits of knowledge (Chapter 5).

GOUT AND ITS URICOSURIC EFFECT

Probenecid came to be the first useful drug for the management of the basic problem in gout — the imbalance in podagrous patients between the production and excretion of uric acid that leads to its accumulation in blood (hyperuricemia) and other tissues. Uric acid is a poorly soluble end product of purine metabolism that precipitates as deposits or tophi about joints, as in the hands and feet, or in soft tissues of patients who have gout, such as the lobe of the ear. Our approach to the basic problem was the inhibition of uric acid reabsorption by the renal tubules. The work was done in dogs, including the dalmation coach hound which handles uric acid more like birds than other dogs or man.

That the work leading to probenecid started out as a project for the physiological conservation of penicillin and ended up to have its greatest benefit for the gout patient is often cited, by others, as a prime example of serendipity. This, we cannot claim to be so, for our uricosuric research on carinamide anticipated that for probenecid. Perhaps the initial observation by Wolfson *et al.* that carinamide was uricosuric (inhibited uric acid reabsorption by the kidney) might be considered serendipitous. The less one knows about the circumstances of discovery the more plausible the suggestion that it was serendipitous, but "fortune favors the prepared mind."

COLLATERAL LITERATURE

Beyer, K. H. (1943): Relation of molecular configuration to the rate of deamination of sympathomimetic amines by aminase, *J. Pharmacol. Exper. Therap. 79:* 85–95.

Beyer, K. H. (1950): Functional characteristics of renal transport mechanisms, *Pharmacol. Rev. 2:* 227–280.

Beyer, K. H. (1950): Pharmacological basis of penicillin therapy. Charles C. Thomas, Springfield, Illinois.

Beyer, K. H., Flippin, H., Verwey, W. F., and Woodward, R. (1944): The effect of *para*-aminohippuric acid on plasma concentration of penicillin in man, *J.A.M.A. 126:* 1007–1009.

Beyer, K. H., Miller, A. K., Russo, H. F., Patch, E. A., and Verwey, W. F. (1947): The inhibitory effect of caronamide on the renal elimination of penicillin, *Am. J. Physiol. 149:* 355–368.

Beyer, K. H., Painter, R. H., and Wiebelhaus, V. D. (1950): Enzymatic factors in renal tubular secretion of phenol red, *Am. J. Physiol. 161:* 259–267.

Beyer, K. H., Russo, H. F., Tilson, E. K., Miller, A. K., Verwey, W. F., and Gass, S. R. 1951): 'Benemid', *p*-(di-n-propylsulfamyl) benzoic acid: its renal affinity and its elimination. *Am. J. Physiol. 166:* 625–640.

Beyer, K. H., Woodward, R., Peters, L., Verwey, W. F., and Mattis, P. (1944): The prolongation of penicillin retention in the body by means of *para*-aminohippuric acid, *Science 100:* 107–108.

Potter, V. R., and Elvehjem, C. A. (1937): The effect of inhibitors on succinoxidase, *J. Biol. Chem. 117:* 341–349.

Quastel, J. H., and Wheatley, A. H. M. (1931): Biological oxidations in the succinic acid series, *Biochem. J. 25:* 117–128.

Smith, H. W., Goldring, W., and Chasis, H. (1938): Measurement of the tubular excretory mass, effective blood flow and filtration rate in the normal human kidney, *J. Clin. Invest. 17:* 263–278.

Wolfson, W. Q., Cohn, C., Levine, R., and Huddleston, B. (1948): Transport and excretion of uric acid in man. Physiological significance of the uricosuric effect of Carinamide, *Am. J. Med. 4:* 774.

8.
Tailoring a Third New Drug

GENERAL CONSIDERATIONS

The story of a successful discovery, development, and delivery of a new drug can be approximated by the orderly sequencing of five words: these are (1) concept, (2) confirmation, (3) confusion, (4) completion, and (5) competition. The chlorothiazide (Diuril) story can be used to illustrate these points and a great deal more that goes into the tailoring of a new drug. But, before we get into the details of that work as source material for portraying research on new drugs, the seven factors set forth in Chapter 4 on designed discovery deserve to be reread (also Chapter 1). Unless or until they are fulfilled, the likelihood of completing a complex project successfully is not very good. Restated briefly, the basic physiological correlates of the clinical situation should be capable of being explored quantitatively with available methodology and instrumentation. If the physiological correlates of the clinical situation are only vaguely conceived, the methodology must be sufficiently general to admit discovery beyond those limits of knowledge. These points about designed discovery are illustrated by the story of Prontosil.

THE PRONTOSIL STORY

It was the discovery of the dye sulfamidocrysoidine (Prontosil Rubrum) by Gerhard Domagk and his associates at the I. G. Farbenindustries in Germany, or more particularly the way they went about the discovery, that

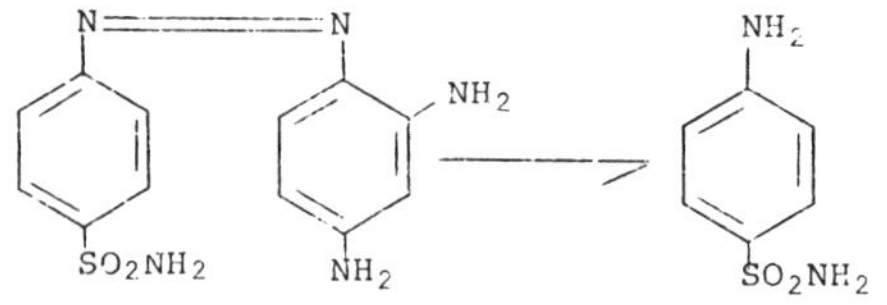

PRONTOSIL   SULFANILAMIDE

FIG. 1.   The structures of prontosil and its metabolite, sulfanilamide.

showed the way to modern drug research. This discovery led to the first sulfonamide drug. Their discovery, Prontosil, was split by the body to yield an active metabolite, sulfanilamide.

As the story goes, German scientists had been intrigued since the latter part of the nineteenth century by the capability of some dyes to stain live bacteria, the process called vital staining. (Actually, the German chemical industry had a history of preeminence in dye chemistry.) Paul Ehrlich and K. Shiga had found that the dye trypan red was active against certain trypanosomes, such as those causing sleeping sickness in cattle and people in some parts of Africa. Later, in 1910, Ehrlich and Hata found the yellow dyes arsphenamine (606 or Salvarsan) and neoarsphenamine to be effective treatment of syphillis in animals and patients. When they synthesized new dyes, chemists at the I. G. Farbeindustries had their compounds screened for antibacterial activity *in vitro*. Those dyes that seemed to be active *in vitro* then were tried *in vivo*, in infected animals, usually to no avail.

In 1929, when Gerhard Domagk, a pathologist, joined I. G. Farbeinindustrie, he insisted on subordinating the *in vitro* tests to the direct assessment of compounds in infected animals, or so the story goes. If one wanted to treat streptococcal infections in people, it made sense to Domagk to test the dyes against streptococcal infections in animals (mice). I suspect this could not have been a very popular decision for the chemists. *In vitro* tests (e.g., where bacteria are grown on broth in a test tube) have an appeal for chemists, even today. Usually, such tests are relatively easy to establish and are much easier to interpret. A technician can test many more compounds *in vitro* at a time. Such tests take so much less of the chemist's compounds than do mice or still larger animals that may take days to get well or die. Whether the mice survive or die depends, moreover, on the size and strain of the bacterial innoculum and when the compound is given with respect to when the mice are infected. The dosage, the frequence, and whether the compound is administered orally or some other way are also important. These and so many other things the pathologist or microbiologist seem to understand can determine whether the animals survive. There must have been times when the biologist insisted on determining whether the compound was so toxic that it was killing both the streptococci and the mice. To settle this quandary about toxicity would take even more of the dye, which may have been hard to come by.

As it turned out, it really was not the chemist's dye, Prontosil, that cured the mice. Its metabolite, sulfanilamide (Fig. 1) was responsible for curing the mice. Sulfanilamide was bacteriostatic, it did not kill the streptococci. It held the bacteria at bay so the natural defenses of the body could destroy them. Domagk's discovery of Prontosil was announced in 1935. He was awarded the Nobel Prize in 1939 for this discovery. In retrospect, 1935 was when the so-called Golden Age in drug discovery began or was introduced.

DOING THE RIGHT THING THE RIGHT WAY

The story of Domagk's discovery relates to the importance of doing the right thing the right way, not necessarily the easiest or fastest or the most direct way. Instrumentation, equipment, was not his problem, but it can make a great deal of difference in how one goes about research and the facility or precision with which progress can be made. For instance, we would have been seriously hampered in our diuretic research that led to the thiazides if the practical commercial flame photometer for the measurement of sodium and potassium had not been made available just before we needed it.

CHLOROTHIAZIDE (DIURIL)

General Considerations

This example of designed discovery is being introduced, for it illustrates more of the elements that go into the tailoring of a new drug than any with which I am familiar. In his book on research in the pharmaceutical industry, L. Earle Arnow recites parts of this story and indicates that the project took 14 years from inception to marketing of chlorothiazide in 1958. He was Director of Research at Sharp and Dohme when our diuretic program started. He had to defend the program to corporate management much of that time, so it must have seemed that long, anyway. Clearly, our work on penicillin that led to probenecid started in 1944. During its first several years that project took priority over all else in the renal laboratory. Just as clearly, were it not for the way we came to think about the functions of the renal tubules during that time the conceptual basis for a saluretic carbonic anhydrase inhibitor may have been no more evident to us than to others.

Fortunately, the management of both Sharp and Dohme and Merck and Company (the two organizations were merged in 1953) understood research. At the time chlorothiazide was marketed in 1958, the total sales of all kinds of prescription diuretics in the United States was something over eight million dollars, including the organomercurials and acetazolamide (Diamox). Even if the saluretic drug we were searching for was worth the whole eight million dollars, the marketing people of the company could think of any number of new drugs they would rather have, so far as well definable market potential or sales potential was concerned. However, the marketing potential of a new product such as chlorothiazide that tied together in an unprecedented way both diuretic and antihypertensive therapy cannot be reliably anticipated by market analysis. Such a product finds (even creates) its own market, with a great deal of help from seemingly everyone, of course. A capable marketing management understands these things; so, back to an account of the designed discovery of this new drug.

In every example of a successful designed discovery mentioned heretofore, the concept on which it was based was sound and methodology for the work was extremely relevant to the physiological correlates of what the new drug was expected to do, clinically. The same is true of this example. To a point, both edema (dropsy) and hypertension are but manifestations of underlying causative diseases. Either condition can be destructive in its own right, edema or high blood pressure. On the other hand, each can be caused by any number or combination of aberrations of function of one or more organs. Some of the causes find their ultimate expression in both hypertension and edema. The two conditions can be interrelated etiologically and in their pathogenesis or development, but this is not necessarily the case.

SALT RETENTION, THE COMMON DENOMINATOR FOR EDEMA AND HYPERTENSION

The concept that formed the basis for the research leading to chlorothiazide was that it should be possible to discover a diuretic agent that was also antihypertensive if it would increase the excretion of sodium (chloride), salt, by the kidney. The sum of the information scattered through the literature (some of it highly controversial) and our own experience made a rational approach to this attractive problem seem feasible. To emphasize our objective to increase the excretion of salt by the kidney, we coined the term saluretic. This was a simple, clear expression of our objective, a saluretic agent for the relief of edema and hypertension.

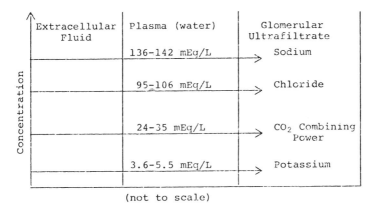

(not to scale)

FIG. 2. Essentially equivalent concentrations of electrolytes in extracellular fluid, plasma water, and glomerular ultrafiltrate.

SALT AND WATER DISTRIBUTION AND EXCRETION

Edema is the presence of abnormally large amounts of fluid in the intercellular tissue spaces of the body. This fluid accumulates in the course of kidney or liver disease or heart failure. *The amount of such extracellular fluid may increase greatly,* even accumulating in the abdominal cavity as ascites. However, *its composition need not change.* Its composition is the *same as that of plasma water. Sodium and chloride are the predominant ions, cation and anion, respectively.* The ratio of their concentrations approaches 1.0 (more nearly 1.35), there being more sodium than chloride. Potassium and "bicarbonate" are the other two principal ions present in considerably lower concentrations in extracellular fluid. Like ships at sea, the cells of the body have pumps in their membranes that keep out the sodium and chloride and which maintain a high intracellular potassium concentration, which is essential to their function. As illustrated in Fig. 2, that same extracellular composition of electrolytes, sodium, chloride, potassium, and bicarbonate ions, persists in the plasma water ultrafiltered at the glomeruli of the kidney. Thus, the glomerular ultrafiltrate (protein is not normally filtered at the glomeruli) has the same concentration of these important electrolytes as in the extracellular fluids, including plasma water. That this generalization holds in health and disease was important to the success of this venture. So was a knowledge of how the kidney works on the glomerular ultrafiltrate.

The functional unit of the kidney, the nephron, is diagramed in Fig. 3. The nephron is made up of a glomerulus, a proximal (convoluted) portion of the

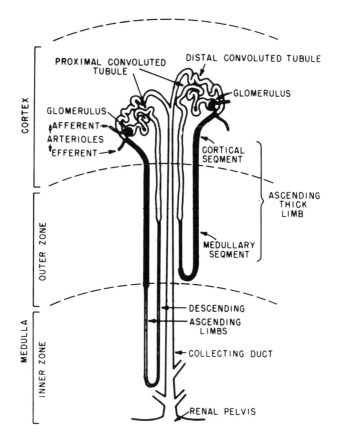

FIG. 3. The nephron, the functional unit of the kidney, oriented with respect to the outer (cortical) and inner (medullary) zone of that organ in transection.

tubule, a long loop (of Henle), a distal (convoluted) portion, and a collecting duct that drains into the pelvis of the kidney (where the composition of urine is the same as in the bladder). Since one needs a dissecting microscope to visualize the nephron, it must be evident that there are many nephrons, for they mostly make up the mass of the kidney. Actually, they are large enough that with microequipment one can puncture the tubules and analyze their fluid at accessible points.

By microanalysis, others showed that as the glomerular filtrate passed along the lumen or bore of the proximal tubule most of the sodium, potassium, chloride, and bicarbonate was reabsorbed and with them an osmolar equivalent amount of water was returned to the body by back diffusion.

The process for reabsorbing sodium was considered an active one on the part of the cells lining the proximal portion of the tubules; the anions, and water followed or accompanied its movement. As a matter of fact, it seemed to us there must be at least two such active sodium-reabsorbing mechanisms. These two mechanisms served to support rationally the chemical program for this research as will be discussed. [Sodium and potassium active transport mechanisms were also known to exist in the distal convoluted tubule, but they were not the object of our primary interest.]

SALT RESTRICTION IN HYPERTENSION

A saluretic agent also made sense as an antihypertensive drug. Both Kempner's rice diet and the low salt diets hypertensive patients were made to tolerate seemed to indicate a need to restrict the consumption of salt by the patient who had high blood pressure. Although the relevance of salt intake to hypertension was controversial at the time, there was no question about the patients' disdain for the unexciting and unpalatable fare entailed in any low salt diet. Thus, we reasoned that if salt restriction was good for the hypertensive patient, it made better sense, and surely a more cooperative patient, if one could liberalize his salt intake somewhat and take away any unneeded sodium chloride, as with the aid of a saluretic agent.

BIOLOGICAL METHODOLOGY EMPLOYED

The technical objective was to inhibit the active reabsorption of sodium, primarily sodium and chloride, so as not to disrupt the normal electrolyte composition and concentration in extracellular fluids. It was reasoned that to induce an increased excretion of sodium and chloride in a normally hydrated animal would assure an increased fluid excretion in the edematous patient where the volume of retained extracellular fluid was excessive. The effect of increased salt excretion should be equivalent to a low salt diet in the hypertensive patient.

Trained unanesthetized dogs (Fig. 4) and renal clearance techniques that gave excellent and quantifiable control of electrolyte and water excretion were employed. The first-line protocol employed for this purpose is illustrated in Table I. The incorporation of both control and drug phase in a protocol that includes all essential parameters is evident. The experiment represented in Table I will be discussed as the first one wherein chlorothiazide was administered to a dog.

FIG. 4. Patricia received from the National Society for Medical Research, its award for the Research Dog Hero of the year. She had been with "the Company" some 15 years by that time and several of her canine associates had been part of the team for from 5 to over 15 years. She is shown with her master, Horace F. Russo, research associate.

CHEMICAL APPROACHES TO THE PROBLEM

It was agreed that two chemical approaches to finding a useful drug would be made. (1) The *organomercurials* were attractive as a lead because they did increase sodium, chloride, and water excretion. They were thought to work by inhibiting sulfhydryl catalyzed dehydrogenase enzymes in the kidney. By doing so they were thought to block the reabsorption of sodium, inhibiting its exchange for hydrogen ions in the proximal portion of the renal tubules. Our objective was to find a nonmercurial compound that would form inactive adducts or combinations with the critical sulfhydryl groups of such dehydrogenases and so inhibit the exchange secretion of hydrogen ions for the reabsorption of sodium. For this purpose, the phenoxyacetic acid moity found in some organomercurial diuretics was made to serve as the carrier of α, β-unsaturated acyl substituents that were capable of reacting with sulfhydryl groups.

(2) Sulfonamides were known to be natriuretic, from the days of the chemotherapeutic use of sulfanilamide, and to be carbonic anhydrase inhibi-

TABLE I

Protocol and First Clearance Experiment Pertaining to the Effect of Chlorothiazide on Electrolyte Excretion by the Dog[a,b]

Time (min.)	Sodium Excretion µEq./min.	Sodium Percent reab.	Potassium Excretion µEq./min.	Potassium Percent reab.	Chloride Excretion µEq./min.	Urine pH	Urine flow ml./min.	Creatinine clearance ml./min.
-60	500 ml. water, orally							
-30	500 ml. water, orally							
-20	3.0 gm. creatinine, subcutaneously; 1.5 mg./kg. 0.14 M phosphate, intravenously, prime, and venoclysis of 0.023 M phosphate containing 0.23 M mannitol at 3 ml./min. (pH 7.41)							
Control phase:								
0-10	8	99.7	14	84.1	6	5.8	1.5	25.8
10-20	6	99.8	12	89.7	5	6.0	1.0	35.7
20-30	8	99.8	13	87.1	4	6.0	0.9	32.7
Chlorothiazide phase: 6.25 mg./kg., intravenously, prime; 7.5 mg./kg./hr. in phosphate-mannitol venoclysis (pH 7.53)								
50-60	285	93.8	55	44.7	134	7.9	2.4	33.8
60-70	311	93.6	55	46.8	142	7.9	2.7	36.1
70-80	241	93.7	42	48.9	119	7.9	2.1	28.2

[a] Dog No. 804 weighing 14.1 kg.

[b] From Beyer, K.H. (1958): Mechanism of Action of Chlorothiazide, *Ann. N.Y. Acad. Sci. 71:* 364.

tors.* Actually, only the sulfonamides that have a "free" sulfamoyl group ($-SO_2NH_2$) inhibit carbonic anhydrase.

Within the limits of knowledge at the time our work on these compounds began, all sulfonamides that inhibited carbonic anhydrase generally were thought to do the same thing in the kidney, one being more potent than another as the essential difference. Acetazolamide (synthesized and evaluated in the early 1950's) was more potent and better tolerated than sulfanilamide, but the effect of the two compounds on the kidney and on carbonic anhydrase elsewhere in the body was essentially similar. It was more active as judged by dosage to the patient and by its inherent *in vitro* carbonic anhydrase activity. Although acetazolamide has been used to some extent as a diuretic, the enhancement of bicarbonate excretion instead of chloride along with sodium caused a self-limiting metabolic acidosis (a compensatory hyperchloremia). (Acetazolamide is employed frequently today in the management of glaucoma.)

RATIONALE FOR SALURETIC SULFONAMIDES

It seemed to us that if a saluretic agent was to be found among the sulfonamides that were carbonic anhydrase inhibitors, either its predominant site of action had to be different from sulfanilamide or its activity had to be due to something other than a primary effect on that enzyme.†

The physiological concept on which we rationalized exploring this type of chemistry was the likelihood that we could find sulfonamides that were secreted by the proximal portion of the nephron, in the manner of p-aminohippurate and penicillin. Ordinarily, compounds secreted by such proximal cells are accumulated therein in concentrations considerably greater than in

*Carbonic anhydrase is an enzyme that is ubiquitously distributed to facilitate the transport of carbon dioxide (CO_2) formed in the course of cell metabolism. For example, it facilitates the release of CO_2 from the bloodstream to the alveoli of the lungs. Inhibition of the enzyme carbonic anhydrase in the eye reduces intraocular tension as in glaucoma. Its inhibition in the brain may give relief from some forms of epilepsy. Its inhibition in the distal portion of the renal tubule renders urine, which is normally slightly acid, basic or alkaline. The enzyme is present in cells of the proximal convoluted segment of the tubules as well, which is particularly important to this research project.

†The work by Pitts and his associates having to do with inhibition of urine acidification by sulfanilamide was thought to place its site of action in the distal portion of the tubule. Grossly, this relationship would be reflected in the increase in pH of urine due to carbonic anhydrase inhibition there. The increased pH would reflect the decreased reabsorption of sodium and bicarbonate ions. We thought the net effect on chloride and bicarbonate excretion would depend on where and how much the enzyme was inhibited, not just how the compound worked. In 1954, we published our thesis that the saluretic compound for which we searched should be secreted by the proximal portion of the nephron, should inhibit carbonic anhydrase at that site, and should be poorly reabsorbed by the distal portion of the renal tubule.

blood or glomerular filtrate. If their accumulation as such coincided with where carbonic anhydrase was present in the proximal tubule, then there was a chance that one could inhibit the enzyme at that site to the greatest extent. (Such a predominant site of action of a compound was anticipated to yield a net increase in excretion of sodium, chloride, and water, whether or not it was a carbonic anhydrase inhibitor. A secondary consideration was that the extrarenal general distribution of the compound for which we searched should remain extracellular, to minimize toxicity attributable to inhibition of the carbonic anhydrase ubiquitously distributed in other tissues.

STRUCTURE/ACTIVITY STUDIES LEADING
TO SALURETIC SULFONAMIDES

Having developed a suitable biological procedure, the first thing was to find an analog of sulfanilamide that would increase the excretion of chloride ions, along with sodium and the expected bicarbonate.

The chemists provided the simplest of analogs varying at first by classic substitutions for the para amino group of sulfanilamide. No attempt was made at that point to influence enzyme activity by using such things as a heterocyclic nucleus instead of the benzene ring. The sulfamoyl group was left strictly alone once we reaffirmed its seeming essentiality.

This simplistic approach to the problem paid off in the first half dozen or so compounds examined in the dog clearance studies. The acid, p-carboxy-benzenesulfonamide (CBS) increased the excretion of sodium, bicarbonate, and chloride ions. This was the first key compound. It was chloruretic, it was rapidly excreted, and it was secreted by the renal tubules. To us, this meant that CBS was being handled by the kidney as we had hypothesized would be

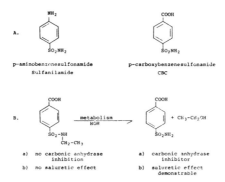

FIG. 5. Sulfonamide structures (A) and relationship of structure to carbonic anhydrase inhibitory effect (B).

the case for a saluretic carbonic anhydrase inhibitor — our objective seemed technically feasible, though the compound was not suitable for development. The structures of sulfanilamide and CBS are given in Fig. 5A to illustrate their similarity yet profound difference. [The para amino group reduces toward neutrality (as to litmus) the acidity induced by the sulfamoyl group in sulfanilamide. The para carboxyl group, being acidic, has the opposite effect of the amino group in sulfanilamide and so increases the total acidity of CBS.]

The CBS results were published in 1954, but it took years and many compounds to get from CBS to chlorothiazide. Each compound, made and tested in such structure/activity research, yields some information, positive or negative, that is helpful to guide the way toward the desired compound. So long as the sulfamoyl group was unsubstituted, or the substitution thereon was removed metabolically (Fig. 5B), retaining some degree of natriuresis (increased sodium excretion) was no problem. However, the presence of chloruresis (increased chloride excretion) and its proportionality to bicarbonate excretion differed considerably from compound to compound. This would be expected if the site of preponderant effect along the renal tubules varied among the compounds being compared, regardless of their relative carbonic anhydrase inhibitory activity. In other words, it was as important to control the physical characteristics of the compound that determined lipid solubility, binding to plasma protein, accumulation in the secretory cells of the nephron, and diffusion from the lumen of the tubule if it was to retain a useful level of enzyme inhibitory activity.

From a structure/activity standpoint, two sulfamoyl groups on the benzene ring were better than one if optimally placed. Introduction of chlorine into the molecule impressed still greater activity, and two chloride substituents

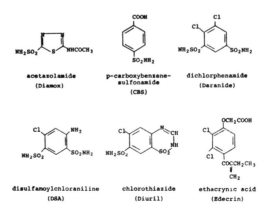

FIG. 6.   Structures of diuretics mentioned in the text.

were better than one in that the resulting carbonic anhydrase inhibitory activity of dichlorphenamide (Daranide) was as great as for acetazolamide (Diamox). Daranide retained both chloride and bicarbonate excretory capability (whereas Diamox was not chloruretic). The corresponding disulfamoylchloranaline (DSA) was less active than dichlorphenamide in the dog but when DSA was subjected to acylation the structure cyclized to yield the benzothiadiazine nucleus and the compound chlorothiazide (Diuril).

Representative structures are presented in Fig. 6. The first renal clearance experiment conducted on chlorothiazide is presented in Table I. The chemists on the team who were responsible for this fascinating work were James M. Sprague, Frederick C. Novello, and their associates. John E. Baer was responsible for the ongoing biological research on this project.

CHLOROTHIAZIDE: ITS SALURETIC CHARACTERISTICS

This first chlorothiazide experiment characterized the compound as we had envisioned the designed discovery of the desirable saluretic agent (Table I). The compound increased the excretion of primarily sodium and chloride ions. Potassium excretion was increased to some extent, and so was bicarbonate as judged by the increased urinary pH when the drug was administered. More lipid-soluble thiazides, including hydrochlorothiazide, that have a greater avidity for accumulation in the cells of the proximal portion and which have moderate carbonic anhydrase inhibitory activity do not increase urinary pH and do not increase bicarbonate excretion under clinical conditions of use. In Table II, the equivalent clinical dosage of several thiazides, their lipid solubility, and carbonic anhydrase inhibitory activity is presented to illustrate over a thousandfold dosage range, the greater association of dosage with solubility characteristics than with enzyme inhibition.

At the outset of this case history, the rationale for an antihypertensive effect of a saluretic agent was set forth. Actually, no serious attempts were made in the laboratory to assess the antihypertensive potential of the compounds that led to chlorothiazide or of that agent either. The laboratory methodology for assessing antihypertensive effects of such a drug seemed unimpressive at that time. Whether or not it would be antihypertensive seemed best evaluated at the clinical level.

It was planned first to establish the credibility of the saluretic effect of chlorothiazide in edematous patients. Once this was done, and the clinical investigators had become familiar with the drug, the intent was to assess the antihypertensive effect in patients having high blood pressure. This proved to be a satisfactory course of action. The antihypertensive effect of the compound was established easily.

TABLE II

Ether/water partition coefficients, approximate order of activity and carbonic anhydrase inhibitory activity.

Compound	Natriuretic Activity	Partition Coefficient	CO$_2$-ase Inhibition (M) x 10^{-5}
chlorothiazide	1	0.08	.17
hydrochlorothiazide	10	0.37	2.3
trichlormethiazide	100	1.53	5.5
cyclopenthiazide	1000	10.2	1.3

Merck Sharp & Dohme—Typo—15018—2-13-62

METHODS VERSUS MODELS

In closing this chapter, an added word of comment may be worthwhile. The concepts and emphasis placed on methodology that formed the biological basis for this project served us well. Both the saluretic potential of the carbonic anhydrase inhibitors and the likelihood of influencing hypertension by an agent that increased salt excretion were concepts not likely to be accepted with one accord. The compound, chlorothiazide, could stand on its own merit both for the reduction of edema and hypertension. It was allowed to do so. The same biological approach and methodology subsequently yielded a useful discovery from the alternative of the two chemical approaches to the problem mentioned on page 76. [The sulfhydryl inhibitory phenoxyacetic acid, ethacrynic acid (Edecrin), synthesized later by Everett Schultz and his associates had a greater inherent saluretic potency than the thiazides.]

One might ask whether the methodology employed in the research on the thiazides and ethacrynic acid was critical to their discovery; this seems likely. Other procedures were available. None seem likely to have given the moment-to-moment assessment of drug effect on precisely what we wanted to know, its saluretic effect, on so quantitative a basis compared with a predrug control phase in the same experiment. Hemodynamic and toxic effects of the drug could be adjudged as well by the procedure we employed. Had one employed a model of cardiac decompensation or renal insufficiency adequate to induce fluid retention, the technical difficulty of maintaining a uniform colony of such animals adequate to control and quantify a drug effect on fluid retention might be defeating. Even under optimal conditions, much of the control features inherent in the clearance technique would not have been contained in the other procedures. We did study the effect of thiazides on steroid-induced fluid retention in dogs but only as a supportive experiment.

Had such other measures been employed as first-line procedures in dogs, both chlorothiazide and ethacrynic acid may have been missed if they had been administered as a single (daily) dose, because of their short duration of action. Weighing the animals once a day or measuring 24-hour urine collections, with or without electrolyte determinations, might not have shown a drug effect, because of the rebound retention of fluid and electrolyte after the effect of the drug was over. Giving the compounds orally more than once a day would have required more compound and more knowledge about the individual compounds (and perhaps more dogs, due to toxicity) than are likely to be available at such a time.

If these same models of cardiac insufficiency, etc., were prepared in rats and were employed as first-line assays of new compounds, the thiazides might have been discarded as insufficiently active to be interesting. The phenoxyacetic acid compounds, like ethacrynic acid which is so potent in dogs and man, would have been found to be inactive. Rats hardly respond to ethacrynic acid and its analogs even when administered intravenously. (Mice respond more satisfactorily.)

OTHER USES FOR CARBONIC ANHYDRASE INHIBITORS

Returning to the *in vitro* carbonic anhydrase inhibition assay; it does have a relevance to tissue fluid accumulation, but it is an unlikely way to discover a saluretic agent. Hence, we did not employ it except to determine the inherent carbonic anhydrase inhibitory activity of specific compounds. Its real virtue is a broader relevance to possible clinical utility (side effects, too, for that matter). For example, carbonic anhydrase activity is critical to the maintenance of intraocular pressure. Acetazolamide (Diamox) finds its greatest usage in the reduction of excessive intraocular pressure, so important to the patient who has glaucoma. Dichlorphenamide is as potent a carbonic anhydrase inhibitor as acetazolamide, but it is intermediate between that compound and the thiazides in the proportion of chloride to bicarbonate excreted. It seems to be preferred for the management of respiratory disorders pertaining to the control of carbon dioxide tension in the blood.

ELECTION OF A NEW COMPOUND FOR
PRECLINICAL ASSESSMENT

The discovery of a potentially useful new compound needs to be affirmed and needs to be supported before its preclinical assessment described in the next chapter (Chapter 9) can be justified. Beginning with the election of a new compound for preclinical, then clinical, assessment the scope of technical personnel involvement and the costs of research escalate. The new compound needs to be a discovery worth the effort. For instance:

(1) The election of metaraminol (Chapter 6) for development rested on a great deal of laboratory and clinical data for analogs of the compound that were in the pharmacological literature. This was in addition to the investigator's knowledge of the metabolism of such agents.

(2) The decision to invest the time and effort to bring probenecid to clinical trial rested on the prior experience with p-aminohippuric acid and carinamide, i.e., the ways they were handled by the body and their effect on penicillin excretion (Chapter 7). This was in addition to assessing the metabolism and excretion of probenecid, itself.

(3) Although that first clearance experiment (Table I) taught us the saluretic characteristics of chlorothiazide, there was a great deal more that needed to be "right" about the compound. The need for it to remain extracellularly in the tissue fluids (other than in the cells of the proximal segment of the renal tubules where chlorothiazide should accumulate in the course of its secretion) was important conceptually. Models, like heart failure or impaired renal failure sufficient to induce edema formation might have been employed as supportive procedures. Instead, 9-a-fluorohydrocortisone was employed to induce fluid retention in dogs, for the procedure was definitive and could be managed precisely. Chlorothiazide reduced that steroid-induced edema in dogs. It increased salt and water excretion under these conditions. Had the agent induced substantial shifts in acid—base balance of blood or if its efficacy had been substantially depressed by acidosis or alkalosis, its clinical utility would have been materially reduced. Its inherent carbonic anhydrase inhibitory activity was of interest, but since the compound was effectively saluretic and remained extracellularly, it was immaterial to potential clinical utility whether chlorothiazide inhibited that enzyme.

Transition from the augmentative aspects of discovery to the collateral preclinical assessment varies with the situation. It is a matter of judgement as to when one has arrived at sufficient evidence to support the decision that an important new compound has been discovered. Thus, it is not remarkable that many seemingly promising chemicals fall by the wayside of preclinical and clinical investigation, at considerable cost of time, money, and effort, as is discussed in the following chapters.

COLLATERAL LITERATURE

Arnow, L. E. (1970): *Health in a Bottle: Searching for the Drugs That Help,* J. B. Lippincott, Philadelphia, Pa.

Beyer, K. H. (1954): Factors basic to the development of useful inhibitors of renal transport mechanisms, *Arch. Int. Pharmacodyn. 98:* 97–117.

Beyer, K. H. (1977): Discovery of the thiazides: where biology and chemistry meet, *Persp. Biol. Med. 20:* 410–420.

Beyer, K. H., Baer, J. E., Russo, H. F., and Noll, R. (1958): Electrolyte excretion as influenced by chlorothiazide, *Science 127:* 146–147.

Beyer, K. H., and Baer, J. E. (1961): Physiological basis for the action of newer diuretic agents, *Pharmacol. Rev. 13:* 517–562.

Beyer, K. H., and Baer, J. E. (1975): The site and mode of action of some sulfonamide-derived diuretics, *Med. Clinics North Amer. 59:* 735–750.

Domagk, G. (1935): Ein beitrag zur chemotherapie der bakteriellen infectionen, *Deutshe Med. Wochenschr. 61:* 250–253.

Ford, R. V., Moyer, J. H., and Spurr, C. L. (1957): Clinical and laboratory observations on chlorothiazide (Diuril), *Arch. Int. Med. 100:* 582–596.

Freis, E. D., and Wilson, I. M. (1957): Potentiating effect of chlorothiazide (Diuril) in combination with antihypertensive agents: Preliminary Report, *Med. Ann. District of Columbia 26:* 468–516.

Gilman, A., and Brazeau, P. (1953): The role of the kidney in the regulation of acid-base metabolism, *Amer. J. Med. 15:* 765–770.

Hollander, W., and Wilkins, R. W. (1957): Chlorothiazide: a new type of drug for the treatment of arterial hypertension, *Boston Med. Quarterly 8:* 69–75.

Lyght, C. E., ed. (1968): A decade with Diuril, chlorothiazide, Library of Congress Cat. Card No. 68–14018, Merck & Co., Inc., Rahway, New Jersey.

Mountcastle, V. B. (1974): *Medical Physiology:* Vol. 2, Part 8, The kidney and body fluids, Chapters 46, 47, 48, 1974, 13th edition, C. V. Mosby Co., St. Louis, Mo.

Novello, F. C., and Sprague, J. M. (1957): Benzothiadiazine dioxides as novel diuretics, *J. Am. Chem. Soc. 79:* 2028–2029.

Pitts, R. F., and Alexander, R. S. (1945): The nature of the renal tubular mechanism for acidifying the urine, *Amer. J. Physiol. 144:* 239–254.

Richards, A. N. (1938): The Croonian Lecture. Processes of urine formation, *Proc. Royal Soc. London (Biol.) 126:* 398–432.

Saxl, P., and Heilig, R. (1920): Ueber die diuretische wirkung von novasurol und anderen quecksilberinjektionen, *Wien. Wchnschr. 33:* 943–944.

Sprague, J. M. (1958): The chemistry of diuretics. In chlorothiazide and other diuretic agents, *Ann. New York Acad. Sci. 71:* 328–343.

9.
Preclinical
Pharmacology

GENERAL COMMENT

There is a great deal more to the preclinical assessment of a new drug than documenting its discovery. In the course of affirming the discovery, a new compound will have been found sufficiently promising to warrant the tremendous amount of work that usually is done to see if clinical trial is justified. At this point, one may have an interesting new chemical, but it is not a new drug — it has not yet been proven useful for any medical purpose. It is at this point that one should determine as much as possible about the new compound, its primary attributes, its secondary pharmacodynamic characteristics, its pharmacokinetics, and its metabolism — what is good about it, what is bad about it. The preclinical assessments of new compounds do need to differ, depending on their individual anticipated utilities. What is described herein is intended to be representative, not comprehensive nor is it supposed to be a pattern for the preclinical assessment of any particular compound or class of compounds. Exploratory safety assessment may be carried out concurrently in order to reinforce the interpretation of results. If it is decided on the basis of these data to study the compound in man, still other safety studies, such as those discussed in Chapter 10, need to be conducted.

Some of the older clinical pharmacologists and clinical investigators were intolerant of the time and effort needed to carry out the preclinical assessment of a new drug, claiming such effort was irrelevant to the likely use in man.

They felt that the transposition of information from laboratory animals to man was unreliable at best. One does not hear such derogation of the usefulness of preclinical information so frequently today. The important reason is that the preclinical work up of a new compound prior to clinical trial is a great deal more complete, better designed, and more relevant to the information desired for clinical trial than it was apt to be not long ago. Time was when some investigators were inclined to rush through a superficial preclinical assessment in what was called a "quick and dirty" manner. In the subsequent clinical trial, such superficial data were useless or misleading and the compound was just as likely to be abandoned for lack of understanding of the agent and, hence, inadequate direction of the clinical study.

To be sure, there is a great deal of variability in the quantitative effect of a drug in different species. The better this is understood for a specific compound the more helpful the information might be for establishing initial dosage ranges in humans. What is less well understood is that in some cases there is as much difference between the various strains of primates. Indeed, the difference between humans also, with regard to dosage and side effects of drugs, may be as great as between different species of more commonly employed laboratory animals. This variability is especially so for drug metabolism and for hypersensitivity — genetically influenced attributes.

The better preclinical assessments were quite adequate for their purpose even years ago. Today, some regulatory agencies require their concurrence that the preclinical assessment is adequate before a new drug is explored in man in the countries in question. This has tended to raise the overall comprehensiveness and level of excellence of such preclinical work, also.

WHY A GOOD PRECLINICAL ASSESSMENT

There always comes a time in the clinical assessment of a new drug when the study runs into trouble. This can be for any number of reasons that will be considered in the chapters on clinical trial (Chapters 14 and 15). Sometimes the problem is hard to ascertain, much less assess. Almost inevitably the compound is deemed at fault. This is the simplest, not necessarily the soundest, assumption. At such a time, the basis for faith in the agent cannot be better than one's understanding of it. As mentioned in a previous paragraph, potential drugs (good as well as worthless) could be cast aside for lack of understanding at such times. Thus, when working up the pharmacology of a new compound do not be dissuaded from the most relevant physiological test in favor of others less relevant but faster or easier to conduct.

Relevance of Laboratory Tests for the Acquisition of Useful Information

What is meant by most relevant and less relevant? What distinguishes a sophisticated experiment from just a difficult one? The degree of relevance has to do with how closely the preclinical protocols encompass the basic correlates of the clinical situation. Perhaps an example will illustrate what is meant.

Before the days of sulfonamides, pneumococcal meningitis was a dreaded disease. The sulfonamides brought a whole new outlook on this serious disease to patient and physician alike. If one inoculated mice with pneumococci they would die unless the sulfonamide was administered. Sulfonamides worked against pneumococcal infections in man or mouse whether the tissue involved was blood, the meninges, or the lung. Such experiments were most relevant to the clinical situation. Equally important for efficacy, there needed to be a sustained bacteriostatic concentration of the sulfonamide, hence the emphasis on an adequate blood level. The development of the sulfonamides did much to create an awareness of the need to know the relationship of chemical structure to the rate of absorption, distribution, metabolism, and excretion, of drugs, for these characteristics were important to an adequate dosage regimen. Fortunately, the sulfonamides were capable of being assayed in tissue fluids rather easily. This chemical method, named for a distinguished pharmacologist, E. K. Marshall, and his student, A. C. Bratton (The Bratton Marshall Method), was a tremendous stimulus not only to the rational use of sulfonamides in therapy but to the development of pharmacokinetics and pharmacodynamics – how drugs behave in the body. Under the *in vitro* circumstances where prontocil is inactive because it cannot be metabolized to sulfanilamide, penicillin-G, bactericidal as well as bacteriostatic, is active; that efficacy being reduced by drug binding on protein. Penicillin-G would have been effective *in vivo* as well against a streptococcal or pneumococcal infection in mice. In other words, as one works beyond the limits of knowledge about a compound, the choice of laboratory methodology should be adequate to encompass the unknown. In that way the compound and the procedure might contribute to knowledge.

Internal Audits as a Part of the Design of Experiments

Frequently, it is impractical to use statistical methods in the initial experiments leading to the discovery or the substantiation of the pharmacodynamic action of an interesting compound. This was the case for protocols such as

TABLE I

Inhibitory Effect of 'Benemid' on Renal Clearance of Penicillin[a,b]

| Time | Urine Flow | Creatinine Clearance | Penicillin-G | | Penicillin/ Creatinine Clear. Ratio |
			Plasma Conc.	Clearance	
min.	cc/Min.	cc/min.	u/cc.	cc/min.	
-115	600 cc. H_2O, p.o.				
-55	400 cc. H_2O, p.o.				
-30	Control urine sample for sterility check				
	Penicillin venoclysis started; 39.2 u/cc. in 5% glucose at 3 cc/min.				
-25	Penicillin prime 9300 u., i.v.				
-22	Creatinine 3.0 gm., s.c.				
0-15	2.3	55.0	0.50	230.7	4.17
15-25	3.1	68.2	0.46	303.2	4.35
B*-0	*'Benemid' prime 12.5 mg/kg., i.v.				
	venoclysis 15 mg/kg/hr. added to the penicillin-glucose solution				
	Penicillin venoclysis continued at 37.2 u/cc. in 5% glucose at 3 cc/min.				
B20-30	5.3	72.2	0.68	69.8	0.97
B30-40	5.0	73.0	0.78	59.1	0.82

[a]Dog 240, wt. = 18.1 kg., exper. 258
[b]From Beyer et al. (1951): *J. Pharmacol. 166:* 625-690.

were employed for probenecid or chlorothiazide. Whenever possible, the reliability of such important protocols should be enhanced by building into the tests *internal audits,* variables that need to change in a manner consistent with one another. For example, in the protocol shown in Table I for the effect of probenecid on penicillin excretion, not only did the amount of penicillin excreted per minute have to decrease if a compound was effective but the antibiotic plasma level had to rise. Its clearance (amount excreted per minute/ plasma concentration) had to decrease as did the ratio of its clearance to glomerular filtration rate (creatinine clearance) if the individual experiment was to be considered reliable. Substantial decreases in other parameters such as urine flow and glomerular filtration rate would render the results suspect. Which is to say, the experiment had to be technically satisfactory as well as consistent within itself. We have made it a practice to introduce this concept of internal audits into protocols where both control and drug response phase could be combined in a single experiment.

Multiple Experimental Approaches to a Salient Effect of a Compound

Where control and drug response cannot be assessed in a single protocol, more than one type of experiment plus good statistical design and control are needed to measure drug effect and to gain as much insight into its action as possible. For instance, several types of tests would be necessary to learn how broad or restricted the actions of antiinflammatory steroids or nonsteroids might be. To design such practical protocols requires some knowledge of the pathology of inflammation and repair.

One should expect to have to demonstrate oral efficacy of a compound by one or more tests in at least one species if a new compound is intended for use by mouth. Moreover, the oral dosage needed to induce a desired effect should be a reasonably practical one. A large difference (say, tenfold) between oral and intravenous acute toxicity (LD_{50}) of a compound may suggest poor absorption when administered by mouth, in the absence of more direct evidence of satisfactory absorption to the contrary.

Statistical Approach

Today, most young people might wonder why the statistical design of good experiments does not stand at the top of the list in this sequence. They have been taught statistics, they think of statistics as the proper basis for measuring, comparing or expressing an effect with another or with a unit of measurement. They see the application of statistics to biological research in the journals and there are excellent texts and reference books to help them use statistics. They probably have never heard of "internal audits." Sequencing control and drug phase in short-term experiments may seem suspect unless performed in such numbers as applicable to statistical analysis. Employing multiple experimental approaches to the assessment of a salient effect may seem a waste of effort and resources. The reason statistical analysis is not set forth as the first of these several approaches to anticipating that a noteworthy effect is soundly based in the assessment of a compound is explained in the next paragraph.

The proper use of statistics is to delimit the numerical generalization of a set of data. This sentence says that a set of data has to be reduced to a few numbers (the generalization) that can form a basis for a conclusion or decision. In addition, statistics should make possible a mathematical expression of the reliability or risk with which the generalization can be employed as a basis for conclusion or decision. To use statistics most reliably, the experiment has to be designed so as to accommodate their application optimally. Note that a well designed experiment from a statistical standpoint does not have to be relevant to its intended purpose. That relevance is the biologist's responsibility. The elegant statistical analysis to which the data may be put may give no indication as to the relevance of the experimental design to its purpose. The statistical analysis indicates only how well the data have been controlled and executed. There are many experiments especially involving large numbers of animals (or patients) that are best handled statistically. When this is the case, it is helpful to have the biologist and the statistician discuss the protocol *before* the experiment is started. However, in doing so be sure not to compromise the purpose of the experiment in order to improve the applicability of the data to good statistical analysis. The statistician is no more in favor of this than the biologist, and if a little more thought is given by both to this common problem it usually can be resolved. (This is not the place to discuss further the use and abuse of statistics.)

The Dose/Response Curve

The dose/response relationship between the amount of a compound administered and the quantitative nature of the response is of fundamental importance. This relationship can be graphed in various ways. The classical way is usually represented by an "S"-shaped curve, as in Fig. 1, where the response at lowest effective doses increases gradually at first, becomes steeper in the middle of the curve, and gradually flattens out as the maximally effec-

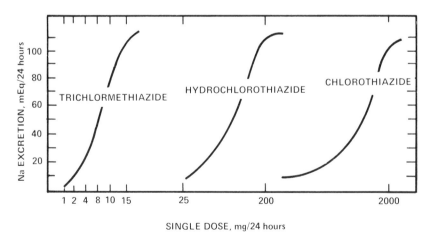

FIG. 1.   From Fuchs *et al., Ann. N.Y. Acad. Sci.,* p. 801, *88*: 795–808, 1960.

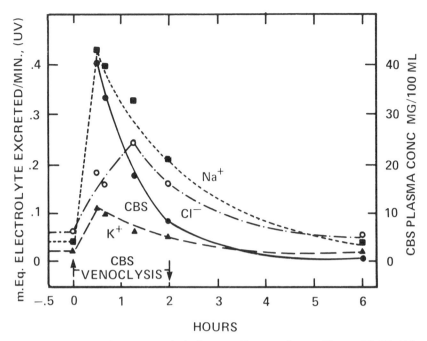

FIG. 2.   Redrawn from Beyer: *Arch. Internat. Pharmacodyn. et Therap. 98:* 97–117, 1954.

tive dose is reached and exceeded. When two compounds can be compared on this basis, where the slope of the two curves is essentially the same but differ in dosage at which they occur, their activity, mode of action, distribution, and elimination may be essentially the same — one being more active than the other. In this unusual example, where three structurally different thiazides have been compared, it is clear that the curves for the two more active compounds are the same and that they differ in activity by tenfold. The least active (1/100 as active as the most active) has essentially the same curve as the others but it differs sufficiently to suggest that a cause should be sought. Actually, this compound, chlorothiazide, differs sufficiently in its solubility characteristics that it has some effect on sodium transport in the distal portion of the nephron in addition to a predominant effect in the proximal segment to which the activity of the other two (hydrochlorothiazide and trichlormethiazide) is limited. This difference in activity is due to the relationship of increasing lipid solubility of the compounds to increasing activity. On the other hand, the maximal potency, the greatest amount of sodium that each compound can cause to be excreted is the same, as is evident from these data. All available thiazide drugs have much the same maximal effect, so when the response of the patient to these drugs is inadequate, drugs having a greater maximal effect, a greater potency, should be prescribed.

Another type of dose/response curve is represented in Fig. 2. The information obtained in this manner was important to the anticipation of saluretic activity in the sulfonamide structure. That is, the excretion of both sodium and chloride ions was increased by the intravenous injection of CBS, potassium being affected to a much lesser extent. When the infusion of *p*-carboxybenzenesulfonamide (CBS) was stopped and its plasma concentration (the amount reaching the renal tubules) was allowed to decrease, there was a gradual return of sodium, potassium, and chloride excretion to the initial control level. The effect of the compound was of a nature that was immediately reversible when it was withdrawn — a safety feature important to the practical clinical use of such compounds.

Figure 1, Chapter 10, represents still another type of dose response curve whereby the acute toxicity of a compound can be calculated. It is discussed in greater detail in that chapter on *safety assessment.*

Even when a fair amount of information is at hand about congeners of the agent that is to undergo preclinical assessment [such as was available prior to the work on metaraminol (Chapter 6)], that specific compound should be evaluated in more than one species for what it is expected to do. The studies should include the dose/response relationship for efficacy and for acute toxicity by the intended route of administration, preferably in the same species. Frequently, the early biological studies can be designed so as to allow some appreciation of onset and duration of action of the new agent. This may be important for the design of subsequent studies if a suitable chemical analytical method for the compound is not available for that purpose at this point in its assessment.

TRANSPOSITION OF LABORATORY DATA TO THE CLINIC

Variability of Response Between Species

Actually, it is seldom that a compound is uniformly active across various species. This should not seem remarkable. By adaptation, some of the animals we use, like the mouse, are herbiverous and others, like the cat, are carnivorous by preference. Whereas the rat is to be found wherever man is, nevertheless, its omnivorous appetite and associated enzyme adaptation seems better suited to its own survival than are those of the dog whose friendship man prefers. The ape seems to differ most quantitatively from man metabolically in our experience. The lesser primates seem as different among themselves as do the more earthbound vertebrates.

Whereas the differences with which categories of animals respond to a chemical may be real sources of error when anticipating its utility in man, nevertheless, they also constitute means for anticipating genetic differences among people and the way they respond to drugs. In this connection, the idea that one should find an animal that responds to a compound metabolically like man for safety assessment, to assure the transposition of results to patients, is as naive as it is popular (see Chapter 10). Perhaps this paragraph can be summarized by saying that the less uniform the response to a compound administered to several animal species by the same mode or modes of administration, the less certain the anticipation of an effect in man or any other species in which it has not been tested.

Variability of Response of Strains and Individual Animals

Within a species of animals, variability of response due to strain (genetic) differences may be considerable. When variability of response is to be minimized, as for assaying and comparing activity or toxicity of different batches of a compound, the use of a single strain of, say, mice is important. This is not particularly different from the variance in response between races of people exposed to the same compound. Various strains of particularly mice and rats are maintained for research purposes such as the development of breast cancer in certain strains of mice, the spontaneously hypertensive strain of rats, etc.

A certain amount of variability of response of a specific animal to a drug on a day-to-day basis is normal, just as it is for people, for reasons of environmental variability of diet, exposure, rest, etc. However, when that variability in response to a compound is substantial for an individual animal or strain of animals from day to day, it is likely that the experiment is not being fully controlled. For example, the rate of excretion of mecamylamine, a secondary amino basic compound, can differ from almost none when the urine is alkaline to a rapid rate equivalent to renal plasma flow when the animal's urine is acidic. As another example, dehydration of mice increases the acute toxicity (lowers the LD_{50}) of some compounds, ethacrynic acid for instance. On the other hand, some animals of the same species and source do absorb or respond to a drug more rapidly or markedly than their counterparts. At the two extremes, such animals of the same species may be referred to as "slow absorbers" and "fast absorbers" when referring to "oral activity" of a drug or to its blood levels.

Variability and the Slope of the Dose/Response Curve

The significance of this variability for anticipating uniformity of clinical response is greatest toward the initial portion of the dose/response curve, at lowest effective dosage. Transposed to the clinical situation, if a minimally effective dose of a compound for one patient is the same as half its maximally effective dose for another, then enthusiasm for the agent would be considerably less than if it were more uniformly effective at a given dosage. This is because of the extra care that might be needed to individualize the dose for a patient.

Also, the slope of the dose/response curve is an indicator of uniformity of response. More potent compounds tend to have steeper dose response curves (the slope is greater) than do less potent drugs. Thus, compounds with steep dose response curves are thought to be less safe somehow than those with flatter curves. This impression (if unsupported by toxicity data) is not warranted in any specific instance. The proximity (and the magnitude of variance of response at the coordinates) of the dose response curves for activity and toxicity relate more properly to safety. My impression is that the more precipitous the dose/response curve for activity or toxicity the fewer the different sites of drug binding (at least in kind) and the fewer or less important the divergent factors that influence the availability and activity of an agent.

Assuming that a new compound has withstood a critical assessment of its primary activity, that for which it is to be used as a drug, its secondary pharmacodynamic characteristics and safety need to be determined. (See Chapter 10 for safety assessment.)

SECONDARY PHARMACODYNAMIC CHARACTERISTICS

The secondary characteristics of a new compound must be assessed and found suitable if it is to merit clinical trial. Generally, the broader the utility of a chemotherapeutic agent for systematic infections in man and/or the more narrowly the activity of a pharmacodynamic agent can be defined, within useful limits, the better. (Conceptually though, a chemotherapeutic agent that kills all microorganisms might well be useless, and a pharmacodynamic agent, such as a prostaglandin, that cannot be restricted in its potent activity seems destined to be more interesting than useful.) As the availability of procedures for evaluating the effects of compounds on increasing numbers of organs becomes greater, the complexity of the "Preclinical" is likely to increase, also. Thus, it is important to weed out early those agents not likely to make the grade and to get to know quite thoroughly those in which so much time and effort are to be invested in the course of their conversion into new drugs.

The nature and extent of assessment of the secondary pharmacodynamic characteristics of a new compound should vary from one type or purpose to another. The idea of doing "everything" on every drug is as absurd as it is extravagant. Assessment of a topical local anesthetic to be used for sunburn or insect bites would be quite different from a topical antiinflammatory adrenocorticoid, for instance.

Appropriateness of Secondary Studies

An appetite depressant, a psychic energizer, and an agent for benign orthostatic hypotension might come from the same genera of compounds but their preclinical laboratory assessments should differ considerably in some respects and not in others. A number of reasons can be cited why this should be so. For example, an appetite depressant for weight loss might be assessed in young adults, clinically. The teratogenicity studies undertaken would be comprehensive before clinical trial, because ultimately young women of child-bearing age are apt to be a market for such an agent. (Even though the preclinical tests including teratogenesis were reassuring, one would anticipate conducting the initial clinical studies in young males or preadolescents. If the compound seemed effective and really worthwhile, the clinicians might then decide to try the drug in postmenopausal women. Finally, it might be assessed in women of child-bearing age if the investigator were willing to risk confusing a drug effect with the common occurrence of abnormalities in the newborn.)

The compound for benign orthostatic hypotension would receive substantial attention in the laboratory with respect to the reflex modulation of systemic blood pressure, cardiac output, and cerebral blood flow with change in posture. The experimental psychologist might check out the compound for similarity to tranquilizers, antidepressants, etc. in his tests and it would be assessed for effects on common organ functions. The teratogenic studies might not be emphasized. The clinical assessment is likely to be carried out in a population of patients beyond the child-bearing age.

The psychic energizer would present another problem, actually two problems that need to be anticipated in the preclinical assessment. It would most likely be studied in elderly patients where the incidence of spontaneous cardiovascular troubles and death are naturally high. The psychic energizer just might also be useful for the management of young hyperkinetic children. Thus, one might expect to see emphasis on behavior studies in the preclinical examination of such a compound. In addition, one would be inclined to add to a reasonably broad laboratory assessment of the compound (including the cardiovascular system) such other tests as might seem sensible to pediatricians knowledgeable about the current practices when evaluating compounds for study in children. (Conceivably, a study in children could change from noble to ignominious quickly in the public eye whether or not the drug is at fault.) Added to all those imponderables would be the requirements of the regulatory agencies within whose jurisdictions it was planned to conduct the clinical research.

PHARMACOKINETIC CHARACTERISTICS, METABOLISM, AND EXCRETION

To this point, we have discussed the need to establish the primary attribute of a new compound by more than one procedure and the need to adapt the assessment of secondary attributes to the purpose for which it is intended. There remain to be established the biophysical conditions for optimal activity, the distribution, binding characteristics of the agent, and its physiological economy (i.e., metabolism and excretion). A number of examples might be cited to illustrate these points. These attributes can be illustrated conveniently by staying with the broad category of carbonic anhydrase inhibitors discussed in Chapter 8.

Prior to the advent of chlorothiazide, the more active diuretics required the coadministration of ammonium chloride (organomercurials) or sodium bicarbonate (sulfonamides) to create an acidic or alkalotic condition optimal for their respective action. Thus, ammonium chloride was prescribed with the organomercurials; they were most active at acid urinary pH and least effective when urine was alkaline. Conversely, acetazolamide was maximally active when coadminsitered with sodium bicarbonate and was all but ineffective under conditions of acidosis. Chlorothiazide was found to be active under conditions of acidosis or alkalosis, the anion accompanying the natriuresis being predominantly chloride under conditions of ammonium chloride acidosis and bicarbonate when alkalosis was induced by the co-administration of sodium bicarbonate. This reliability of the thiazide under these extremes of variability was important. Its use in diuretic therapy could be initiated simply and promptly whether or not the electrolyte status of the patient was normal.

Prior to the advent of the thiazides, we realized that a generally useful carbonic anhydrase inhibitory diuretic should have its volume of distribution limited essentially to extracellular fluid (except for secretion by the renal tubules) if side effects attributable to carbonic anhydrase inhibition in the brain, the eye, erythrocytes, and elsewhere were to be avoided. The thiazides have a volume of distribution essentially extracellular, they are generally effective as diuretic agents and they do not have the extrarenal side effects common to carbonic anhydrase inhibitors that have a broader than extracellular distribution.

The binding of drugs to protein, such as plasma albumin, is an important aspect of their use and physiological economy. Whereas the proportion of total drug plasma concentration bound to plasma protein cannot be ultrafiltered by the glomeruli, neither is it directly available for pharmacodynamic or chemotherapeutic activity. It must dissociate from an inert bound form to be active. Ordinarily, the equilibrium between free and bound drug in plasma is easily reversible. It varies so that the lower the total drug plasma concentration, the higher the proportion bound to albumin. The binding of thiazides to plasma proteins varies from some 60% to well over 90%. Their dosage varies inversely with the extent of their binding, though this attribute does not account entirely for the marked range of equivalent (effective) dosage among them. Other physical factors, such as lipid solubility, dissociation, metabolic stability, and relative activity of metabolites contribute to drug dosage, to where the agent acts, and to duration of its effect.

Metabolic degradation of chlorothiazide or hydrochlorothiazide is not important to their duration of action. The thiazides are secreted by the renal tubules, their dosage being inversely related to rate of excretion, grossly.

Unless the effects attributable to the inherent characteristics of the new compound are anticipated and examined in its pharmacological assessment, they are likely later to obfuscate its safety assessment in animals or man. For example, if a new compound ever affects the capability of the bowel to sustain its role in the conservation of water and electrolytes, this had better be noted and explored by the pharmacologist in the preclinical studies, for he is likely to be the only one to view the finding with curiosity. The clinical effect might be a diarrhea, as in cholera.

The kaliuretic effect of chlorothiazide was noted from the beginning of its study. Drug-induced potassium loss, why it occurs, under what circumstances it is greatest, what to do about it and how, has figured in the use of the thiazides since the inception of their clinical trials.

The fact that chlorothiazide was secreted by the renal tubules, apparently in the same way as p-aminohippurate, penicillin, and the probenecid family of compounds, made it likely to affect uric acid secretion; it might be uricosuric like probenecid or it might produce uric acid retention by the kidneys, like most uricosuric agents do when they are administered at low dosage. Chlorothiazide turned out to be uricosuric when administered intravenously (when the amount presented to the kidneys was sufficient, as by intravenous administration) and to cause uric acid retention under ordinary clinical conditions of use (i.e., oral saluretic dosage).

WHAT NOT TO DO

Within the scope of these pages, a more detailed delineation of the preclinical pharmacodynamic assessment of a new compound by classes of drugs, by organs, or by "do's" and "don'ts" seems excessive. This is not intended to be a manual of pharmacology in the first place and the requirements of the regulatory agencies do need to be met (Chapter 17) if the compound is to be assessed clinically with their concurrence. In this connection, though, there is one "don't" that may not seem like good science, but it is good sense. Don't, *do not,* subject an interesting new compound needlessly to (interesting) new procedures in the laboratory while the interpretation of the results from such new procedures can be more controversial than conclusive. By Federal Regulation all data need to be incorporated in the preclinical report to the regulatory agent prior to undertaking its clinical assessment. With the best of intentions on the part of all concerned, such information of uncertain significance could become cause for delaying or denying clinical trial and so become a source of conflict and embarrassment to the discoverer, the sponsor, and to the agency as well.

So as to give the reader a better idea of the scope of preclinical assessment of a new compound prior to its clinical evaluation, I have reproduced as Table II, the Table of Contents of the *Preclinical Evaluation of Indomethacin,* an important nonsteroid antiinflammatory agent used principally in the management of arthritis. This "Preclinical" does not include *Safety Assessment* (see Table of Contents at the end of Chapter 10).

TABLE II

Table of Contents from the Preclinical Evaluation of Indomethacin (Indocid)
Pharmacology Section (May 15, 1964)[a]

(continued)

Table II *(continued)*

(continued)

Table II *(continued)*

(continued)

Table II *(continued)*

[a]Permission granted by Merck & Co., Inc.

COLLATERAL LITERATURE

Armitage, P. (1971): *Statistical Methods in Medical Research,* 3rd Printing, Blackwell Scientific Publications, London, England.

Colton, T. (1974): *Statistics in Medicine,* 3rd Printing, Little Brown and Co., Boston, Massachusetts.

SECTION II
DEVELOPMENT

10.
Safety Assessment

TO ASSURE SAFETY FOR ALL

"To assure (drug) safety for all is to deny therapy to any." Beyer (1965): *Proc. Western Pharmacol. Soc. 8:* 68–71. From Theory to Therapy: Today and To-morrow.

The quotation cited above was first used in a speech before The Western Pharmacological Society in 1965. It was intended to teach the reality of safety assessment in a single sentence. ". . . to deny therapy to any" while everything possible is being done to assure a new drug's ". . . safety for all . . ." can be a quiet tragedy, hard to assess, easy to ignore, and known to few at the time, usually.

I put the statement together one evening in Washington during a dinner conversation with other members of the, then, Drug Research Board. That group had been brought together under the auspices of The National Academy of Sciences to help resolve some of the problems that inevitably followed the 1962 legislation pertaining to new drugs. The statement is a summing up of what people knowledgeable of the field know to be a realistic attitude about the safety assessment of a new drug. Even if "everything" known at any time was done, a politically attractive attitude, safety for all could not be assured. People differ a great deal, qualitatively and/or quantitatively, in their reactivity to drugs. Trying to assure safety for everybody would be a little like trying to tailor a pair of trousers to fit exactly all men (and women) over the age of 21, for example. Insistence on doing everything is a waste of resources and a handicap to the advancement of toxicology because of the superfluous diversion of resources that might better be used to gain new knowledge about safety assessment to advance the field. Even if everything the toxicologists knew how to do at the time could have been done, the teratogenic effect of thalidomide would not have been noted during its preclinical safety assessment.

THE DIFFERENCE BETWEEN SAFETY ASSESSMENT
AND TOXICOLOGICAL ASSESSMENT

Only in the past decade or so has the term safety assessment come to supersede toxicological assessment as more fitting to new drug evaluation. The terms are not synonymous. The safety assessment guides the clinical investigator to dosages with which he might proceed with caution to use the new drug. The toxicological assessment tells him what to expect when the dosage has exceeded the bounds of caution, or, what might happen to the occasional patient unusually sensitive to the agent. All this presupposes a reasonable transposition to man of results (dosage and effects) found in laboratory animals, which is generally but certainly not always the case.

PROFESSIONAL STRUCTURE OF THE
SAFETY ASSESSMENT AREA

Before we get too far into the safety assessment of new drugs, it might be helpful to introduce some more general aspects of the subject. Toxicology is a seldom-taught aspect of a pharmacology curriculum; so few pharmacologists have much insight into what safety assessment is all about. Pharmacologists may differ sometimes as to their role in the medical curriculum. There is no doubt about the essentiality of well trained toxicologists to the chemical industry. Industry's toxicologic problems include pollution, food preservation, packaging, drugs, and cosmetics.

Actually, members of the Society of Toxicology are scientists with differing technical backgrounds who have been trained in the ways of inducing and recognizing aberrations in structure or function of organisms by chemical or physical force. With rather few exceptions, the people we refer to as toxicologists will have been trained in one or more of the following disciplines: physiology, pharmacology, biochemistry, pathology, electron microscopy and, more recently, in teratology, oncology, or mutagenesis. All these capabilities are needed today for what may be considered adequate safety or toxicologic assessment of a new drug. Their special training in toxicology is usually on-the-job, under the supervision of more experienced professionals.

Pathologists may form the backbone of the toxicology or safety assessment group in industry, just as they are in forensic medicine,* or their role may be more a supportive one, depending on the institution. Usually, all the records and hundreds of slides from many animals and tissues end up on the pathologists' desks. The recommendation of the senior pathologist (whatever his title), supported by staff and consultants, usually is needed before the new compound can be made available for systematic trial in man, or domestic animals if it is an animal science product. The pathologist may be an M.D., trained in human medicine, or a D.V.M., a veterinary pathologist. Frequently, today, the pathologist, regardless of his professional degree will also have a Ph.D. degree.

The overall design of a safety assessment may require the collaboration of several specialists, each of whom accepts responsibility for a specific segment of the study. Thus, physiologists and pharmacologists are trained to design and handle the drug—animal aspects of the study up to the demise of the animal and its inspection in the autopsy room. There the pathologist takes over the gross and histological examination of the animals and their tissues.

The biochemists are responsible for the clinical chemistry and special chemical studies conducted on the animals during a safety assessment. In a good sized pharmaceutical research laboratory, there may be as many as a thousand animals on test that require routine and special chemical analysis of blood and urine. The routine analyses can then be handled directly through computers to final printout of results. Many other aspects of safety assessment data handling have also been adapted to computers.

The staff in teratology has been a part of safety assessment for many years, since the thalidomide tragedy. Their procedures are reasonably well developed and accepted within that discipline. Their investigations are collateral and supportive to the large chronic toxicity studies. The shorter duration of such studies makes it possible to schedule them early or late in the overall safety assessment. They have very special requirements from beginning to end.

Today, the research oncologist has pretty well accepted the premise that drug-induced false cell mutation will lead to death of the cell involved or to tumor production. (There may be other ways of inducing carcinogenesis.) Consequently, the relatively rapid ways of assessing mutagenesis become immensely important. Even so, the adaptation of that methodology to safety

*Perhaps it should be made clear that the subject matter of this chapter is not what is known in forensic medicine as toxicology. In that instance the toxicologist is concerned with identifying a cause of death – the identity of a compound, the likely dose, mode of administration and such other relevant information as may be needed. The forensic toxicologist makes use of knowledge about drugs that has been created in the course of their development and use. It is not his purpose to contribute to the safety assessment of a new drug except by chance.

assessment will seem more credible as it becomes better developed and as the relevance of such animal studies to man becomes better accepted.

As recently as 1950, the laboratory assessment of drug safety was really intended to give some assurance that the compound was unlikely to cause serious trouble at the outset of the clinical trial. In those days, it was considered evident that the best study of man was man. The staff and space needed to conduct that work in animals were quite modest, for three reasons: (1) The duration of the "chronic" toxicity test was only 3 to 6 months. (2) The study was not so elaborate. (3) The scope of the testing was not so inclusive. By the late 1950's the duration of the studies had begun to increase for no better reason than that many thought it the "safe" thing to do.

The advent of the thalidomide fiasco gave more sensible direction to safety assessment – broadening the scope of testing. It seems that teratologic methodology of that day (1961) was not adequate to have revealed the proclivity of thalidomide to induce phocomelia nor was it generally employed. That lesson has served to motivate the development of still other collateral tests as adjuncts to the long-term toxicity studies. It is interesting that when the thalidomide tragedy struck it was not from the need to do more of what was being done for longer periods of time, but because of something that was not being done – adequate teratogenic studies.

Since 1960, the safety assessment area of the pharmaceutical research laboratories has become the most rapidly growing in space, facilities, and personnel of any part of the research organization. In the larger institutions, only modern methods of advanced planning and scheduling keep such a complex structure functioning smoothly. Only the computer assimilation, processing, and reporting of results make the careful use of such volumes of information manageable. Now to the core types of tests for safety assessment.

SAFETY ASSESSMENT – WHERE IT BEGINS

What is generally called safety assessment relates to the more structured studies carried out by a group of toxicologists and pathologists on a compound being worked up for clinical study. Actually, the safety assessment of a compound may have begun with the structure – activity assessments from which it was selected for further exploration. It may be recalled from Chapter 9 on Preclinical Pharmacology that the presentation of data from the original renal clearance protocol by which chlorothiazide was discovered (Chapter 9, Table I) provided for an assessment of whether the compound was effective, whether the experiment was technically satisfactory, and whether there was any evidence that the compound may have been toxic. Toxicity in this instance may have been reflected in a more or less sudden decrease in urine flow, a reduction in glomerular filtration rate, restlessness, cutaneous vasodilation, salivating, or any aberration in behavior of the dog. More compounds are likely to be abandoned in the course of their pharmacological work up than subsequently for reasons of toxicity. In the pharmacological assessment, toxicity might be no more than an inability to separate two pharmacodynamic actions of an agent sufficiently (in terms of dosage) to make it likely that the patient would tolerate the compound for its intended purpose. Gastric intolerance is another form of toxicity that may be observed in the course of the initial pharmacodynamic studies, whether the compound is given orally or intraveneously to the animals.

ACUTE TOXICITY STUDIES

The first thing people associate with safety assessment is the determination of a compound's acute lethal dose (LD). For example, the LD_{50} is the amount calculated from a dose-response curve to kill 50% of a given population of animals. The value is usually accompanied by some expression of variability, like the $LD_{50} = 50 \pm 5.0$ mg/kg (standard deviation*) of body weight. The animal may be a mouse, rat, dog, chicken, or some other creature. Usually, one obtains an LD_{50} when the compound is given orally, subcutaneously, intramuscularly, or intravenously, as in Fig. 1. Frequently, several species of animals are employed for the determinations, if there is enough of the compound. An LD_{50}, LD_{10}, or even an LD_1 value may be calculated, especially for pesticides, to give some idea of individual sensitivity to the agent. However, the numbers of animals needed for reliable determination of such values as the "LD_1," with usefully low variance usually are so great as to preclude such estimates.

Figure 1 is a dose-response curve for indomethacin administered by stomach tube as single doses to mice. The "curve" (A) is a plot of the dose/death coordinates at the end of 14 days. Curve B is a plot of the dose/death relationship at the end of 24 hours. In each instance the data can be plotted as straight lines on the log probit scale from which the LD_{50} (or most any other LD value) can be obtained by inspection. From the difference in calculated slope of the two curves and the lesser value for the delayed death LD_{50}, it should be evident that the cause of death was different when it

*Standard deviation indicates that in 2/3 of 100 trials the calculated LD_{50} will be between 45 and 55 mg/kg.

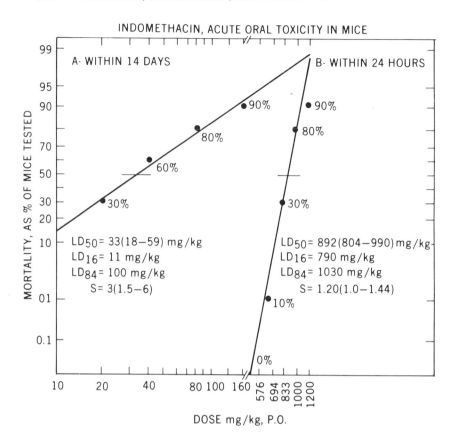

INDOMETHACIN, ACUTE ORAL TOXICITY IN MICE

occurred within the first 24 hours of drug administration as compared with when it occurred later. Variance is represented by the numbers (in parentheses), such as LD_{50} = 33 (18–59) mg/kg.

HOW ACUTE TOXICITY STUDIES ARE USED

Actually, the acute lethal dose (LD) values, *per se*, are apt to be more useful to the pharmacologist than to the toxicologist. A very low LD_{50} value (high acute toxicity) simply means that the compound is very active, but not necessarily unsafe. It is the compound with the high LD_{50} (low acute toxicity) that is apt to be less interesting if that is all that is known about it. The slope of the toxicity dose—response curve may give some anticipation of a similar slope to its pharmacodynamic activity with respect to dosage, but this projection is not reliable. Good oral absorption may be anticipated by values for oral and intraperitoneal or intravenous acute toxicity data that closely approximate each other (a low oral/intravenous ratio of LD_{50}'s). If the values for the acute toxicity determinations on a compound (i.e., oral LD_{50}) are essentially similar for several species then the likelihood of extrapolating such results to still other animals is good. Such may mean that the processes of absorption and elimination of the compound are not profoundly different in these animals.

Let me illustrate this use of the LD_{50} values by the pharmacologist before going on to other aspects of acute toxicity information. As recited in the mecamylamine story (Chapter 5) one day an interesting record of an experiment suggested that the cycloaliphatic secondary amine being studied was a ganglionic blocking agent. Ganglionic blockade was not known to exist outside the quaternary ammonium compounds.

The available quaternary drugs, such as hexamethonium and pentolinium, were difficult to use, though very effective against severe hypertension. The reason they were difficult to use was largely because of their poor and erratic absorption when administered orally. Amines are usually much better absorbed from the gastrointestinal tract than their quaternary counterparts. With no better immediate way to check the oral absorption of the exciting new secondary amines, we requested a comparison of oral to subcutaneous LD_{50} values in the mouse. These LD_{50} values came out to be quite similar, indicating that the compound was well absorbed from the gastrointestinal tract. A comparison of the acute toxicities of this amine and several quaternary ammonium ganglionic blocking agents is illustrated in Table I. Actually, the second of many compounds in the series studied was marketed as mecamylamine (Inversine).

[The decision to recommend that this compound be worked up for clinical trial in anticipation that it might be our first new drug in the important hypertension field of therapy was based on simple acute blood pressure tracings that reflected its ganglionic blocking action (see Chapter 5, Fig. 3) and the low ratio of oral to intravenous LD_{50}'s. That decision was made about the data during the Fall Meetings of the Pharmacology and Physiology Societies in 1954. Perhaps one of the factors that made the decision appealing was a symposium at one of those meetings that had to do with the optimal characteristics of the quaternary ammonium structure that bestowed maximal ganglionic blockade on such a molecule. Listening to those papers did not seem nearly so exciting as the new findings that I have just described. Obviously, the new compound needed a lot of support and so did the recommendation to management. The drug did a lot to introduce the company to the potential for still better antihypertensive therapy, the saluretic thiazides.]

TABLE I

Acute Toxicity of Mecamylamine and Other Ganglionic Blocking Agents[a,b]

Compound	Species	Route				Ratio P.O. LD_{50}/I.V. LD_{50}
		I.V.	P.O.	S.C.	I.P.	
Pentolinium	mice	29 (26-33)	512 (430-610)	—	36 (34-37)	18
Chlorisondamine	mice	24 (21-27)	401 (366-438)	—	—	17
Hexamethonium	mice	21 (19-23)	484 (385-608)	—	42 (37-46)	23
Tetraethylammonium	mice	29 (27-30)	655 (534-806)	—	56 (52-75)	23
Mecamylamine	mice	21 (18.8-23.5)	92 (80-107)	93 (82-105)	39 (36-42)	4.4
Mecamylamine	rats	—	171 (147-199)	145 (127-165)	54 (51-58)	—
Mecamylamine	guinea pigs	—	144 (122-169)	127 (112-144)	52 (48-57)	—

[a] The values in the table are LD_{50}'s calculated along with the 95 percent confidence limits, according to the method described by Weil (1952). Ten animals at each of 4 dose levels were employed. All values are in terms of mgm. of ion or base/kgm.

[b] From Stone et al. (1956): *J. Pharmacol. 117:* 169-183.

114

Another use of acute toxicity data is for estimating a likely safe but effective dose when a new compound is given in single doses to highly trained very valuable unanesthetized laboratory animals. No one wants to hurt such friends that actually seem to enjoy being a part of the action, so to speak. Some of the dogs used in our renal program were around for as long as 15 years before they were retired to the farm.

When doing acute toxicity studies, a checklist of signs of induced changes is helpful lest some subtle effect of the compound escape notice, but the technician should be trained to search for and record any other signs or symptoms that may not have been listed. The time of onset of signs of toxicity and death may indicate whether the mortality is due to an acute overt pharmacodynamic effect or to a slower degeneration of some organ or function. This feature of Fig. 1 was noted at the time it was discussed. Such information may also be helpful when the dosage range-finding experiments are undertaken for the more protracted toxicity studies.

Ordinarily, animals subjected to the acute toxicity tests are not autopsied for gross and histologic examination, for such studies may be more misleading than helpful. They may mislead because the profusion of profound effects induced at symptomatic to lethal doses can obfuscate important findings. The important signs and symptoms are induced more reliably by subacute to chronic administration of the drug at lower doses that may or may not produce outwardly apparent change in the animals. They may also mislead in that at subsymptomatic acute doses the effect may not persist long enough to induce well defined aberrations of structure or function. In other words, such acute toxicity studies may be more confusing than helpful when pressed to provide information better obtained in more appropriate experiments. To know whether such information was helpful or misleading, additional toxicity studies required of compounds being prepared for clinical assessment would have to be done anyway. It cannot be overemphasized that in toxicologic assessment of a new drug each experiment should be so carefully selected and designed as to yield useful information instead of adding confusion to ignorance.

ADAPTING SAFETY ASSESSMENT TO INTENDED CLINICAL UTILITY

If an interesting new compound is to be assessed clinically, it should be subjected to safety assessment appropriate and adequate to the purpose of the study in man. Thus, if one wanted to see whether the new drug was a local anesthetic when injected subcutaneously into the arm of a person, a

3-month oral toxicity study in laboratory animals would be wasteful at that point and neither appropriate nor adequate for the intended study. More to the point would be (1) acute intravenous and subcutaneous toxicity studies in several species, (2) experiments on the reversibility of local functional and structural effects, (3) local irritation studies together with (4) a cardiovascular workup in laboratory animals wherein the compound was administered intravenously. If the compound proved interesting as a local anesthetic, then one would want to undertake more protracted studies wherein the agent was administered however it need be (orally or parenterally) to assess its inherent systemic, not just its local, toxicity.

SELECTION OF ANIMALS FOR STUDY

The first line basic toxicity studies for compounds that are to be employed systemically are the subacute and chronic administration to two or three species of animals. Usually, the animals employed are rats and dogs. If a third species is employed, it is usually selected for a specific purpose from among those animals on which a considerable body of background toxicological data is available. This diversification of species is to lend perspective to the interpretation of results. Thus, the mouse might be preferred to the hamster which in turn is better understood than the gerbil in the toxicology laboratory. Whereas the immunologist has developed a useful working knowledge of the guinea pig, this species is more apt to be avoided by the toxicologist except for the purpose to which the immunologist might put it. Highly inbred strains of animals give for many measurements (assays) a more uniform or reproducible response. The outbred animals are more apt to demonstrate greater variability of toxicity. Thus, both are useful, but the outbred strains are preferred for toxicity studies.

There is a certain popularity to the notion of finding a species for toxicity studies that most closely approximates the metabolism of a specific drug by man. This gives an aura of authenticity or credibility that the results will more certainly resemble an effect in man. This illusion is apt to be more fiction than fact in my experience, for there is a great deal more to the interaction of subject and drug than the metabolism of the compound. Indeed, something is to be said for selecting one of the species for the safety study that is dissimilar in the metabolism or overall elimination of the drug. Man is about as heterogeneous a species as we are likely to encounter with respect to both numerous genetic and environmental factors that affect drug disposition and action.

DOSAGE RANGE-FINDING STUDIES

The selection of dosage for a subacute or chronic toxicity study on a new compound is a serious business. Usually, at least three dosage levels are selected for each type of animal. These should range from no toxic effect at the lowest dosage to sufficient toxicity at the highest dosage to assure that some of the animals will not survive the duration of the study.

Thus, the range-finding studies should make use of the acute toxicity information and should employ sufficient dosages over a broad enough range to assure:

1. that the dosage range for the long-term study is not so low that no manifestation of toxicity is seen; and
2. that the dosage range is not set so high that all the animals manifest toxicity or that so many die during the test as to reduce the numbers surviving to the point that the subsequent study of tissues is inadequate.

Often, what appears over a few days to be a satisfactory dosage range becomes too much or too little as the metabolism of the animal adjusts or adapts to the drug over a period of time. The range-finding studies must anticipate that the duration of administration of the drug may be for a period of weeks to months for the subacute tests to the lifetime of a mouse (18 months), or rat (2 years), and 2 years or longer in the dog or monkey for the chronic studies. The studies are started in young adult animals.

An equivalent number of identical control animals (not given the drug) are carried through the same procedure concurrently in the subacute and chronic toxicity studies for comparative purposes.

SUBACUTE TOXICITY STUDIES

The subacute toxicity study is designed to suffice for the support of clinical studies wherein the drug is administered for a few days to 2 weeks in man. The drug is usually given orally once or twice a day at some three dosage levels to dogs and white rats for 7 days per week. Clinical chemistry, hematology, and microscopic urinalysis are performed during a control phase prior to starting the drug phase of the experiment. These chemical studies are repeated periodically during administration of the compound and then again after the agent had been withdrawn, if a recovery phase is part of the protocol. More frequently, the animals are sacrificed while still being administered the drug. In any event, they are autopsied and examined thoroughly both grossly and histologically; special stains, electron microscopy, etc., being employed where they may be thought to be useful.

CHRONIC TOXICITY STUDIES

The chronic toxicity studies are performed in much the same way as the subacute trials. Special procedures are introduced as required. Enough animals are employed at each dosage level so that the rat studies may continue for 2 years if desired to incorporate assessment of carcinogenesis and the dog studies for as long a time or longer depending on the compound and for what purpose it is intended. These studies have become so expanded with respect to numbers of animals, numbers of test procedures, and duration that the data are best handled with the aid of computers and by automation of as much of the technical work as possible.

These chronic toxicity studies usually run concurrently with the clinical trial but are initiated well in advance of the protracted clinical studies. They serve to supplement and extend the subacute animal studies. They may be monitored periodically by sacrificing a portion of the animals after 6 and 12 months for gross and histomorphic examination of various tissues in addition to the daily observations and the chemical and hematology laboratory studies.

SUPPORTIVE STUDIES

Three other types of studies have been introduced as part of the safety assessment over the past 15 years. These include teratogenesis, mutagenesis, and carcinogenesis. The purposes of the studies are suggested by their names. To describe the various types of tests in each category and the current stage of their development would be unnecessary for present purposes. The teratogenic studies have been a routine part of safety assessment since the early 1960's. The carcinogenicity studies are more or less accepted as needed for the assessment and approval of a new drug. They may or may not be incorporated in the chronic toxicity trials. The mutagenicity assessment is not yet standardized sufficiently for the preference of specific procedures over others that seem as well founded. This is bound to settle down in the next several years.

In the past and today, important aspects of the mutagenic tests have been and are anticipated by the practical multigeneration tests, usually in mice or rats. The drug is given to the males, usually over a period of time. They are mated and the resulting litters are divided into those young that will be given the drug to maturity to repeat the mating process for multiple generations. Those young not chosen to continue the study are autopsied at each generation to search for changes in structure of various organs. These tests can be modified to suit better the purpose of the new agent.

ANTICIPATORY SAFETY ASSESSMENT

There is a trend today toward the concept of anticipatory safety assessment. Where this "anticipatory" concept is employed, the initial acute toxicity, teratogenic, and mutagenic studies, and the first part of a subacute toxicity test in rats and dogs will have been completed before the compound is given to man. Performed concurrently, they give so many of the signs of impending trouble (if any) with the compound that the few weeks and reasonable amount of chemical required seem well invested. All this information must be obtained anyway, and so a prudent attitude might be *the sooner the safer,* from any point of view.

THE PRECLINICAL SAFETY ASSESSMENT REPORT

All of the safety assessment studies are required to be reported to the Food and Drug Administration and to be made available to the clinical investigator as part of the preclinical report. The writeup also must include the names and qualifications of those who took part in that research. As important new data are obtained, the preclinical reports are revised and distributed as above.

At the end of this section the Table of Contents for the Preclinical Report on the safety assessment of indomethacin (Indocin) is reproduced as Table II. This is the same antiarthritic compound on which the Preclinical Pharmacology Table of Contents was reproduced at the end of Chapter 9 (see Chapter 9 Table II). In order to give some idea of the size of the report as well as the complexity of the work, the pagination, some 595 pages, is left beside the items. This also helps to give an idea of the number of tables, data summary tables, in each part of the study.

On the other hand, the Table of Contents can give only a superficial impression of what modern safety assessment is all about. This report does not reflect work on the compound since that time. Mutagenic studies specifically identified as such were not performed at that time (1964). Mutagenicity and carcinogenesis were covered realistically in the scope and depth of reproduction studies including teratology and the two year trials in rats and dogs.

120

Table II *(continued)*

(continued)

Table II *(continued)*

(continued)

Table II *(continued)*

OVERSIGHT AND THE MISINTERPRETATION OF FINDINGS

Undoubtedly, the safety assessment of a new drug is the most demanding of the preclinical biological studies. This is not because the technical aspects are any more sophisticated than the pharmacological or microbiological, etc., evaluation. The assessment is demanding because of the judgmental aspects of the work and the consequences of oversight or misinterpretation of findings. This is the "last step" in the preclinical biological assessment. An oversight or under-estimation of the significance of an observation may be catastrophic at worst and at best wasteful of time and effort at the clinical level.

PHYSIOLOGICAL CHANGES IN STRUCTURE
AND FUNCTION

On the other hand, the toxicologist and pathologist must be ever mindful that what might seem a serious adverse affect may actually be an artifact due to a technical error in handling the study, or real but irrelevant, being peculiar to a single species or even a strain of animal. As the studies become increasingly complex, the opportunity to introduce error or misinterpret observations becomes more frequent. A few examples may suffice to illustrate this important point.

When chlorothiazide and then hydrochlorothiazide were first studied, the top dosage for the chronic toxicity studies was set very high. This could be done with impunity for their rate of absorption following oral administration simply was not great enough to alter electrolyte balance profoundly and their acute toxicity was low (lethal dose was high). After the initial diuresis in dogs and rats, body weight and electrolyte balance stabilized in spite of the continued administration of either chemical. Superficially, this return of urine volume to control values might seem to indicate that the compound had ceased to be effective. This was not so.

The way we determined that the compound continued to be effective during the long-term studies was to give a loading dose of salt and water occasionally. In the dogs given the thiazides, this replacement of salt and water resulted in a prompt saluretic–diuretic effect. The kaliuretic effect seen to accompany the saluresis in the acute renal clearance studies did not persist, since the laboratory diet of the animals provided potassium endogenous to the food and they did not lose their appetite. Hypokalemia was not a problem.

The situation differed for ethacrynic acid, a more potent saluretic agent. The dogs could not sustain their salt and water balance in the subacute or chronic studies when provided with food and ordinary drinking water. They drank copiously to sustain their blood volume but ceased to eat and became moribund at the top oral dosages of the drug. When the dogs were provided saline to drink, they were actually able to return their electrolyte balance to normal. The animals began to eat again and in so doing obtained sufficient potassium from their food. Thus, unless saline was provided to the dogs, we observed the adverse effects of dehydration and loss of electrolyte balance, a physiologic not a toxic effect of the drug, per se.

In either instance, thiazide or ethacrynic acid, it was the pharmacodynamic effect of the agent on sodium, potassium, chloride and water output that made it possible to anticipate what would happen to a digitalized patient or to the debilitated individual whose homeostasis was inadequate to handle over-dosage of the compounds. Both compounds, chlorothiazide and ethacrynic acid, caused a hyperuricemia due to the competitive inhibition of uric acid elimination by these saluretic agents. Again, an immediately reversible physiologic effect on renal function.

Two more illustrations should suffice to show that the safety assessment of each new drug is a problem unto itself.

(1) Fortunately, cortisone came along before the present attitudes about safety assessment prevailed. For one thing, it would have been impossible to make cortisone available to all the patients in need and still have enough for what would be done today to assess a new adrenocorticoid. For another, a chronic toxicity study on such a steroid is a very complicated problem, some of the animals dying from intercurrent infections due to the steroid suppression of host resistance (an immunosuppressant effect). The endocrine effects reflected in the clinical chemistry and histopathology make an interesting or alarming study, depending on one's familarity with such work. Other observations from osteoporosis to gastric ulcers and teratologic abnormalities are enough to give one pause, but these are the overt physiological effects of such steroids and are accommodated by proper adjustment of dosage to a safest level for patients.

(2) Fortunately, Vitamin B_{12} came along when the question about chronic toxicity would not have been raised since it, too, was a natural product. I have wondered at times whether there has been enough B_{12} made since it was first identified to conduct one full fledged toxicity study, not that it is needed.

TRANSPOSITION OF FINDINGS FROM
LABORATORY ANIMALS TO MAN

The basis for judgment as to the likely transposition of findings from laboratory animals to man has increased greatly in complexity and thoroughness over the past quarter century. Earlier, the duration of the chronic toxicity was apt to be 3 months, for instance. Since those days, the credibility of the preclinical assessment has improved as has its thoroughness. Still, there are areas where the capability to anticipate trouble remains unreliable, as for hypersensitivity reactions. The scope of predictive reliability of the mutagenicity tests remains unsure. On the whole, safety assessment is in a dynamic state of development. The experienced investigator in this area knows full well that he must assess the new compound within the limits of knowledge and methodology. Should catastrophy strike one of his agents, it is most apt to do so where the state of relevant methodology is inadequate to the purpose.

"Experience can complement the effective use of knowledge, but it is not an adequate substitute." K. H. Beyer: (1966): Perspectives in toxicology. *Toxicol. Appl. Pharmacol. 8:* 1–5.

COLLATERAL LITERATURE

Committee 17, Environmental Mutagen Soc. (1975): Environmental Mutagen Hazards, *Science 187:* 503–514.

Goldberg, L., Ed. (1973): Carcinogenesis testing of chemicals, CRC Press, Inc., Cleveland, Ohio.

Lowrance, W. W. (1943): *Of Acceptable Risk: Science and the Determination of Safety,* William Kaufman, Inc., Los Altos, California.

WHO (1966): Principles for Pre-Clinical testing of drug safety: *World Health Organization, Technical Report* Ser., No. 341, World Health Organization, Geneva.

WHO (1967): Principles for the testing of drugs for teratogenicity. *World Health Organization, Technical Report* Ser., No. 364, World Health Organization, Geneva.

11.
Chemical
Development

IMPORTANCE OF PROCESS DEVELOPMENT

When I joined the pharmaceutical company of Sharp and Dohme in May, 1943, fresh out of the University of Wisonsin's graduate and medical schools, I brought with me an interesting new compound – a potential new drug. The story in back of the discovery of that compound, metaraminol, was discussed in Chapter 6. Through its introduction to the market by Sharp and Dohme I was taught my first lessons in drug development: Where to get a kilogram or so of an optically active form of the agent for safety assessment? How to meet the needs of the pharmaceutical chemists for supplies with which to develop suitable stable formulations? How to get the much larger amounts, kilograms of material, for clinical trial? These were hard lessons. Actually, the amount needed for safety assessment and clinical trial of that compound was not of the magnitude that would have been required of a new sulfa drug, but it might as well have been. The problems encountered were not all that different, for we did not have either suitable development or production facilities for the product.

Without experienced development chemists and facilities for process development, we were dependent on any chemical company to which we went with a request that they make the amounts that were needed for product development. Such a company, if it accepted a contract to make the supplies would necessarily have to work out something larger than bench scale synthesis. This experience put them in the position to write process patents on our compound. Consequently, the rights to use such patents needed to be negotiated even before the structure of the compound was revealed. Without such agreement, their process patents (or any other process patents) were as useful to our suppliers as the product was to us. Moreover, the organization that controlled the most practical process patent was likely to control who was going to make the compound and at what price.

As we foresaw the future, either we had to acquire a chemical plant, or we had to merge with a chemical company. Happily, the merger of Merck and Sharp and Dohme to form the new Merck and Co., Inc. solved the process development problem.

WHEN PRODUCT DEVELOPMENT BEGINS

For practical purposes, product development begins with the effort to make a drug out of a compound. That interesting compound may have been arrived at by the efforts of one or a team of organic chemist(s), to synthesize however many chemicals needed to be made to arrive at an exceptional one for development. On the other hand, it may have been obtained by isolation from a natural source, be it from plant (Rauwolfia serpentina for hypertension) or animal tissue (ACTH, adrenocorticotropin, for arthritis). It may have been obtained by manipulating the conditions of a certain microbiological fermentation process with subsequent isolation and characterization of a new antibiotic agent. So far as the development chemist is concerned, his interest and responsibility begin when there is something to develop.

DECISION TO DEVELOP A DRUG

The development people may or may not have participated in the management decision that a particular compound was worth trying to develop into a drug. What management of a pharmaceutical company requires by way of information about the compound, the form, and who makes the decision that something is worth developing varies greatly from one company to another. The better and more thorough the biological work up of a compound to this point, regardless of where it comes from, the more likely the decision to develop or abandon the agent will have been a good one.

The adequacy of this basic workup cannot be over emphasized. If the scope of a company's research program is very broad, it may be that only one of every six or seven compounds brought to development will reach the market, will become a new drug. Of those that do reach the practicing physician, still fewer are of sufficient economic importance to help pay for the synthesis and testing of thousands of compounds each year.* Such an economic failure would be a new drug that grossed a million dollars in sales. A different situation is the compound developed and marketed for a relatively rare but medically important purpose with no anticipation of profit, such as actinomycin-D for Wilm's Tumor, a rare cancer of the kidney that occurs in children. The twenty million dollar product more realistically represents a drug that physicians find frequently useful in their practice. The defense of such a statement is better documented elsewhere. These figures are mentioned here to emphasize the importance of the care that should be taken with the decision to develop a new drug. The budget for drug development in a research institute that generates interesting new compounds may be as great or greater than for the more fundamental research. The dollars that can be ascribed directly to the development of a new drug are so great as to render the cost of initial synthesis and preclinical research on it a very modest proportion of the twenty to thirty million dollars or so that may need to be spent on making it a new drug ready for the expense of marketing the product.

INITIAL STEPS IN PRODUCT DEVELOPMENT

When the decision is made to develop a compound, it is given a special code name or number that will stay with the agent until it receives a trademark and a nonproprietary name. (Trademarks are dealt with in Chapter 16.) The compound may be assigned to a coordinator whose function is to see that the schedule that interlocks the many aspects of development into a time frame is held to or that revision thereof is communicated to those who need to know. That master plan for development commits manpower such as toxicologists, pharmaceutical chemists, those responsible for clinical research, and patent lawyers at specific stages in the plan.

It seems the larger the organization the more formal this effort to coordinate the interactions of these separate groups needs to be. Very likely, the coordinator for development will be in contact regularly with a counterpart in marketing. In turn, marketing will see that their sales estimates are transmitted to chemical development in terms of the amount of drug that should be produced and at what rate to fulfill their needs as soon as the regulatory agency approves the new drug. In a large company there may be many concurrent demands on the time of each of these special groups. Each is likely to

*The Pharmaceutical Manufacturers Association reported that in 1970 its members obtained, prepared, extracted, or isolated 126,000 compounds and conducted 703,900 pharmacological tests.

have its own assignment of priorities among projects that require attention. Moreover, this complex central planning and coordination must be done in an atmosphere conducive to the growth and professional satisfaction of the best attainable personnel in the several areas of specialization that have been mentioned.

Whereas the medicinal chemist may have made a few milligrams or grams of a compound for the pharmacologists or microbiologists, etc. to study in laboratory animals, still larger amounts are needed for the initial safety and pharmaceutical explorations. Actually, the chemist who synthesized the compound the first time is more interested in getting it than in the cost or availability of starting materials. The chemist is not concerned with whether the process can be scaled up safely for the preparation of equally pure drug. The initial job is to get the compound regardless of how it has to be made.

HOW AND FOR WHAT PURPOSE THE INITIAL
DEVELOPMENT MATERIAL IS MADE

The first of the compound made by the development chemists will probably be synthesized by the same process and in the same kind of bench scale glassware, etc., as was used in the original synthesis, assuming that we are dealing with a synthetic material. That first material made by this group is apt to be for the use of their physical chemists so that product specifications and analytical methods can be initiated. The compound is shared with the biologists and pharmaceutical chemists. If the agent is tremendously active, milligrams or grams may suffice to help the biologists. Otherwise, the estimate of initial needs by the toxicologists will run to hundreds of grams or a kilogram or more for acute toxicity and dosage range-finding. If need be, the process for synthesis may be the same but larger glassware may be used to make sufficient material. Or, the synthesis may have to be repeated time after time if it cannot be scaled up. Again, the compound has to be made on schedule almost without regard for cost or effort.

THE IMPORTANCE OF CHEMICAL FORM AND FORMULATION

As soon as possible, the pharmaceutical chemists need to be supplied a few milligrams or grams for their initial studies. Before the chronic toxicity studies that may require kilograms of compound are started, analytical control procedures must have been worked out and a judgment made as to the form and composition of the agent that will be best suited for use in man. That decision must also be acceptable to the marketing people. For example, a stable succinate may be preferred to a hygroscopic or otherwise unstable chloride of the agent, or the tartrate may yield a more suitable crystalline structure than the succinate. Several considerations make this earliest possible choice of a suitable form and structure of the compound important. Not the least of these is that the safety assessment and the ultimate formulation for marketing needs to be on the same form of the drug as that on which the bulk of the clinical study is gained prior to the new drug application.

INTERMEDIATE PILOT PLANT PRODUCTION

From the prechronic dose range finding studies an estimate of chemical quantities needed for the chronic toxicity and collateral research can be estimated. This quantity plus that needed to establish the dosage form(s) and the amount estimated for Phase I clinical trial usually force the development chemists to the practical adaptation of the original process to pilot plant equipment. Usually, there is no need to develop a practical production-type synthesis until clinical utility is established. This is particularly true today when the time from selection of a compound for clinical trial to approval (or rejection) by the regulatory agency may take years.

PROCESS DEVELOPMENT FOR PRODUCTION

Once the clinical studies have demonstrated initial activity and utility and the long-term (2 years or so) chronic toxicity studies are in progress, work should be underway to develop a practical production type synthesis. Thought should be given to costs of material, the source and availability of raw material and of equipment. If some of the clinical studies are performed abroad before they are initiated in this country, the final steps in the synthesis must be accomplished outside this country for reasons relating to the restrictions on shipment of investigational new drugs.

Factors that Relate to the Process

The new production synthesis needs to be safe with regard to explosion hazards and the corrosion of metal or glass lined vessels. Workers need to be protected from direct contact with highly active or sensitizing agents. Air pollution and water contamination can be serious problems. The chemical engineers and plant health people are important in resolving these problems.

Sometimes microbiological (fermentation) synthesis of material, either as partial or total synthesis, is the most practical and least expensive means to the end. This is usually the case for complex chemicals such as antibiotics and steroids. Such processes are frequently amenable to substantial improvement in yield through genetic mutation and transformation of the microorganisms. But rapid disposal of, say, 45,000 gallons of broth that contains both chemicals and microorganisms can be a serious problem.

Availability and Development of Intermediates

If chemical intermediates are not available or can only be obtained from a single source, it may be prudent to produce at least some of what is needed. This can constitute a source of still other development problems.

Problems with Process Development

If special equipment is needed for the factory, it may have to be designed and made to order. If the anticipated bulk compound needed to satisfy marketing estimates is not large, the process may be developed to fit equipment already in the factory, thereby reducing costs and increasing the efficiency with which facilities are utilized. On the other hand, formulations like penicillin products can only be produced in equipment specifically assigned for that purpose because of the risk of contaminating other products produced in the same equipment, hence sensitizing people to the antibiotic, unwittingly. If the marketing needs for bulk drug are huge, it may be cheaper to build a production facility for that compound. Automating the factory process represents a challenge for the chemists and chemical engineers assigned to develop the synthesis.

Problems with the development of a factory process for a new compound are not always one-of-a-kind. If in the course of a few years the research biologists in a laboratory find two or three compounds in a chemical series to be importantly different from one another from a therapeutic standpoint, the purchase of common intermediates and starting materials on an increased scale may make savings possible. So might the use of common production facilities. The benzothiadiazine nucleus common to chlorothiazide and hydrochlorothiazide might be an example where common starting materials could be employed. Such might be the case for the related benzodiazepinones, chlordiazepoxide (librium) and diazepam (valium), likewise.

QUALITY CONTROL

Each step in a process presents its own problems to the physical chemists who must develop the analytical methodology to assure in-process controls on purity and the nature of impurities. Quality control is a great deal more than just the stated purity of the final product. If the process yields the wrong size crystals for pharmaceutical production of the tablet or if optimal gastrointestinal absorption (bioavailability) of the drug depends on a specific crystal size then any other size or variability in size from production batch to batch becomes unacceptable to quality control.

ALTERNATIVE PRODUCTION PROCESSES

It is not enough to work out a process for the production of a new drug at the level of 100,000 kg. per year that must be just as good or better than the few milligrams or grams that were first made for biological evaluation. The development chemists must work out and patent all conceivable alternate processes that might be suitable for production. If some other chemist here or abroad works out and patents a simpler, cheaper synthesis that was overlooked, one might end up paying royalties on a product to someone else who owns the patent on a better process. It might be more economically feasible to produce the drug by that process. This is not an hypothetical situation. It does happen. There are those who make a practice of trying to improve and sell production processes to the owners of important new drugs. Thus, a series of patents pertaining to the continued improvement of process for the manufacture of an important product (i.e., yield improvement, process simplification, use of cheaper starting materials, etc.) may be the most effective way to sustain control of it long after the initial patent on the drug has expired.

PRODUCT UNIFORMITY AROUND THE WORLD

Whatever the process, the development chemists and engineers of an international corporation will have to adapt it to the availability of equipment and materials at a foreign production site. Materials may be procurable locally or may need to be shipped half way around the world. The product itself will need to meet the different and increasingly stringent standards set for a drug and its impurities in the various countries where it is marketed. Some countries require that some or most of the steps in the manufacture of a drug sold there must have been conducted there. Quite apart from meeting the standards of various countries is the assurance through quality control that the same product produced in various countries of the world meets the same standards of uniformity set by the development chemists.

Most people outside the chemical industry have no insight into the contributions of good development chemists to the well being of mankind. The chemist who synthesized a compound the first time is the one who gets the product patent and the public acclaim, if any. For the development team there is the pride and satisfaction of having made possible the production of a new drug inexpensively and at least as pure as the first time on a scale sufficient to supply the worldwide demand for the product which is no mean accomplishment!

COLLATERAL LITERATURE

Abraham, E. P., Chain, E., Fletcher, C. M., Gardner, A. D., Heatley, N. G., Jennings, M. A., and Florey, H. W. (1941): Further observations on penicillin, *Lancet 2:* 177–188.

Fieser, L. F., and Fieser, M. (1959): Steroids, Reinhold Publishing Corp., New York.

Kendall, E. C. (1971): Cortisone, Charles Scribners' Sons, New York.

Link, K. P. (1943–1944): The anticoagulant from spoiled sweet clover, *Harvey Lecture 39:* 162–216.

12.
Pharmaceutical
Development

PHARMACEUTICAL DEVELOPMENT

The technology of pharmaceutical production has come of age. Many developments have made this so: high speed equipment for compressing tablets, for filling, sealing, and labeling capsules and high speed equipment and new materials for packaging, better control of labeling, on-line quality control, safety measures for the protection of personnel from exposure to the drugs, and automation of warehousing. A trip through one of these facilities is an interesting experience. Gone are the days when the pharmacist in the corner drug store compounded the prescriptions written by the physician and brought to them by the patient. It seems doubtful that anyone really regrets the change because of the greater assurance of product uniformity and quality control available today. About all that remains of the myths about the old ways is the prejudice held by some physicians and regulatory agencies about combining drugs in a single formulation. This, too, is losing ground, for such rational combinations are generally employed in the management of hypertension, for instance.

INITIAL SOLUBILITY AND STABILITY STUDIES

It is the pharmaceutical chemist who must prepare the first formulation of the new compound for study in patients. These chemists must demonstrate the production formulation of that new drug to the people who are to produce it for the market. This is a complex job.

Those first few milligrams or grams of the chemical available to the pharmaceutical chemists will be used to explore its solubility and stability characteristics. These tests are generally referred to as preformulation studies. Hardly ever is a compound as stable as the pharmacist would like, or so it seems. The accelerated stability tests at elevated temperatures are intended to anticipate drug stability problems that might not show up otherwise until years later at ordinary conditions of shelf life. Usually, it is preferred that the compound be stable in its final formulation for a shelf life of 3 to 5 years. One may have to settle for less than this, but 2 years generally is the minimum to satisfy marketing conditions. Partly, this is because conditions of storage in the drug store or in the home may vary tremendously in temperature, humidity, exposure to sunlight, and in climatic conditions — as in the tropics, the desert or at the sea shore.

SELECTING THE PREFERRED FORM
AND CRYSTALLINE STRUCTURE OF THE COMPOUND

In order to get the proper conditions of stability, solubility, disintegration, bioavailability, etc., one may need to study both the parent compound and various salts of it. Crystal structure and particle size may be critical to the type of formulation desired and to its optimal absorption from the intestinal tract. Decision as to the most suitable form of the chemical should be made before the long term chronic toxicity studies are initiated, for the long term safety studies and the clinical trials should be performed with the form that is ultimately marketed.

DOSAGE FORMS

Solutions of the compound for injection may present problems related to solubility, stability, irritation to tissues and compatbility with preservatives. Suspensions for oral administration are also apt to be difficult, when it comes to patient acceptability of taste, odor, the way they feel in the mouth, aftertaste, even color, in addition to stability, compatibility with other drugs, and preservatives.

One of the most exasperating dosage forms to develop, but a popular one outside this country, is the suppository. Getting the right size, shape, hardness, melting characteristics, and optimal bioavailability of the suppository so that it may be employed interchangeably with other equivalent dosage forms sometimes seems to border more on art than science. Then, too, this dosage form is relatively slow to produce compared to tablets, and the conditions for storage may be exacting.

The most common dosage form is the compressed tablet, followed at some distance by the capsule, but the capsule is likely to be the more convenient form for clinical pharmacology, the phase I and II clinical studies. Early in a development project the small amount of drug available does not permit the formulation of a tablet dosage form. For this reason hand-filled capsules or a simple solution of the drug in water may be used for the phase I studies.

When comparing formulations of the drug in capsules and tablets for bio-availability, it is difficult to predict which may be superior. Capsules may be more readily formulated, frequently requiring simply the compound and a small amount of diluent or filler. However, there are real disadvantages to capsules besides the fact that they necessarily are more expensive, even to the few companies that make the actual capsules. The size capsule needed for a given drug dosage will vary with the dosage, size, and conformation of the crystal structure which influences the bulk density of the compound. These latter characteristics influence the extent to which it can be compacted into the capsule. To a point, the smaller the capsule the more acceptable it is likely to be to the patient. This matter of crystal size and shape may be an important determinant for the manufacturing process that is developed for the compound.

CAPSULES VERSUS TABLETS

There are several encapsulating machines available. Each requires that the drug formulation be adapted to its use. They all have the common disadvantage that drug encapsulation is a slower process than tabletting. Such encapsulating machines run at speeds up to 150,000 capsules per hour versus 500,000 tablets per hour that can be compressed on a tabletting machine. (Actually, this rate for capsules represents a tremendous technical advance from some 30,000 per day only 6 or 8 years ago.)

The tabletting of a drug is a much faster, cheaper process, but it does require more excipients than a capsule formulation. These materials include lubricants, such as magnesium oxide, that keep the material from sticking to the high speed punches, binding agents or gums that hold the tablet together, and disintegrants that facilitate tablet disintegration in the stomach or beyond. These excipients and the drug itself must be stable under conditions of instantaneous heat and pressure of compression that must be controlled for product uniformity.* Moreover, the physical characteristics of the excipients as well as those of the compound itself can markedly influence the bioavailability of the drug. Thus, quality control includes not only the drug and its impurities but the physical and chemical characteristics of all the materials (and their impurities) contained in the formulation.

To this point, we have discussed the factors that determine the physical suitability of dosage forms. Factors that influence the choice of dosage forms may be less tangible in part but no less important. The ultimate dosage form should be used for the greater part of the clinical (phase III) studies. It is of even greater concern to the marketing people. It must be attractive and practical, as well as possessing the physical characteristics the chemists and biologists would optimize.

DOSAGE SCHEDULE: PHARMACOKINETICS

In the past, most drugs other than aspirin and cathartics seemed to be prescribed for administration morning, noon, and night (t.i.d.). This practice persists to some extent today. Actually, outpatients who work prefer to take a drug once or twice a day if need be, when he or she is going through the ritual of dressing for work in the morning or retiring for the evening. Most drugs can be adapted to such a regimen, but by no means all of them. Hence, the pharmacokinetics of the drug need to be worked out in patients (how it behaves with respect to absorption, distribution, and elimination). Absorption, excretion, drug half-life, or effective duration depends on both the chemical and physical characteristics of the drug and the formulation, as well as the condition of the patient. Very young infants and very sick or elderly patients may not be able to eliminate (metabolize or excrete) the drug as rapidly as older children or normal adults. This latter aspect of therapeutics becomes more a matter of patient care.

DOSAGE FORMS: PATIENT ACCEPTANCE

Usually, the problem is to get the proper amount of drug in as small a tablet or capsule as possible, or in a small volume, preferably less than 1 or 2 ml for injection, or in a teaspoonful instead of two tablespoonfuls, depending

---

*Today, many tablets are imprinted with a name or code to identify product, dosage, and manufacturer. This is done either as part of the act of compressing the tablet or printed after compression. Most patients prefer colored dosage forms. Also, color coding as well as tablet size of different dosages of a drug is important. The choice of colors is becoming more and more restricted. This is due to the increasing number of dyes that have been subjected to carcinogenicity assessment.

on dosage form. This is not always so. Where the daily dose of a steroid is 0.75 mg. and it is to be administered half in the morning and half in the evening, the compound must be diluted or made up in some preferably inert ingredient sufficient to yield a convenient tablet or capsule size, for example. If the steroid is for rheumatoid arthritis patients, whose hands may be stiff, the tablet size must be large enough to be manageable. Also, such patients may not be able to open some of the bottles with fancy tops that children are not supposed to be able to unscrew.

People, sick or well, tend to respond positively to warm colors and attractive but not necessarily elaborate packaging of drugs. In the international markets, care must be exercised with the choice of colors. In some cultures, blue is associated with death — hardly an association one would want to have made for the dosaage form of a new drug. Abroad, medicine is more apt to be prescribed in an original container of only a few tablets or capsules to prevent substitution. In this country, products that require an elaborate dosage regimen also may be packaged by the manufacturer for the convenience of the patient. Some of the birth control pills are so packaged to prevent error by the patient. [Actually, as a common dosage form, the *pill* went out of favor along with prescription formulation by the drugstore pharmacist who used such a small (pill) mold to shape the formulations that the doctors prescribed and he compounded.]

DRUG COMBINATIONS

The combination of two or more active ingredients in a single dosage form presents many very real problems, technical and otherwise.

As mentioned in a prior paragraph of this chapter, the attitude of the Food and Drug Administration (FDA) and that of the academic physician with whom the agency consults is usually quite negative toward drug combinations, though not invariably so. Prior to the 1962 amendments to the New Drug Act in this country, a combination of drugs only had to be safe, theoretically. It did not have to be rational. Today, each active component of the dosage formulation must be proven to contribute to efficacy or safety, which is not unreasonable.

The academic physician is usually at odds with the practicing doctor when he insists that the doctor is in a better position to optimize the dosage of the individual drugs he prescribes in combination for his patients. This might be true of any two drugs commonly prescribed together by the doctor if he has sufficiently few patients, enough time and a better than usual understanding of the pharmacokinetics of each drug as influenced by the state of the disease, patients' age, sex, etc. By analogy, a tailor should be able to fashion a jacket to his clients figure better than if the coat were bought "off the rack," so to speak. Few of us can afford the luxury of tailored clothes, any more. The busy practicing physician who must prescribe the drugs and the patients who must remember how the doctor said to take them find useful combinations the simpler more reliable form of therapy, frequently.

COMPOSITION OF MATTER PATENTS

It should be mentioned that it is possible to patent unique dosage forms of drugs as "compositions of matter." Such patents are apt to be less valuable than a process patent for the manufacture of a compound or the basic patent on the drug itself. Nevertheless, there are occasions where it is prudent to file for such patents. This is mentioned again in Chapter 16 on Patents.

QUALITY AND PRODUCTION CONTROL

Beyond the development of suitable formulations of drugs, the pharmaceutical chemist must concern himself with devising controls to assure that the processes he has demonstrated to production result in a clean, uniform product reaching the patient. Just the table of contents of the 1975 WHO Expert Committee Report on Specifications for Pharmaceutical Preparations is enough to give some insight into the complexity of the problems with which these scientists deal. The diversity of methodology and sophistication of analytical instrumentation make it possible to write specifications for quality control of products that simply could not have been met a decade or so ago. Specifications for radiopharmaceuticals, the prevention of microbial contamination of nonsterile drugs, quality requirements for plastic containers, guidelines for the establishment, maintenance, and international distribution of chemical reference substances all represent special yet common technical considerations. Pharmaceutical aspects of drug evaluation for registration, even good practices in manufacturing and quality control of drugs need be set forth in detail. From time to time, these may need to be revised as new manufacturing facilities are designed to reduce cost, to accelerate production, or to adapt to important restrictions on materials such as are set forth by various countries.

BIOAVAILABILITY AND NEW FORMULATIONS
OF MARKETED DRUGS

It may be of interest to close this chapter with what at first may seem a paradox. Many formulations presently on the market were developed before the extent of their bioavailability became known. Thus, the physician will have become familiar with the dosage and duration of action of an oral dosage form of the drug from which only, say, 70 percent was available to the patient by gastrointestinal absorption. Any new formulation of that drug submitted to the FDA will not be approved unless it has essentially the same bioavailability as the original product or unless the dosage of the new product is proven clinically. The rationale for this attitude is that if the bioavailability from the new formulation is less than the product on the market, the patient's response to a usual dosage of the drug would be less than expected; therapy might be unintentionally inadequate. If the bioavailability of the new formulation is better than that on the market, say 100 percent instead of 70 percent, then the customary dosage might be excessive. If the new product were a cardiac glycocide, digitalis for instance, the greater availability of the drug from the formulation (100 percent instead of 70) might induce serious toxicity. In other words, with today's technology it is possible to express dosage statistically to account for what is available to the patient in addition to what is incorporated in the formulation. Even so, it would be unreasonable to expect the individual patient to respond to a prescribed dosage of any drug precisely the same way as the "average" patient for still other reasons beyond the control of the pharmaceutical chemists.

COLLATERAL LITERATURE

WHO Expert Committee on Specifications for Pharmaceutical Preparations (1975): World Health Organization Technical Report Series No. 567, World Health Organization, Geneva.

13.
Clinical Pharmacology

WHAT DOES IT DO? WHAT IS THE DOSE?

Only 3 decades ago, when the pharmacologist turned over his laboratory data to support the clinical study of a new drug, two questions were likely to be asked of him. What does it do? What is the dose? Both were reasonable questions, but it has always been the extrapolation of dosage from laboratory studies to the clinical situation that has bothered the conscientious preclinical investigator as well as the clinician, that and safety assessment. This estimation of an initial dose was and still is a responsibility of the preclinical investigator, in consultation with colleagues who have conducted the safety assessment, for between them they know most about the compound at that time.

Years ago, the clinical study was initiated with that recommended dosage unless the clinical investigator decided on another. Thus, there has always been good reason for the pharmacologist to want to know as much as possible about the new compound recommended for clinical trial. If, in the interest of safety, the dosage recommended was too low to be effective in man, enthusiasm for the compound might be lost prematurely. If the dosage recommended was set to assure efficacy without due regard for safety, an effective compound might soon gain an image of being unsafe. Once established, these clinical impressions of safety or utility can be most difficult to change. For example, an antihypertensive agent, hydralazine, gained a reputation for being effective but having a high incidence of untoward reactions at the dosage introduced for general use. Years later, the dosage was recognized to have been set too high. Lowering the generally recommended dosage reduced considerably the incidence of side effects, but the image that hydralazine is an effective but hazardous drug persists. Whereas dose-response curves were conducted in the laboratory animals, they were seldom established in man until the advent of the clinical pharmacologist.

There have always been pharmacologists who were only interested in what we call, today, molecular pharmacology (molecular pharmacologists) or who were most interested in the behavior of drugs in patients (clinical pharmacologists). In the past 2 decades, the role of the clinical pharmacologist has become sufficiently differentiated from that of the internist or clinical investigator that the place of clinical pharmacology in the development of new drugs seems clear enough.

DEVELOPMENT OF CLINICAL PHARMACOLOGY

Clinical Pharmacology as a specialty that combines the disciplines of pharmacology and medicine for the assessment and teaching of drug therapy is only in its second generation of such medical scientists. European-trained pharmacologists have generally been M.D.'s who were more interested in the theory than the practice of therapeutics. They, usually, assumed little or no responsibility for patient care. In the United States, pharmacology developed as a laboratory discipline for which the Ph.D. seemed a more appropriate degree for those not directly interested in patient care. A generation or so ago, the chairman of a department of pharmacology in a medical school almost invariably was a medical graduate, an M.D. But as this vestige of a common professional bond between medicine and pharmacology lost favor, the pharmacologist lost his way to the patient. The clinical investigator likewise found it beyond his element to seek out the pharmacologist in the laboratory.

With the onset of a profusion of new drugs since the mid 1930's, their clinical assessments were conducted for the most part by investigators tutored in clinical observation but essentially unschooled in many instances in the discipline of research. This weakness in the scientific basis for new drug research plagued clinical trials, especially through the 1940's and 1950's. This was an important factor that ultimately led to the reappraisal of pre-1962 "new drugs" by the Committee of Experts of the Drug Research Board, The National Academy of Science following the 1962 revision of the Food, Drug and Cosmetic Act and the concomitant more stringent regulations.

During that quarter century when the greatest progress in drug research took place there were centers in this country, England and elsewhere, where pharmacology retained its clinical orientation. Such was the case at Cornell and at the University of Pennsylvania. Schools like Wisconsin and Michigan encouraged their graduates to seek both the M.D. and the Ph.D. At the Johns Hopkins Medical School, E. K. Marshall, Jr., and his students taught so soundly the relationships between sulfonamide dose, blood level, and *bacteriostatic* effect that the principle has been applied beyond its usefulness ever since. (Although penicillin is *bactericidal* as well as *bacteriostatic* the most popular formulation of that antibiotic, early in its clinical use, was designed to sustain little more than a determinable plasma penicillin concentration for hours.)

During the 1950's and since, the teaching of pharmacological principles and proper design of the clinical assessment of new drugs by Walter Modell, Louis Lasagna, Albert Sjoerdsma, and others led to an increasing group of young physicians who found such research fascinating. They called themselves clinical pharmacologists. Some of these, such as John Oates' group at Vanderbilt, Daniel L. Azarnoff, Leon I. Goldberg, and still others are capable of guiding sophisticated laboratory research as well as teaching therapeutics at the patient's bedside and conducting clinical research.

THE CLINICAL PHARMACOLOGISTS' ROLE

By 1962, the position of clinical pharmacologists in the development of new drugs was sufficiently clear (though still controversial) that the proposed New Drug Regulations in the USA identified that role particularly with Phase I or Phase I and early Phase II of the three phases into which the Commissioner of the Food and Drug Administration proposed to divide the research on new drugs in man. (See Chapter 17 for a description of the three phases of clinical investigation.)

IMPORTANCE OF "THE PRECLINICAL"
TO THE CLINICAL INVESTIGATOR

This responsibility of the clinical pharmacologist under Phase I amounts to the affirmation, qualification, and extension of the essential laboratory pharmacology by corresponding studies in patients or volunteers. Obviously, *The Preclinical* monograph that summarizes both laboratory activity and safety data, such as was discussed in Chapter 9 and 10, are important to his effort.

Such a document represents the elements of research of hundreds of scientists prior to more formal publication of the information in various journals. Preferably, that document should not only be studied by the physician at any level he undertakes to investigate the new drug, it should be discussed thoroughly by him with someone intimately familiar with the laboratory research described therein. Knowing this information well may save the clinical investigator false starts, the wasteful use of patient material, and on occasion this may save embarrassment to all concerned by what might have been a needless mishap.

What the clinical pharmacologist may want to know or need to know before he puts the new compound into man may be more than what the preclinical writeup teaches about its primary and secondary attributes. He may need to know what safety precautions should be taken especially with regard to top dosage, how much compound is available, how directly the anticipated clinical utility can be approached or simulated, the intended mode of administration, and whether there is a suitable analytical method for measuring the drug and its metabolites in blood and urine. The list is by no means complete.

TYPES OF CLINICAL PHARMACOLOGICAL STUDIES

In turn, what the clinical pharmacologists may be expected to contribute is information obtained in patients or human volunteers about:

(1) The absorption and excretion of the drug
(2) The identity and rate of formation of metabolites
(3) Pharmokinetics of distribution and elimination of the drug
(4) The dose/response relationship, when that is feasible
(5) Some indication of the agent's activity, preferably on a comparative basis
(6) Interactions with other drugs
(7) Mechanism and site of action.

Since little of this information is available on most drugs in general use, it represents more what one would like to know than what is needed to get on with the more elaborate clinical assessment. Like the comprehensive preclinical assessment, though, the more thoroughly these clinical pharmacological aspects of the new compound are understood the better is the basis for managing the extended, Phase III, clinical studies.

INITIATION OF THE CLINICAL PHARMACOLOGICAL ASSESSMENT

Some Admonitions

There are at least two frequent serious faults in the initiation of the clinical pharmacological assessment of a new compound that could be stated as admonitions. First, study carefully "The Preclinical" writeup on the compound. Don't just glance at it and turn the volume over to the resident physician in the hospital who may or may not be interested in the project; who may or may not remember the basic sciences in this particular area. The second admonition to be kept clearly in mind as one designs a protocol for studying the drug is to *keep it simple!* There never was an experiment that could not be wrecked by adding just one more parameter or maybe one more blood or urine collection. For example, more than once an apprehensive investigator has made the alarming observation that the subject's hemoglobin value had fallen markedly not long after a new compound had been administered to volunteers. Actually, the trouble was not due to the drug, except indirectly. The problem was due to the inordinate amount of blood the overly enthusiastic investigator had withdrawn. Plasma volume had been replaced acutely, physiologically, by more tissue water than blood cells at the expense of the hematocrit. No harm done, just a hapless error; the hematocrit soon readjusts.

The Dose-Response Curve

The dose-response curve, that is, the relationship of increasing dosage to the magnitude of a specified effect, is the backbone of laboratory pharmacology (Chapter 9) and the calculation of acute toxicity (Chapter 10). It is a very useful concept, the discussion of which could easily be expanded into a chapter or a book.

Today, the clinical pharmacologists will have worked this dose-response relationship out in humans before the Phase III studies are undertaken. Preferably, the investigation will have been conducted in mildly hypertensive patients, if the compound is a blood pressure lowering agent, and the mode of administration will have been that which is to be used in practice. Enough different dosages should be employed (perhaps 4 or 5) to cover the range from minimal activity at the lower level to the maximally tolerated dose at the upper limit. For the data to be very reliable, enough subjects have to be employed at each dose level to yield a reasonable expression of variability in response.

In planning the study, a decision needs to be made as to whether the same subjects will be used for all 4 or 5 dosages or whether different persons will be employed at each dose level. Preferably, both male and female subjects will be chosen in approximately equal numbers for the experiment. This is likely to increase the statistical expression of variability of response unless separate dose-response curves are developed for men and women, which in this case probably would not be worth the effort unless the agent were some sort of antihypertensive estrogen, for example. It might be hard to get enough patients for the study who have reasonably uniform "mild" hypertensive status. If (to get sufficient numbers to satisfy the statistician) the age spread among the patients has to be from, say, 25 to 65 years, or if one has to incorporate both black and white patients, or if the study has to be extended over a period of months in order to randomize the distribution of these and other variables, the complexity of such a simple thing as a dose-response curve begins to be bothersome.

Clinical studies of such a nature need still other measures of control. The various dosages and placebos need to be randomized over the duration of the experiment, but the appearance, taste, and packaging of the dosage form need to be identical so the patient cannot knowingly relate the way he feels to dosage. Regardless of motivation to keep the dosage schedule scrupulously as prescribed, patients are notoriously indifferent to the details of when to take what, so the more fastidious investigators incorporate in the protocols of their experiments some means for revealing such lack of cooperation. Data on such patients should be discarded, for it is likely to be misguiding. If this happens, so that by such deletions the investigators end up with unequal numbers of patients at the several coordinates of the dose-response curve, using the mean or median response may be misleading and the statistician may be obliged to subject the data to certain transformations that may or may not be acceptable to the next statistician who sees the data.

Thus, the actual design of and directions for so objective a test as the blood pressure response of mild hypertensive patients to different doses of a drug becomes a research project in its own right. Today, these dose-response curves are best conducted on so-called metabolic wards where the conditions of the experiment can be carefully monitored. Anyone who tried to do such careful work in the days before such facilities were available may remember the saying that the hardest thing to get in a hospital was a reliable 24-hour urine collection from a patient.

COMMENTS RELEVANT TO PHASE I AND
EARLY PHASE II STUDIES

A great deal of thought should go into how to get the maximal amount of useful information in the first few "simple" experiments. For example, a dose response curve for chlorothiazide in human volunteers is represented in Fig. 1. A new saluretic agent is apt to be sufficiently potent even by oral administration that an analytical method may not be needed except to measure bioavailability of the drug. Simply following cumulative urinary electrolyte and water output (by hydrated volunteers) periodically for 6 or 8 hours over a modest range of single oral doses of the compound is sufficient to give considerable information. From such experiments, potency, the effect of the compound on individual electrolyte excretion, onset of action, duration, secondary retention of electrolytes (if the experiment is prolonged to 24 hours), tolerance by the subject and useful information about dosage should be clearly evident. The data should be compared to experiments conducted by the same protocol in the same well hydrated subjects given a placebo (an essentially similar dosage form of inert ingredients) instead of the drug. If drug absorption, renal clearance, half-life, metabolism, and optimal frequency of dosage are to be determined, then an analytical method for the compound

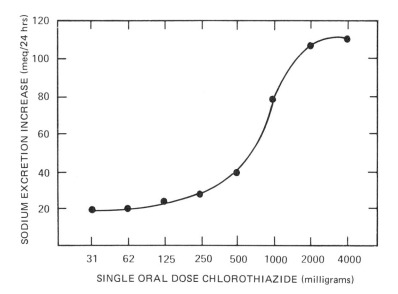

FIG. 1.   Dose response curve for single oral doses of chlorothiazide, showing sodium excretion as the parameter of measurement. Redrawn from Ford, R. V. *et al.* (1957): *Arch. Int. Med., 100:* 582–591.

will be needed. Since the conditions of the patients for whom such a drug may be indicated vary so greatly, these studies should be extended reasonably in late Phase II of the clinical program to nephrotic, cirrhotic, and cardiac decompensated patients as experience with the drug accumulates. The assessment of utility in such patients might better be left to Phase III clinical studies.

An antibacterial chemotherapeutic agent would require considerably more work-up than mentioned for the diuretic. Initially, drug blood concentrations attained at increasing individual doses might be obtained, then the corresponding response to multiple daily doses up to the maximal amount suggested by the preclinical safety studies should be gotten. It would be helpful to keep in mind the prior laboratory conditions, dosage, and kind of therapeutic effect when animals infected with a strain of organism sensitive to the agent received the drug. Such problems as scarcity of drug produced by a relatively undeveloped fermentation process, the possibility of inducing patient hypersensitivity to the drug, and the ethical considerations of investigating such an agent in subjects other than those who conceivably could derive some benefit from it seem inevitable.

Where a protracted period of drug administration is required before a beneficial effect can be anticipated, as for an antidepressant drug, and where the analytical method is not sufficiently sensitive to follow the small dosage usually required, the initial dosage regimen may have to be worked out from what is known about the half-life of the drug in animals, from secondary pharmacodynamic effects that can be observed (such as dryness of the mouth) and from the upper limits of dosage placed by the safety assessment scientists in animals.

On the other hand, dose-response estimation of a new glucocorticoid adrenocortical steroid dosage for clinical study may be expressed biochemically and clinically, usually promptly and clearly. (This is not to say that the Phase III clinical assessment is easy. The multiplicity of their actions, good and bad, are legend.) The protocol need not be complicated to establish the dosage regimen for the initial trial of drug utility. The amount of steroid needed usually is relatively small, which is apt to be fortunate considering the chemistry and the cost involved in the synthesis of most active compounds of this general category.

In today's climate of clinical trials wherein any misadventure is likely to be interpreted as a drug-related adverse reaction, it is folly to initiate clinical studies on the utility of a new compound until the likely dosage regimen has been worked out by the clinical pharmacologist. Actually, this Phase I clinical research should help define the conditions of the subsequent clinical research. For example, how well a new antiarrhythmic compound was absorbed from the gastrointestinal tract following oral administration to man could determine whether one initiated assessment of its utility by the oral or the intravenous route, regardless of how well it was absorbed by dogs or other animals. If the agent were well and uniformly absorbed when given orally to normal individuals, one might elect to initiate clinical trial of antiarrhythmic activity by this route. If gastrointestinal absorption of the compound was poor or erratic, one might prefer to study first its ability to suppress a less serious cardiac arrhythmia by intravenous injection of the new drug. It should be recognized that these two protocols are by no means equivalents. Each tells more about the compound than that it is active. Whichever route of administration is employed first, the dosage regimen should have been worked out carefully and the patients selected meticulously, for it is drug action that is being studied at this point, not drug utility.

SELECTION OF PATIENTS FOR CLINICAL STUDIES

To select patients for this study carelessly and have one or two die of ventricular fibrillation while receiving the drug is apt to raise more questions about the agent's safety than can be answered at the outset of the clinical work. Since the deaths must be reported to the regulatory agency the compound may have been put at jeopardy thoughtlessly, needlessly, seriously, and understandably. Seriously and understandably, for while the investigator may be able to account for a death by his familiarity with the patient and the special clinical circumstance, those remote from the actual situation but sharing responsibility for permitting the study to continue (as by the Food and Drug Administration or a hospital committee) are not likely to accept the coincidence without further exploration which, at best, is time consuming or may lead to the abandonment of what might have been a useful drug.

There is a great deal more to be said about the choice of subjects and patients for clinical research. The following are a few examples of hazards to be avoided in initiating clinical studies. At the clinical pharmacological Phase I or II one should not knowingly employ patients who have a recent history of peptic ulcer when studying an adrenocorticoid or a nonsteroid antiinflammatory agent. Should the patient develop an ulcer during such a study, it would be hard to rule out the compound as a precipitating factor. Diabetic patients are not to be chosen for early work on a new diruetic agent lest shifts in electrolyte balance easily tolerated by the normal individual affect adversely the metabolic balance of the diabetic individual. There is no need and considerable hazard to exploring in cirrhotic patients a new diruetic agent before it is well understood. To initiate the study of appetite stimulation by a new compound in the very elderly patients, where appetite is a problem, is to court disaster

for the compound because of the inevitably high mortality rate and the uncertain ability of such subjects to cooperate fully. These illustrations simply
serve to reinforce the need to understand the compound, the selection of
proper subjects or patients, and how to avoid needless complication before
undertaking the full-fledge assessment of its clinical utility and safety.

HAZARD OF USING AN INVESTIGATIONAL
NEW DRUG AS A LIFE-SAVING MEASURE

Time was when once the behavior of an important new compound in man
was understood, it was permitted to be used in all sorts of situations where
the knowledgeable clinical investigator thought its administration justifiable
and where current therapy had been found inadequate. Sometimes this use of
a new drug took place in terminal situations as a physician's last hope of helping the patient. Often enough, one did save a life, but often the patient died
as was to be expected. In the record of a new compound today, "a death is a
death is a death," a macabre paraphrasing of Gertrude Stein's famous poem
about a rose. To accumulate a needlessly high number of deaths in the clinical assessment of a new drug is to delay acceptance of that new drug application by a regulatory agency seemingly endlessly. In effect, this can delay the
availability of a useful new drug to the medical practitioner at a cost of needless inconvenience, illness or death to patients who might have benefited from
the agent. Indeed, the choice of subjects and patients in the course of assessing
a new drug is a most serious matter, having profound ramifications.

To recapitulate, the clinical pharmacological assessment is to learn how to
use the new drug to its greatest advantage. In the clinical trial this knowledge
is employed to assess the utility of the agent for the purpose it was intended
to serve.

COLLATERAL LITERATURE

Melmon, K. L., and Morelli, H. F. (1972): *Clinical Pharmacology. Basic Principles in
Therapy,* The MacMillan Co., New York.

14.
Clinical Trial —
Its Structure

"Interesting new compounds are discovered.
Interesting new drugs are developed."

Today, the clinical assessment of a new drug is the most expensive, most time consuming, most exciting, most frustrating, most complex and most regulated aspect of new drug development — by far. (KHB)

CLINICAL ASSESSMENT IN FORMER DAYS

Time was when important new drugs were mostly discovered and developed through the initial establishment of identity and/or utility in an academic environment. This was between 1900 and 1950 as an approximation. The discovery of important drugs, such as insulin, heparin, penicillin, dicoumarol, and, for that matter, liver extract and various endocrine organ extracts, required only the number of clinicians and physiologists or biochemists needed to make enough of something or other to give to a few patients. Usually they worked as a team. To be sure, these materials were natural products derived, as were our most ancient drugs, from natural sources. Then, and among some of the "old timers" still, drugs derived from "natural" sources (animal or plant) were generally considered safe and so there seemed to them to be no need for elaborate safety studies. To give such precious materials to animals for studying more than their physiological effects would have been thought a waste of substance better saved for a needy patient. The very word, vitamin, characterized a whole category of compounds as essential to health, not harmful; though Vitamins A and D were subsequently recognized to need clinically prudent management to be safe.

Surgeons might have required informed consent to operate on their patients in the old days, but the motivation for clinical and preclinical collaboration then was more an intellectual avocation that attracted a relatively few high minded individuals of principle. Fortunately, they were spared the development of today's regulations, labors and imponderables that surround the introduction of anything to clinical trial, even a new use for an old drug.

TIMES HAVE CHANGED

Although many modern drugs are made by fermentation (such as B_{12}, most antibiotics, and many steroids) this is a matter of more favorable production cost. (Semisynthetic was the term introduced for some of these compounds that were produced in part by fermentation and partially by chemists.) As the pharmaceutical companies organized their research effectively, their effort yielded a host of new drugs that needed clinical investigation.

The period from, say, 1935 to 1965 probably saw the discovery and development of more new kinds of useful drugs than those of us who have been involved are likely to see repeated. These products included congeners of natural products that for one reason or another seemed better suited as drugs. (The synthetic steroids that replaced cortisone and hydrocortisone substantially in the management of arthritis illustrate this point.)

Enthusiasm for these many categories of new drugs did outstrip on occasion the acumen with which some of their potential uses were explored. Necessarily, some physicians were encouraged to conduct clinical studies who might better have left this exacting work to others better trained. The concurrent need for both more clinical studies and better studies to satisfy regulatory agencies that in turn have found themselves almost constantly harassed (ostensibly to sustain the public's safety) has created a difficult environment in which to work. Thus, today the clinical investigator, regardless of aptitude or objective, needs to be intimately familiar with regulations and requirements with which he works.

On the other hand, the individuality of the clinical investigator can still be expressed. For example, he may discover an important new use for a marketed drug. He and his professional associates may establish satisfactorily the conditions for that new use as they communicate that experience to each other by way of meetings of professional societies, publication in appropriate journals (and by news releases which may or may not be appropriate). Lest the investigator defy good judgment, such studies might better be done with the knowledge of the manufacturer of the drug and of the regulatory agency. They both will need to become involved if the new use is to be applied for and approved for addition to the claims structure (approved uses) for the drug. Whether or how the new claim is set forth in the package circular and how it is called to the attention of the physician will involve all three in negotiation. In many countries where drug investigation is conducted, law or regulation prescribes the process from the first involvement of a patient to approval of the old drug's new use or the new drug for marketing.

MAKING A NEW DRUG OUT OF A DISCOVERY

The process for discovering new compounds that are importantly saluretic or anti-inflammatory, for instance, is one thing. Making important new drugs out of them for cardiovascular-renal diseases or for the management of the arthritides has become a complex development problem. If the company that commits itself to develop a new compound into a drug is global in its resources and in its delivery or marketing of new drugs, then the complexity of what needs to be done around the world is fantastic. The more complex this situation becomes the greater the risk of ruining in the process what might have been a valuable new drug. (This last statement is explained toward the end of this chapter.)

Today, the clinical trial of a new drug relates particularly to what the Food and Drug Administration (FDA) of the United States of America would call Phase III of the total clinical assessment (Chapter 17). The clinical assessment may encompass the latter half of Phase II when one transitions from the Clinical Pharmacology Phase I and early Phase II (the pharmacodynamic and metabolic interactions between body and compound) to Phase III. Phase III of the trial is the expanded, protracted phase wherein the therapeutic aspect of what the new drug does to the body, be it an antihypertensive or anti-arthritic effect, is measured. In other words, today, the clinical trial goes beyond the assessment of its pharmacology in man to taking the measure of the new drug from the standpoint of utility and safety in the appropriate patient. This may sound like a reassuring statement. It is not. For instance, taking the measure of a new drug, such as chlorothiazide, from the standpoint of utility might have meant the difference in time and resources between showing that it lowered blood pressure in the hypertensive patient and then proving that lowering blood pressure or arresting its progression by use of the drug was beneficial. That difference, that delay, in this instance could have been measured in many years, much involvement of resources and many lives that were prolonged usefully by virtue of its early release for this use. It was a decade between the first clinical reports of its antihypertensive action and the first reports by E. D. Freis and the Veterans Administration that documented the beneficial effects of the agent in reducing morbidity and mortality of hypertensive patients. It would have been tragic to have withheld the drug from hypertensive therapy for that decade.

Transitioning from Laboratory to Clinic

I have been writing about the relevance of the preclinical data to the clinical situation and the reliability of its transposition to man for the past 30 years or more. The similarity of response of laboratory animals and man to drugs, is sound but not infallible; so is its practical application where the preclinical work-up has been appropriate and adequate. [For instance, from the laboratory data the anticipated clinical dose for probenecid prior to its clinical trial was two grams or less per day (Chapter 7). That was in 1949. The clinical dosage is still $1-2$ grams (20 mg/kg) per day. The compound is safe and effective. Its preclinical assessment was relevant to the clinical situation. Its clinical trial was adequate to affirm its pharmacodynamic activity, hence its utility. Today in this country, very likely neither that preclinical nor its clinical assessment would suffice for regulatory approval even for Phase III clinical trial to which it would have to be submitted prior to the new drug application. In those days the preclinical safety assessment consisted of acute toxicity and a 3-month administration (chronic) to rats and dogs, and this was the case for probenecid. Preclinical pharmacology was definitive and clinical trial consisted of affirming the pharmacodynamic effects in man. All the pre-NDA animal and clinical work on probenecid was done within the time and cost it would take to conduct the animal safety assessment that would be required for such a compound today.]

It is easy to understand the lack of credibility with which the transposition of laboratory data to the patient was held before we developed much insight into the absorption and physiological disposition of the agent. Then, too, the importance of approximating closely the clinical situation (of obtaining a good laboratory correlate of the clinical situation) when assessing a new potential drug at the laboratory level, such as has been discussed in Chapters 5 through 9 was not well understood. Consequently, in the laboratories of some companies, the new compound received a superficial preclinical appraisal and was then sent to the clinic to see whether it was sufficiently active in patients to warrant the investment of further time and effort. Actually, the custom of a cursory laboratory workup and then clinical exploration worked reasonably well for the development of "me too" drugs subsequent to the first of a kind, such as the many antihistaminic agents and anticholinergic compounds, a number of which have reached the market as useful drugs.

Well before the historic 1962 new regulations of the Food and Drug Administration (FDA) pertaining to the assessment of new drugs for both safety and utility, the workup of a new drug prior to clinical trial was generally a great deal more sophisticated in those institutions where it was recognized that good research at a preclinical level was more important than a superficial clinical experience for the selection of compounds for development to new drugs. Then, too, the more sophisticated clinical investigators demanded more and better preclinical data as they learned to use that information.

Twenty-five years ago, the clinical pharmacologist did not seem to exist outside this country except in England, and his very existence was debated in the United States as well. Then, when the preclinical assessment of activity and safety of a new compound had been completed and described, the monograph describing those results (*The Preclinical*) customarily was given to the clinician experienced in the use of drugs in the field wherein the compound was expected to be useful. The clinician tried it out in such patients as were available and at a dosage suggested by the preclinical workup of the agent as likely to be safe and possibly effective. In those days everyone knew that if one gave more or less of a drug to a patient the effect should vary correspondingly between the limits of toxicity at excessive dosage and no effect if the regimen prescribed was too low. Thus, if the dosage selected initially turned out to be well within these limits as the clinical study evolved, it was seldom that an actual dose-response curve was worked out carefully. Today, the dose-response curve is likely to be established as part of the clinical pharmacologists' efforts prior to the full scale (Phase III) assessment of the utility and safety of the new drug. This role of the clinical pharmacologist is discussed in Chapter 13.

The Purpose of the Clinical Trial

The purpose of the clinical trial has always been to judge the safety and efficacy of the new drug, even though the pre-1962 regulations pertained specifically to safety. How one goes about that assessment and what one requires of supportive data continue to change. Five or ten years from now, the purpose of the clinical trial will be the same, but how one goes about it will have changed. Judged by the past, the clinical assessment of a drug will become more complex. It may be better.

The Clinical Investigator's Responsibility

When a clinician becomes an intended investigator of a new drug, his or her curriculum vitae must be submitted along with the protocol and such additional information as the regulatory agency may require before the clinical study is begun. There are no proscribed qualifications for such an investigator beyond the license to practice medicine. There is no certification of clinical pharmacologists and other clinical investigators, though local hospital peer review boards may set their own requirements. However, if that agency (FDA) decides for any reason that an investigator has not performed reliably in the past this may or may not be published in the Federal Register but is or should be called to the sponsor's attention. That investigator's work will not be recognized by that agency unless or until his or her name is cleared. Thus, whereas there is no certification of clinical pharmacologists or other clinical investigators today, the effect of such censorship, whether or not this is generally known in any specific instance, is a serious matter and one to be avoided.

To be sure, one can participate in a clinical study as an associate of a primary investigator, or, for that matter, as a practitioner. Today, all clinical investigations conducted in other than the doctor's office have to be approved by a board of peers, an Institutional Review Committee, some of whom may not be physicians. The interaction between investigator and such board or committees is a matter of concern to both the National Institutes of Health (NIH), if they support the work, and to the Food and Drug Administration. Since these requirements do change from time to time and the changes are published by the NIH in their communications or by the FDA in the Federal Register, those concerned do need to follow and comply with such announcements.

The details of the study of a new drug must be submitted by the sponsor to the FDA for concurrence before the investigation is undertaken, whether it relates to a new use for a drug or to a new drug or device. If the study is not conducted along the general outline of the work as originally submitted or as revised and resubmitted, then the FDA may insist that the investigation be stopped, that the material be returned to the sponsoring company and that the returned investigational material be destroyed.

The foregoing dicussion regarding the requirements placed on the clinical investigator by the regulatory agency through the drug sponsor, usually a pharmaceutical company, may seem harsh. To the physician carefully trained in clinical research these regulations are more a nuisance than a hazard, if one remains abreast of and complies with their aperiodic revision. Such work should merit confidential inspection and so should plans for the research.

As a condition for undertaking the assessment of a new drug, an investigator must agree to obtain a signed statement of informed consent from each volunteer for the study. The statement is intended to make clear that the investigator has informed the volunteer as to the nature of the proposed study, its purpose, possible benefits, and risks and that by signing it the person truly volunteers to participate. Generally, such a discussion between the physician and the volunteer is helpful and gives the participant a sense of involvement in the advance of therapy. Written informed consent from the patient may afford the physician some protection against suit insofar as informed consent is possible or practicable in a specific situation. There will always be situations where it is not readily evident just who is empowered to give consent. In such cases the problem might more prudently be placed in the hands of counsel familiar with such matters for guidance.

If an investigator contracts to conduct a clinical study for which he accepts a new drug, he should take no license with that study lest he place both patient and the drug at needless risk. Regardless of circumstance, an alarming adverse reaction of a patient to the drug should be reported promptly to the sponsor. The sponsor is required to report the alarming finding to the regulatory agency (FDA), promptly.

The Sponsor's Responsibility

Usually, the sponsor of a new drug is a pharmaceutical company, although this is not invariably the case. [Indeed, it may be agreed between a company and an individual clinician, who has an idea worthy of exploration, that the clinician will act as the sponsor of the clinical trial, the role of the firm being to supply materials and other support requested of it. These are special or exceptional situations for the most part.] In any event, the sponsor must make available to the other parties (usually the investigators) and to the FDA all relevant information known about the compound. As that situation changes materially or alarmingly, the investigator and the FDA should be notified at appropriate times as specified in the published regulations (see Chapter 17).

The clinical investigator who is to assess the safety and utility of the compound will be given the clinical pharmacological studies that contribute to a better understanding of the dose—effect relationships, absorption, distribution, and elimination by volunteers. This is in addition to *The Preclinical* writeup and the information it provides. In some instances, the clinical pharmacologist may himself elect to take the new drug into the Phase III assessment of utility, if it falls within his interests to do so.

TYPES OF CLINICAL TRIALS

There are three types of clinical trials; still more, perhaps, depending on who classifies them and how. For present discussion, these three are: (1) the individual clinical trial; (2) the multi-clinic trial and (3) the institutional clinical trial. We will also deal with international clinical trials, but they are mostly of types 1 and 2 above. The three types will be discussed separately.

INDIVIDUAL CLINICAL TRIALS

The individual clinical trial is apt to be a separate study designed for and conducted by a clinical investigator. It may be one of several similar studies intended to build up a large clinical experience to support the intended claim structure (what it does) for the new drug. It may serve a specific range-finding purpose prior to the more complexly coordinated trials. It may simply satisfy the investigator's own interest and curiosity or that of someone else.

Open Studies

These clinical trials may be "open" or "blind." Open in the sense that the investigator assesses the activity of a drug in terms of and controlled by his own clinical experience and acumen. (The patient may also know that the new drug is being given. In the single blind study the patient does not know and in the double blind study neither patient nor investigator knows whether the new drug, a placebo, or perhaps another drug is being assessed, as determined by the design of the study.) Being more interested in new drugs than the academics of clinical investigation, I like best these open studies at the hands of real experts. This is the way Withering ascertained the usefulness of digitalis, the way Hench and his associations at the Mayo Clinic first studied compound E (cortisone), the way most initial new drugs of a category have been explored.

Today, the open clinical trial is a procedure generally discounted by the inexperienced investigator and the regulatory agency personnel alike, at least for most purposes but not all. Before we leave this type of study, it deserves more explanation. For example, I doubt if anyone would insist on a double-blind assessment of Vitamin B_{12} in pernicious anemia. On the other hand, such double blind, controlled, studies wherein neither patient nor investigator knew whether drug or inert "placebo" was being used would have been appropriate to the examination of some of the many claims for B_{12} that were made at the peak of its clinical assessment. Indeed, better controlled studies might have saved some of the claims that at a later date were retracted by the FDA for B_{12} on the basis of inadequate clinical data.

In my opinion, most compounds should be explored initially in open study by astute clinicians as the first part of their (Phase II) clinical trial.

As a matter of fact, I should prefer that no so-called blind, controlled study be started on a new drug until the experienced investigator has a chance to explore the compound in various types of patients. The open study is where utility is observed and where activity is demonstrated. The blind, statistically controlled study is where its effects are quantitated, for better or worse.

Blind Studies

In the past 2 decades, the blind, statistically-controlled clinical trial has come into its own. It sounds so respectable, so utterly honest and scientific, so unbiased, that any other way of doing clinical trials is considered by its enthusiasts as a waste of time and resources. These studies may be classified as single-blind and double-blind. In the single-blind experiment, the investigator knows whether the patient is receiving a test drug or a placebo (a "sugar pill" that is identical in appearance to the active compound) or a second drug of the same appearance, but the patient does not know which he is getting. In the double-blind clinical trial, neither the clinician who rates the response nor the patient knows which of two drugs (or drug vs. placebo) being employed in the study is being given the patient. The studies in either instance are designed so as to randomize bias on the part of the patient in the single blind study and by both patient and physician in the double blind trial. Also, as many of the accountable variables as possible, such as age, sex, time of year, race, etc., are randomized statistically. What is searched for and assessed by way of effect and side effect is scrupulously and systematically recorded in a prearranged way so that the data may be programmed, if so desired, for analysis by a computer and for ultimate statistical expression. The nature of the experiment and the statistical treatment thereof to arrive at significance of an effect differ somewhat from situation to situation and even from country to country in terms of preference.

Differences Between Individual Trials

The clinical assessment of utility and safety has always been based on more than a single clinical study. Seldom does a single investigator have enough similar patients available to him within a period of a year or so to do the entire study by himself.

When several (say five) clinical investigators employ the same formulation of a drug independently of each other in what is intended to be the same protocol, and one or two reports of results vary substantially from the others, every effort should be made to account for the difference by reviewing the data from all five studies carefully. The difference may be accounted for by patient selection, especially if a side effect such as the occurrence of peptic ulcers is noted in a single clinical trial. Seemingly trivial differences in interpreting or complying with a protocol may be at fault. An overly enthusiastic or indifferent attitude on the part of the investigator can influence the response of patients quantitatively or even qualitatively. Also, the attitude of the physician who monitors the study for the sponsor can make a great deal of difference in the approach of the individual investigator toward the study. I cannot remember an overall trial of a new drug where such differences between individual studies did not occur. Whereas all studies, good and bad, are apt to be counted equally by a regulatory agency when considering adverse effects reported therein, it may be a fairer representation of the new drug's characteristics to report but defer interpreting such accountable, or even unaccountable, aberrant results until they attain individual significance rather than incorporate them into a general analysis of the several studies.

When the studies reported by clinical investigators differ materially from each other in purpose or design, they should be considered on their own merit and not thrown together for analysis, except, perhaps, in a gross sort of way as for the accumulation of experience with side effects. Even though there are enough pitfalls to account for real differences in the individual clinical trials, be they "open" or "blind," they are the keystone of the clinical assessment of a new drug.

MULTI-CLINIC TRIALS

In the multi-clinic trial of a new drug, the investigators from several institutions agree on a protocol that all will use, including the criteria for patient selection, defining and quantitating effect or side effect, the dosage regimen to be employed, and any number of other determinants that help to sustain a uniform, unbiased clinical appraisal of results. The trial may involve several clinics over a period of months to years. From such a study, the numbers available for statistical analysis can be in the thousands rather than tens of patients. The multi-clinic trials are designed so data can be programmed by computer for one or more statistical assessments.

The credibility that is accustomed to these studies (apart from the professional stature of those involved) derives from the magnitude of the trial and the impression that so big a study must have been well conceived and executed. Three such studies that have never been wholly accepted or rejected come to mind. Perhaps the most important, and certainly the most controvertable, was the University Group Diabetic Study on tolbutamide, the oral sulfonylurea antidiabetic drug that at least a third of all maturity onset diabetic patients have taken. Prior to this study that questioned both the utility and safety of such a sulfonylurea, these oral antidiabetic compounds were considered to be effective in about one-half to two-thirds of patients with maturity onset diabetes, although in 1958 Krall *et al.* of the Joslin Clinic placed the overall effectiveness in 1400 patients at 20–25 percent. The report of the University Group Study concluded that it was not only ineffective but that the incidence of deaths from coronary heart disease was greater in patients who received the drug than in those (control) patients to whom the drug was not given.

In another area, an earlier multi-clinic study supported by the British Medical Research Council did not distinguish aspirin from cortisone when given to rheumatoid arthritic patients. A more recent multi-clinic comparison of aspirin with indomethacin in this country met a similar fate. In it the statistical analysis of results was inconclusive but the rheumatoid arthritic patients were reported to have felt worse when they were switched from indomethacin to aspirin.

In my opinion, multi-clinic studies are a useful, important, but a very blunt instrument with which to determine the features of a drug or with which to distinguish between the similar features of two drugs. Perhaps the nephrologist and the consultant on hypertension would support this measure of insensitivity by the following analogy. I believe both the individual investigator with a few edematous patients and a few days of close study or a multi-clinic trial with thousands of patients extending over a few years could distinguish between the diuretic potency of chlorothiazide and the more potent ethacrynic acid or furosemide. I would expect the individual investigator to note the greater antihypertensive effect of chlorothiazide, but this might be less evident in the multi-clinic trial. In other words, the more numerous the individual groups of investigators from different institutions the more frequent and systematic their insensible variation in technic and interpretation of procedure would be, hence the less sensitive their group perception. From another point of view, I would expect the statistical expression of the group perception to be less sensitive or acute, as the case may be, than that of the best investigators in the group.

On the other hand, some assessments can hardly be made except by multi-clinic study, such as the evaluation of therapy for long-term benefit in fibrinous glomerulonephritis, for instance. Fortunately, most clinics do not see sufficient numbers of this variable situation so that pooling their experience with a form of therapy is the more reliable basis for assessment.

INSTITUTIONAL CLINICAL TRIALS

There are the institutional clinical trials that can be set up by a single agency, such as the Veterans Administration study of hypertension therapy. The large Joslin Clinic study of the sulfonylurea antidiabetic compounds was mentioned earlier in this chapter. Still other large medical groups have the resources to handle tremendous studies and this has been done, for example, as the Framingham study of cardiac disease. [These tremendous studies as well as the multi-clinic studies are listed in the selected references.] Usually, these studies are allowed to run for years. The large institutional trials differ from the multi-clinic trials importantly. Such an institution as the Veterans Administration Hospitals is likely to have more uniform practices, procedures, and patient population than one might expect to find among the individual groups participating in a multi-clinic study. Perhaps the best recent publications that would attest to the precision of such institutional studies are those by Freis and his associates from the Veterans Administration that document the usefulness of drug treatment for mild hypertension, to moderate progression of the disease and lower the incidence of stroke and coronary occlusion.

International Clinical Trials

There are features of international clinical research that are of interest but which may be neither well known nor understood in this country.

Sponsors of international clinical research (from this country) find clinical investigations abroad to be different in some respects but there is no difficulty in finding investigators capable of the most sophisticated studies in all countries where there has been a long and modern heritage of excellence in medical education. Today, the fact that many investigators will have had part of their training in another country as well as their own has tended to lend a uniformity to their standards of excellence. Where necessary, clinical protocols and procedures are scrupulously adhered to and such studies are accepted by the FDA and regulatory agencies in other countries in support of a New Drug Application. Indeed, in the past few years it has been possible to obtain excellent multicenter studies abroad.

On the other hand, most clinical studies conducted abroad are of an individual nature. The forces of conformation to the wishes of a strong regulatory agency are not felt so firmly elsewhere, yet. Understandably, then, the investigator abroad is more inclined to individualize his study in order to broaden his experience with the drug. Normal volunteers are not as commonly employed in initial clinical studies abroad as in the United States. Studies on a new drug are customarily conducted in patients who might benefit from its use. Whereas obtaining informed consent is not in the tradition of clinical research it is becoming a more general practice abroad as well as in the U.S.A., especially when it is anticipated that the work will be published in this country. In other words, the sanctions of (1) presenting studies at international meetings, (2) publishing in journals of international esteem, and (3) having the work accepted by various regulatory agencies tend to generalize the pattern and quality of work in many lands.

It is understandable that in every country a new drug must have the appraisal of outstanding clinical investigators and educators of that nation before it is accepted by that regulatory agency. This is true regardless of who has studied the compound or where. The medical profession of any land looks to its leaders for guidance as to what is good therapy. Satisfying this multinational compulsion does lead to considerable redundancy in the world literature on new drugs. Having worked with clinical investigators for many years in many lands I have been impressed by the fact that there is no single road to excellence in clinical research; that excellence is attainable by the many avenues investigators around the world follow in their work.

Clinical Trials in Perspective

Today, the clinical assessment of a new drug may take well over twelve-million dollars, 6 years or more, and a tremendous technical effort of a global nature before it can be delivered to the physician. Was it ever thus? No, the three New Drug Applications (NDA) on cortisone in 1950–1951 were little more than the clinical impressions of a few distinguished men who gave the steroid to a few patients who had rheumatoid arthritis. It took the FDA one to three and one-half months to approve the steroid for marketing. In fairness to all, in the past 25–30 years the pendulum seems to have swung from what everyone would agree were more superficial assessments of new drugs to what today might be considered exaggerated evaluations with respect to need.

The clinical investigation of a new drug can be self defeating today. For some classes of drugs, only a half dozen well supervised clinical studies of a size and complexity that can be easily managed are needed to establish efficacy reasonably and the more common adverse effects of the agent. The management of tens of studies and hundreds of patients is likely to introduce error by inadvertence, and a disproportionate number of what may or may not be side effects of the drug that must be reckoned with.

In Chapters 9 and 13 on preclinical and clinical pharmacology, emphasis was placed on keeping the experiment simple. That principle applies to the assessment of clinical utility also. There is no substitute for the simple direct experiment. The use of computer and statistics cannot make a poorly designed study good. Moreover, repeating a protocol many times at the hands of as many investigators doesn't improve it.

When you get right down to it, at times it is impossible to develop a placebo that the determined patient cannot distinguish from the drug in spite of an identical appearance of the two dosage forms. If the color, size, shape, or taste of a formulation is changed during a study, the work may need to be started over because of the likely psychogenic response of many patients to any change in the appearance of a drug. For that matter, exposure of the patient to new physicians in the course of a study may alter the incidence of side effects or the utility of the compound materially. For the results to be most meaningful, the protocol must be appropriate, adequate, and feasible, and the patients should be exposed to the same dosage forms and management throughout the study. If such rigid criteria are scrupulously observed, there is little reason why the clinical assessment of a new drug needs be as ponderous as it has become.

COLLATERAL LITERATURE

(See Collateral Literature, Chapter 15.)

15.
Clinical Trial —
Its Function

INTRODUCTORY REMARKS

In the preceding chapter we considered the development over the past quarter century or so of the interactions between the clinical investigator, the sponsor of a new drug and the regulatory agency — the Food and Drug Administration (FDA) in the U.S.A. Various types of clinical studies were discussed briefly.

In this chapter, the clinical studies that lead to the fulfillment of requirements to market the new drug will be discussed in terms of their function or purpose.

Years ago, we distributed the new drug and the preclinical information to a number of clinicians who were experienced in the area of medicine and therapy into which the compound was thought to fit. Such busy people communicated (1) their needs for an additional drug, (2) adverse reactions if serious, (3) their appraisal of the drug, and (4) a copy of a manuscript describing the results of the work, unless other help was needed. Of course, sometimes the association between clinician and research or clinical personnel of the company that interested him in the study was very close and exciting, but the relationship was not very exacting of either party, contractually. After the results of a number of clinical studies on a compound were gathered together, perhaps a dozen reports, research management and the medical director of the company decided whether enough information was in hand to write a description of the drug, a package circular that set forth the efficacy, side effects and contraindications sufficiently documented to be accepted by the FDA [FDA does not license a drug, although the Bureau of Biologics licenses biological products for marketing]. In other words, what was submitted by the investigators more or less determined the claim structure that was made for the new drug.

Today, it is mandatory that the important and desired claims of efficacy be anticipated by the time the extensive clinical studies are planned so that the clinical research is adequate to that purpose. This is because of the more detailed and rigorous regulatory requirements, the tremendous cost of clinical studies (that may be reckoned in millions of dollars) and the years needed to accumulate a sufficient experience with the drug to fulfill those requirements. Money, time and personnel need to be budgeted carefully under these prevailing conditions.

THE IND (INVESTIGATIONAL NEW DRUG) STATUS

When the drug is ready for clinical trial beginning with Phase I clinical pharmacology, investigators must be solicited to do specific studies on an agreed number of patients or other personnel, depending on the study, and within a prescribed period of time. The investigators are given all the biological information available on the compound. Their qualifications, the clinical plans, and all laboratory data relating to synthesis, formulation, and the preclinical information on activity and safety together with the qualifications of the laboratory scientists who did the preclinical studies are submitted to the FDA in a form they prescribe. This constitutes an application for Investigational New Drug status, or IND for the new drug. The FDA may accept the IND or ask for additional data or for specific conferences before its approval. Only after the IND is accepted by the FDA may material be sent to the clinicians so their studies may begin. The IND may be supplemented from time to time and new IND's may be submitted, if this seems needed to expand the project.

THE INITIAL CLINICAL STUDIES

The initial clinical studies, Phase I mentioned previously in Chapter 13, usually relate to dose-range finding, dose-response curves, some of the metabolic work, adequacy of the formulation (amount absorbed, for example), in humans. Some early Phase II work may be included in the plans for the initial IND if, say, the response to the increasing dosage is one of increased urine volume and electrolyte excretion (diuretic drug). These studies are usually short term (days, weeks) and involve small numbers of patients or normal volunteers.

Once again though, the most helpful advice as one progresses into the Phase I–Phase II work is the threefold admonition to: (1) choose the subjects carefully to avoid unnecessary, adventitious, bothersome happenstances that can only be handled adequately by preventing their occurrence; (2) keep the design and execution of the first clinical experiments simple and (3) keep the simple experiments relevant to the basic clinical situation for which the new drug is intended.

CLINICAL SAFETY ASSESSMENT

When it appears that there may be enough information to justify taking a new compound into Phase III studies, the clinical safety assessments should be set up. These are as similar as practicable to the corresponding chronic safety assessments initiated on the compund in the laboratory with notable and practical modification. Frequently, an institutionalized population of healthy individuals is needed to supply the numbers of reasonably uniformly cared for people required for the study which may have a duration of weeks to 6 months or more, depending on how long the new drug will be administered. Alternatively, it may be possible to design long-term clinical assessments of utility, of a year or longer, to incorporate the elements of safety assessments.

Whereas it is not prudent to include toxic doses in the study, one would like to incorporate a dosage level or two that are definitely greater than it is anticipated will be needed for maximal therapeutic effect. This higher than maximal therapeutic level would be unrealistic for a digitalis analog where therapeutic-to-toxic dosage ratios are generally low but would be no problem for a thiazide and some antibiotics, for instance, if the studies were monitored appropriately and carefully.

Biopsy material is not likely to be available from these human safety trials but substantial hematology and clinical chemistry would be mandatory and readily available. If the study is strictly a safety assessment, a similar number of subjects who receive placebos identical with the new drug in appearance and taste should be subjected to identical handling including taking samples of blood, urine, etc. on the same day to be analyzed by the same laboratory. If the study is a modified Phase III long-term assessment, another drug may be employed for reference purposes instead of the placebo.

Variations in clinical chemistry and hematology do appear over a period of months in most hospital laboratories as personnel, equipment, time of sampling, etc., change. These aberrant figures, if allowed to stand alone, might appear to indicate drug toxicity. Frequently they cannot be accounted for or even proven to be circumstantial unless control and drug-administered subjects are subjected concurrently to the same analytical procedures. Incidentally, these studies (human safety assessments) are sufficiently costly regardless of who does the analytical work that definitely prescribed specimens of body fluids should be of sufficient amounts and frequency to make possible a check on reliability of the assays by submitting them to another laboratory, if this seems indicated and prudent. Indeed, the likelihood of occasional blemishes in the laboratory data is considerable if for no other reason than the mass of figures that may be accumulated. These data carry the basis for comparing control with drug effect as samples of biological fluids are compared at intervals of weeks or months for perhaps a year or longer. Redundancy, the ability to check such analytical work is highly desirable. The need to protect the basic safety trials by such means cannot be overemphasized. Such procedures do not make a poorly designed study better, but they certainly improve the opportunity to deal with problems credibly.

STUDIES IN CHILDREN

Except for the assessment of vaccines for the infectious diseases of childhood, initial evaluation of potential therapeutic agents is seldom conducted in infants or older children. The testing of attenuated vaccines as for measles, mumps, etc., in young children can be of benefit to the child and usually represents no great risk or problem. Such studies are usually done with the collaboration of the Public Health Service or in institutions responsible for the care of children. Both types of organizations are very sensitive to their responsibilities for minimizing risks to the children as well as for complying with the requirements for informed consent and the use of peer review committees.

New chemical compounds, potential new drugs, are usually established as effective and safe in adults before being administered to children, but this is not always so. For example, early in its assessment probenecid was added to penicillin therapy for children who needed that antibiotic. The effect of raising the antibiotic blood level by that adjuvant seemed likely to be beneficial to the children. In such cases, transposition of dosage data from laboratory animals (dogs) to children on a body weight basis (i.e., mg/kg) is reasonable if done with allowance for incomplete maturation of many bodily systems for a year or more after birth.

Of the commonly employed drugs, the antibiotics are the ones most frequently developed for which the need during childhood suggests that pediatric
studies be conducted as part of the Phase III clinical program. Such compounds as antiepileptic agents logically belong in the Phase III clinical trial
in children, whereas new compounds of infrequent interest to the pediatrician
might better be deferred from study in children until their use and abuse in
adults are understood very well.

PLANNING THE CLINICAL TRIAL

All the Phase I and II studies do not necessarily have to be completed before the Phase III large scale clinical studies pertaining to utility and safety
are planned and actually gotten under way. The intent of developing the
Phase I and II studies to this point is so that the extensive Phase III clinical
assessment can be planned and initiated rationally. Indeed, the FDA needs to
concur with the adequacy of the Phase I and II studies and the plans for
Phase III before these latter clinical trials are begun in the United States.

Plans for Phase III should include such studies as are needed to establish
the claim structure of the new drug — what it is to be used for. These studies
will establish the early image of the drug, its capabilities and limitations. They
will be among the first results on the new drug that are reported at scientific
meetings and in the clinical literature. They will be the early source of information about the drug to appear in textbooks along with the basic preclinical and clinical pharmacology.

The claim structure, what it is good for, is the most important part of the
package circular, the monograph that accompanies each drug package. It is
the most important aspect of the advertising or promotional literature. Regardless of all the other important things in the package circular, the physician prescribes the drug for a purpose, something it is supposed to do, the
claim or claims made for the drug. (The package circular is discussed in Chapters 17 and 18.)

The marketing area of a company may have a lot to say about the basic
strategy of the Phase III program. They should be given opportunity to make
their wishes known at the outset, rather than two-thirds through a 6-year,
twelve-million dollar Phase III program. For instance, one company's marketing area may be content with a single primary claim for a new drug if its scope
of usefulness (what it might reasonably be expected to do) might be evident
to the physician, hoping that thereby it might be made available to them and
to the practitioner in a shorter period of time. The marketing area of another

company might prefer to have the whole likely claim structure for the compound cleared through the regulatory agencies at the time it is approved for marketing, feeling that they might reach a greater market potential, even though they would have to wait longer for the product. Simply stating such problems hardly does them justice. Some such considerations that relate to the Regulatory Agencies appear again in Chapter 17. Other aspects are developed in Chapter 18 and 19 on the delivery of new drugs.

Whatever the plan for Phase III, all this, the preclinical and clinical pharmacology and safety assessment accumulated to this point together with information pertaining to who and where and what is to be done at a clinical level, is filed with the FDA. The selection of investigators, negotiation of the terms and details of their study, assurances of proper peer review committees, and eliciting patient consent, all take time and patience.

MONITORING THE CLINICAL TRIAL

Individual compounds or areas of clinical research are assigned to monitors in the medical department of a pharmaceutical company. The monitor (a dreadful designation) is usually an M.D. who handles the many interactions between the sponsor and the investigators. He or she has a supportive staff that handles the administrative details so that the monitor may give more time to the several clinical investigators. Periodically, the clinical investigators submit reports that are in turn the basis for regular reports from the sponsor of the drug to the FDA. These progress reports include the circumstances and details of adverse reactions that are not alarming (as defined in the Regulations; see Chapter 17) as well as a status report on the projected study.

If the adverse reaction or cause of a death is alarming, or if anything occurs anywhere in the total study that is alarming, this should be reported to the FDA and to the clinicians studying the drug by the sponsor without undue delay. Sometimes a difference of opinion can occur as to what is alarming. When this happens, the person closest to the situation and the facts may be least inclined or the first to holler "wolf" and is most likely to receive blame along with the sponsor if his or her judgment turns out to be wrong. Of course, the clinician may report adverse reactions directly to the regulatory agency as well as to the sponsor of the drug.

In the previous Chapter (Chapter 14) on the clinical trial, various types or procedures of clinical studies were discussed. These procedures hold for the Phase III studies. A difference peculiar to Phase III is that these studies usually are for a long period of time. (It takes a long time to accumulate a series of, say, fifty or a hundred patients of a kind who have been given a drug for 6 months or a year in addition to the many who will have been given the drug for a shorter duration.) The cost of periodic hematology and clinical chemistry in such studies becomes impressive. The likelihood of the study being completed without trouble is not very great. However, the better the studies are designed, supervised by the investigator, and recorded the less likely are unaccountable inconsistencies in drug performance and adverse effects.

BEYOND THOSE FIRST SEVERAL GOOD STUDIES

It has been my good fortune to have worked with many interesting, active new compounds and to have helped shepherd them through their clinical trials and tribulations. After the first several good studies on a new drug are completed, it has seemed to me that we have learned little more that we needed to know by the subsequent trials. After those first few studies, it seemed the more vast and prolonged the studies became the more certain something or several things would happen that would unjustifiably jeopardize that compound ever reaching the market. As mentioned in a previous paragraph, a peptic ulcer, heart attack, hyperplastic mammary nodule, diabetic coma, or death may be clearly unrelated to the drug so far as the investigator is concerned. However, if one or more of these unfortunate occurrences happens several times in a trial that involves perhaps thousands of patients, many of whom will have received the drug for 6 months to a year or more, the net effect may be most unfortunate. It may be more than a perfectly good drug can survive when the data are submitted to one or more of the groups that must judge it.

In the foregoing paragraph it was stated that extending the clinical studies beyond the first several that are well done can be as much a hazard as a help for the total premarketing assessment of a new drug. Such an attitude is certain to be controversial, to say the least, for it is inconsistent with what is being required today. On the other hand, putting more patients on study for longer periods of time does no more for the establishment of clinical utility and safety than does giving the chemical to larger numbers of rats and dogs for longer periods of time assure a better assessment of safety. Broadening the *scope* of the laboratory studies is what has improved safety assessment, not doing more of the same.

In a way, marketing the drug is how the scope of the assessment of a new agent has been and is broadened beyond any reasonable clinical trial, and it seems likely to remain so.

POSTMARKETING CLINICAL EXPLORATION

Actually, the clinical exploration of a useful drug is never over. After it is marketed, the sponsor is likely to continue to encourage clinical studies for at least several years. The purpose may be to expand the usefulness of the drug, if possible. Likewise, many biologists and clinicians who were not part of the initial investigations are likely to find that the new drug happens to fit some idea or lend itself to testing some pet theory. The caliber of the investigators, the quality and variety of their work and publications are apt to be substantial. These studies which will appear around the world, regardless of where the drug is marketed, take their measure in both a practical and an esoteric way.

Regardless of whether a specific regulatory agency has approved it, these studies (sometimes called Phase IV studies) are where and when a drug's usefulness and its behavior when abused or subjected to unusual clinical circumstance are determined. Every day and every way that the public is deprived of a useful drug needlessly by extending the Phase III studies or by picayune negotiations is a very real deprivation to the practice of medicine and a delay in the ultimate assessment of its usefulness for the purpose it was intended. Such so-called protection of the patient is the antithesis of motivation and progress in therapy.

COLLATERAL LITERATURE

Beecher, H. K (1959): Experimentation in man, Publication 352, American Lecture Series, Charles C. Thomas, Springfield, Ill. Catalog card No. 58–14065.

Cooper Clinics Committee of the American Rheumatism Assoc. (1967): A three-month trial of indomethacin in rheumatoid arthritis with special reference to analysis and inference, *J. Clin. Pharmacol. and Therap.* 8: 11–37.

Cornfield, J. (1971): The university group diabetes program: A further statistical analysis of the mortality findings, *J.A.M.A. 217:* 1676–1687.

Dawber, T. R., Kannel, W. B., and Lyell, L. P. (1963): An approach to longevity studies in a community: The Framingham Study, *Ann. N. Y. Acad. Sci. 107:* 539–556.

Friedman, G. D., Kannel, W. B., Dawber, T. R., and McNamara, P. M. (1967): An evaluation of follow-up methods in the Framingham Heart Study, *Am. J. Pub. Health 57:* 1015–1024.

World Health Organization (1975) Guidelines for Evaluation of Drugs for Use in Man: Report of a WHO Scientific Group, World Health Organization Technical Report No. 563, World Health Organization, Geneva.

Kannel, W. B., Gordon, T., and Schwartz, M. J. (1971): Systolic versus diastolic blood pressure and risk of coronary heart disease: The Framingham Study, *Am. J. Cardiol. 27:* 335–346.

Kannel, W. B., Wolf, P. A., Verter, J., and McNamara, P. M. (1970): Epidemiologic assessment of the role of blood pressure in stroke. The Framingham Study, *J.A.M.A. 214:* 301–310.

Knatterud, G. L., Meinert, C. L., Klimt, C. R., Osborne, R. K., and Martin, D. B. (1971): Effect of hypoglycemic agents on vascular complications in patients with adult onset diabetes, *J.A.M.A. 217:* 777–784.

Lasagna, L. (1955): The controlled clinical trial: Theory and practice, *J. Chron. Dis. 1:* 353–367.

Mainland, D. (1961): Experiences in the development of multiclinic trials, *J. New Drugs (J. Clin. Pharmacol.) 1:* 197–205.

Marble, A. (1955): Critique of the therapeutic usefulness of the oral agents in diabetes, *Am. J. Med. 31:* 919–930.

Marsh, B. T. (1974): Clinical trial procedures; a summary of requirements in thirty-three countries, *J. Int. Med. Res. 2:* 26–31.

Medical Research Council and Nuffield Foundation Report (1954): A comparison of cortisone and aspirin in the treatment of early cases of rheumatoid arthritis, *Brit. Med. J. 1:* 1223–1227.

Medical Research Council and Nuffield Foundation report (1954): A comparison of ministration after cardiac infarction, *Brit. Med. J. 1:* 803–810.

Meyler, L., and Peck, H. M. (1972): Drug Induced Diseases, Vol. 4. Excerpta Medica, Amsterdam.

The University Group Diabetes Program (1970): A study of the effects of hypoglycemic agents on vascular complications in patients with adult-onset diabetes, *Diabetes 19:* (supplement 2) 747–830.

Veterans Administration Cooperative Group on Antihypertensive Agents (1970): Effect of treatment on morbidity in hypertension. II. Results in patients with diastolic blood pressure averaging 90 through 114 mmHg., *J.A.M.A. 213:* 1143–1152.

Veterans Administration Cooperative Study Group on Antihypertensive Agents (1967): Effects of treatment on morbidity in hypertension: Results in patients with diastolic blood pressures averaging 115 to 129 mmHg., *J.A.M.A. 202:* 1028–1034.

16.
Patents, Trademarks, and Copyrights

Congress shall have power . . . to promote the progress of science and useful arts, by securing for limited times to authors and inventors the exclusive right to their respective writings and discoveries. Article 1, Section 8, *The Constitution of the United States of America.*

One of the greatest heritages the signers of the Constitution of the United States bestowed on this country was the power given Congress to enact laws having to do with copyrights and patents. The first patent law enacted for this purpose was in 1790. The Patent Office as a distinct bureau is said to date from 1802 when the duties of a separate official in the Department of State (but now in the Department of Commerce) was designated "Superintendent of Patents." Other laws pertaining to patents, trademarks and copyrights have been enacted and revised from time to time.

COMMON FEATURES

Patents, trademarks, and copyrights have two features in common. First, each is a grant of certain exclusive rights to the recipient. Secondly, those rights are granted for definite periods of time and so are more of the nature of a lease than a deed. They assure the designee a right to defend that which is recognized as his under the law. Otherwise, patents, trademarks, and copyrights are quite different from each other in coverage, assignment, duration, and in other details, including the fee for filing or registration.

The purpose of this chapter is to give enough of the generalities of each type of coverage to distinguish between them and to give some appreciation of their scope, importance, and their limitation. Since this book relates particularly to the discovery of new drugs, the greatest emphasis will be put on patents. Occasionally, one hears or reads of arguments to do away with, to shorten the duration or to restrict otherwise one or another of these three rights. Usually, this criticism is without a full consideration of the total purpose of their combined structure. That purpose is to assure a sustained basis for creativity and an image of excellence by writers, inventors, or manufacturers which has been a great source of strength and motivation for growth of this nation since its inception.

Before getting into a discussion of their individual characteristics, the tripartite elements of this chapter may be abridged as follows: (1) A *patent* describes a new and useful invention or discovery. (2) A *trademark* relates to any word, name, symbol, or device used in commerce to identify the source of goods and to distinguish it from the goods of others. (3) The *copyright* goes to the *form of expression* rather than to the subject matter of a writing.

PATENTS

What you say about your new drug might be copyrighted, what you call it might be trademarked, but *it is the new drug that may be patented.*

As mentioned at the beginning of this chapter, The Constitution of the United States recognized in Article 1, Section 8, the importance to this nation of "securing for limited times to authors and inventors the exclusive right to their respective writings and discoveries." Since the first enactment of the patent law in 1790, it has been revised from time to time, the most recent being enacted July 19, 1952. The importance of a strong protective patent policy to a nation is self evident if one compares the patent policy with the creativity of the pharmaceutical industry of various countries. The discovery of useful new drugs within that industry is greatest where patent protection is greatest, least where the patent structure and policy is non existent in a nation. Moreover, recent analyses indicate that some 88% of drug innovation today comes from the pharmaceutical industry. If this association of patent protection with productivity is so real, then it is worth understanding what patents are, for what they are granted, to whom, for how long, and something about their structure.

The front page of a patent is reproduced as Fig. 1 since few people have occasion to see the original of such a document. This page indicates that it is a United States Patent and gives its number. It indicates the inventors, the na-

2,608,509

THE UNITED STATES OF AMERICA

TO ALL TO WHOM THESE PRESENTS SHALL COME:

Whereas James M. Sprague, of Drexel Hill, and Karl H. Beyer, Jr., of Bala Cynwyd, Pennsylvania, assignors to Sharp & Dohme, Incorporated, of Philadelphia, Pennsylvania, a corporation of Maryland,

PRESENTED TO THE **Commissioner of Patents** A PETITION PRAYING FOR THE GRANT OF LETTERS PATENT FOR AN ALLEGED NEW AND USEFUL IMPROVEMENT IN

COMPOSITION CONTAINING PENICILLIN AND AN ADJUVANT OF THE GENERAL FORMULA $R_1CH_2SO_2NHR_2COOH$,

A DESCRIPTION OF WHICH INVENTION IS CONTAINED IN THE SPECIFICATION OF WHICH A COPY IS HEREUNTO ANNEXED AND MADE A PART HEREOF, AND COMPLIED WITH THE VARIOUS REQUIREMENTS OF LAW IN SUCH CASES MADE AND PROVIDED, AND

Whereas UPON DUE EXAMINATION MADE THE SAID CLAIMANT s are ADJUDGED TO BE JUSTLY ENTITLED TO A PATENT UNDER THE LAW.

NOW THEREFORE THESE **Letters Patent** ARE TO GRANT UNTO THE SAID

Sharp & Dohme, Incorporated, its successors   OR ASSIGNS

FOR THE TERM OF SEVENTEEN YEARS FROM THE DATE OF THIS GRANT

THE EXCLUSIVE RIGHT TO MAKE, USE AND VEND THE SAID INVENTION THROUGHOUT THE UNITED STATES AND THE TERRITORIES THEREOF.

In testimony whereof I have hereunto set my hand and caused the seal of the Patent Office to be affixed at the City of Washington this twenty-sixth day of August, in the year of our Lord one thousand nine hundred and fifty-two, and of the Independence of the United States of America the one hundred and seventy-seventh.

Attest:

Karl H. Axline
Attesting Officer.

John A. Marzall
Commissioner of Patents

ture or title of the patent, to whom it has been assigned and the date of issue, all duly attested and signed by the Commissioner of Patents.

A patent for an invention (or discovery) is a grant of certain rights to an inventor by the Patent and Trademark Office of the United States. The subject of the grant is an invention. (Note: invention and discovery, and inventor and discoverer may be used interchangeably in this text.) The person entitled to the patent is the inventor. The duration of a United States patent is 17 years from the *date of issue* of the patent, *not* from the date the patent *application* was filed. (Apparently, this odd duration is the result of compromise between those who felt 15 or 20 years was a proper duration.) The grant extends throughout the United States and its territories and possessions. The right is to *exclude others* from making, using, or selling the invention; it is not the right to make, use or sell the invention.

What constitutes an invention as the term is used here? What makes it patentable? There are four types of pharmaceutical inventions that are patentable. These are (1) a product (the compound, *per se*), (2) a process for making the product, or (3) a "composition of matter" containing the product or (4) a "use" patent, a novel way to use the product. When it comes to new drugs, it is usually the chemical compound that is the "product." One of the two things that determines whether the discovery (product, process, composition, or use) is patentable is its *novelty*; the fact that it did not exist before the discovery and that it is unique with respect to the characteristic(s) described in the patent application. (So-called patent medicines ordinarily do not meet these qualifications and so are not patented.) Ordinarily, natural products are not patentable. However, if through genetic mutation a new flower, such as a rose, or a novel derivative of a bacterial fermentation product, an antibiotic, is discovered, these can be patented. In addition to being novel, the discovery must be *useful*. Usefulness of the compound might be to lower blood pressure; usefulness of the process would be for the preparation of the compound; usefulness of the composition of matter might be to treat hypertension, as examples.

The inventor or discoverer is the only one (or ones) in whose name the patent can be issued, in which respect it may differ from copyrights or trademarks. The inventor may assign the patent. Ordinarily, a condition of employment in a research laboratory is that patents to all discoveries will be assigned to that company. In turn, patents can be reassigned. License to manufacture or sell may be granted to another company or to other companies by the assignee of the patent.

When we get beyond these simple statements, the situation becomes so complex that the Patent Office prefers to deal with patent attorneys registered with that office to handle such matters. Usually, patent attorneys are lawyers who have obtained a technical background in chemistry, engineering, or some other specialty. Companies that have a research and development group of any consequence usually have their own patent lawyers. In turn, these people may seek outside patent counsel to complement their expertise in very important cases. Private inventors, universities, and other groups may employ patent attorneys in private practice if their needs are only occasional. In any instance, the inventor needs to file with the Patent and Trademark Office a power of attorney authorizing his patent attorney to deal with the agency for him. The Patent and Trademark Office usually does not deal with the inventor directly.

The groundwork for patent application may be laid before the invention or discovery is made. In a well run medicinal chemistry group the individual chemists are expected to know reasonably the patent literature as a part of the background for the type of chemistry with which they work. In structure/ activity work such as was dealt with in Chapters 6, 7, and 8, it would be disastrous to limit oneself to making only "new" compounds that might be patentable. Consideration of patentability comes with the "fine tuning" of lead chemistry, the optimal combining of chemical novelty with biological utility. To illustrate this point, it will be recalled from Chapter 7 that p-aminohippurate (PAH) (an "old" compound) would inhibit penicillin secretion by the tubules of the kidney, as did probenecid (Benemid). Whereas PAH was not effective when administered orally and the daily dose given intravenously at constant rate was about 200 grams, probenecid was effective when administered by mouth at a daily dose of 2 grams a day or less. The chemical structure of probenecid combined novelty with utility. It was patentable as a new and useful compound.

The establishment of novelty for a compound may require a great deal of effort before the examiners in the Patent Office, who may or may not be patent lawyers, are convinced. These examiners, or sometimes the courts, decide what novelty is in a specific instance. The one devastating way to destroy novelty is to disclose the structure of a compound to the public over a year before patent application is filed. After a year following disclosure, it is considered an "old" chemical, in the public domain, hence not patentable. Usually, initial patent application(s) is/are filed well before the compound is disclosed by publication or by presentation at a public meeting and in advance of being submitted for clinical investigation. There is a Paris Convention among a number of nations whereby the original filing date for all of them, which is important for the establishment of priority of patent application.

As a step toward establishing novelty of a compound, the patent attorney for the inventor needs to search the patent literature. There are over 3.6 million issued U.S. patents in, of course, a great many fields or categories. In addition, the world literature must be searched for such a disclosure. The Scientific Library of the Patent and Trademark Office is said to have available for public use over 120,000 volumes of technical books in various languages, some 90,000 bound periodicals and over eight million published patents from various countries. There is a Search Room which contains a complete set of U.S. patents and the Official Gazette since it was first published. A Record Room is provided where the public may inspect the records and files of issued patents and other open records.

Frequently, the initial patent application will disclose and claim the structures of several related compounds considered to be novel, a process for synthesis sufficient that one knowledgeable in the art could make the compound(s) and a disclosure of the utility thereof. The inevitable dilemma of the patent attorney in such a situation is to claim the invention as broadly as possible and to define it as precisely as possible in that application, for very good reason. If the attorney discloses and claims only the compound that seems most likely to become a new drug, that patent application might block the possibility of patent protection for other related compounds with subsequent additional applications. If the disclosure is too broad, the credibility of the application or even an allowed patent may be weakened, increasing thereby the likelihood of the application being rejected by the examiner or the patent being invalidated if challenged in court. The synthesis may or may not be the one ultimately employed and the utility may or may not be the ultimate commercial use for the compound. However, the inventor is obliged to disclose the best mode of practicing his invention known to him at the time of his application.

In any event, the initial application is likely to be rejected by the examiner in the Patent and Trademark Office to whom it is assigned because the invention seems obvious from the literature searched by the examiner. The attorney for the inventor has 6 months in which to reply to this "First Office Action" and the interaction with the examiner goes on from there until the "Final Action" that allows or disallows the patent. This can take years of negotiation. If the examiner finds adversely, the inventor through his attorney can appeal to the Board of Appeals of the Patent and Trademark Office. If turned down there, appeal can be made to the Court of Customs and Patent Appeals, which is a special court in the Federal court system.

Whereas product patents are the strongest and most desirable, process patents are very important also. As a matter of fact, some countries allow process patents but not product patents today.

The patent attorney is inclined to write applications on all conceivable processes that might be useful for the manufacture of the compound or compounds claimed in the product patent application. As mentioned in Chapter 11 on Chemical Development, there is no great satisfaction in owning the product patent on a compound and then paying royalties to someone else who owns a patent on a substantially more economical or practical process than those developed by the manufacturer. Thus, process development may continue long after the product patent structure is established. As a matter of fact, the most practical process patents may determine who continues to manufacture a drug on a profitable basis once the product patents have expired.

Composition of matter and use patents are the weaker of the four kinds of patents. These may relate to some unique feature of the formulation that makes the drug useful when administered orally whereas ordinarily it would have to be given by injection. The invention may be a way of solubilizing an otherwise poorly soluble drug so that it might be injected intravenously for prompt effect. A unique formulation of an old drug for an entirely new use might be patentable. The aspect that makes these patents weak is that they are the most easily circumvented if it becomes economically worthwhile to do so.

Sometimes two applications are filed more or less concurrently by different people who claim the same invention. This is likely to happen when a new field of synthesis has opened up and activity among such chemists is greatest. Since a patent can be granted only to the one who is found to be the *first* inventor, a proceeding known as an "interference" is set up by the Patent and Trademark Office to determine who is entitled to the patent. For that matter, an interference can be initiated between a valid patent application and a patent that has not been issued for more than one year prior to filing the conflicting application. Under these conditions the contesting parties have to file evidence as to the date of their respective inventions. There are two important factors that determine priority of inventorship: (1) the date of the "concept of invention" and (2) the date the concept was "reduced to practice." Ordinarily, if the comparison of dates shows that the person who conceived the compound was the first to synthesize and test it, the patent goes to him or her. It is possible for one person to have conceived the invention sooner but to have reduced it to practice (i.e., to have synthesized and tested the compound) after the other inventor. If the time between conception and reduction to practice does not represent "due diligence" (i.e., a reasonable period of time, taking into consideration all aspects of circumstance) then the inventor with the later date of conception but prior reduction to practice may be judged the inventor to whom the patent should issue. Sometimes, to avoid the expense of the interference proceedings the parties involved will agree to an exchange of evidence from which the attorneys judge the first inventor. Usually, such an agreement includes a provision for granting a license to the losing party to the interference.

Once the U.S. patent is issued, the inventor has the right to prevent another from making, using or selling his product in the United States. If the patent is disregarded (violated), the inventor or the company to which the patent is assigned can sue, recover damages and prevent continuation of the infringement. Alternatively, the owner of the patent may decide to license the infringer to continue his operation under the patent protection. The company that has infringed the patent may decide to withdraw and desist or attempt to negotiate a license to continue operating. The license usually carries a royalty expressed as a lump sum and/or a percentage of ongoing sales. Alternatively, the infringer may decide to contest the validity of the patent in court.

If a compound is anticipated to be a substantial contribution to medicine, patent applications for it are likely to be filed wherever (in all countries) possible. The owner of the patent may or may not be or represent an international organization capable of distributing the product worldwide. Alternatively, obtaining the patents in many countries may be for the purpose of licensing another company or agent in such countries to manufacture or sell the drug. The complexity of such actions is too great to warrant consideration here, but in principle their importance cannot be overestimated.

IMPORTANCE OF PATENTS

The ability to obtain patent protection on new drugs does affect profoundly the structure and function of research on drug discovery and development, for very practical reasons. It is this incentive that has brought research on new drugs to its present high state of development in the pharmaceutical industry. To be sure, industry had to learn how to organize and conduct biomedical research for the discovery and development of new drugs. But there was the incentive that this was worth the investment so long as productivity could be protected. It costs millions of dollars a year to run a substantial pharmaceutical research organization. The budget of the research division of a pharmaceutical company may be over one hundred million dollars a year. It would seem unreasonable for a company's board of directors to approve such huge amounts of stockholders' equity in the advancement of medicine if there were no way to protect its investment from all here and abroad capable of making and selling the new drug as soon as approved without having made any investment in its discovery.

Patentability of products does influence the orietation of research for new therapy. For example, the development of new vaccines is a much less frequent aspect of research programs than emphasis on the discovery of useful new chemicals. One deterrent is that such natural products may not be patentable.

The assurance of patent protection makes it worthwhile for a company to encourage research in very difficult areas of chemistry and biology in hopes that a breakthrough would constitute a generally useful contribution to medicine. This was the case for steroid chemistry, for example, when the anti-inflammatory adrenocorticoid activity was discovered. This may come to be true for prostaglandin research in which The Upjohn Company has pioneered.

For that matter, management must have assurance that the return from the tremendous investment in building manufacturing facilities around the world for a new drug can be realized more profitably than safer means for investing such monies. Just the cost of bringing a useful new drug from the laboratory through clinical trial to the market is reckoned today in years of effort and millions of dollars that only private enterprise is likely to handle effectively.

Two other aspects of patents might be of sufficient general interest to consider before concluding this section. Time was when academic institutions and their faculties disdained patents for lack of understanding the role they have played in encouraging progress in drug research. An exception to this generalization is the following:

In 1924, Steenbock and Black, working in the Biochemistry Department of the College of Agriculture at the University of Wisconsin, found that by *irradiating foodstuff* and feeding it to animals they could prevent rickets just as well as by administering Vitamin D to them. The basic patent issued to Dr. Steenbock was turned over to a Wisconsin Alumni Research Foundation, founded for the purpose of encouraging graduate education at that institution. The effect of financial grants from that foundation to the university has continued to have a major beneficial impact on that institution and its graduate students. Today, many research oriented universities have definite patent policies. A number of such research foundations have been organized to handle patents and thereby to support research. Alternatively, some such institutions have turned to The Research Corporation, a foundation for the advancement of science, to handle patent affairs for them.

Finally, although a patent gives its owner the right to protect a discovery, it certainly does not assure that the owner will have that field of therapy to himself. What the patent does is disclose to the rest of the world, by its issuance in the Official Gazette, what was allowed. Moreover, copies of issued patents can be obtained from the Patent and Trademark Office. This helps any other scientist or research group decide how best to circumvent that work as they search for a novel useful product. Thus, far from discouraging others from competing (which might be done more effectively by secrecy) the patent encourages and helps direct competition. This can encourage the synthesis of so-called "me too" products that fall outside the original patent and so may be patentable in their own right. This practice has been disparaged by those least familiar with structure/activity research. One familiar with the profound differences in biological effects that seemingly slight changes in structure can induce is likely to be more tolerant. For example, at least nine thiazide diuretics have been patented and marketed in this country since chlorothiazide (Diuril). More important than the chlorothiazide analogs has been the encouragement to discover other types of diuretics that have extended drug therapy or that possess attributes different from the saluretics. Thus, the physician and the patient have profited by these other drugs from the encouragement chlorothiazide gave to research on diuretic and antihypertensive therapy, even though that drug was a substantial breakthrough in its own right.

TRADEMARKS

A "trademark," as defined in Section 45 of the 1946 Federal Trademark Act, "includes any word, name, symbol or device or any combination thereof adopted and used by a manufacturer or merchant to identify his goods and distinguish them from those manufactured or sold by others."

The primary function of a trademark is to indicate origin. Most physicians and medical scientists are familiar with the trademarks of such companies as Eli Lilly and Co. or E. R. Squibb and Sons, which appear on labels and in advertisements. There are many examples of well-known trademarks such as the keystone symbol for The Pennsylvania Railroad or that for "Chessie the Cat," the Chesapeake and Ohio Railroad. Well known trademarks for drugs that identify them with a specific manufacturer would be Abbott Laboratories' Nembutal brand of pentobarbital and Schering Corporation's Clor-Trimeton brand of the antihistamine, chlorpheniramine.

Trademarks serve to guarantee a uniformity of quality of a product and to sustain an awareness and demand for a product originating from a specific manufacturer. Registration of a trademark in the Patent and Trademark Office does not, of itself, create or establish any exclusive rights. (For that matter, a trademark need not be registered to be protected under common law.) Registration of a trademark on the Principal Register under the 1946 Act is constructive notice of the registrant's claim to ownership. Such registration gives the owner the right to sue in the Federal courts and to prevent importation of products bearing an infringing mark. Thus, the owner of the registered trademark can sustain more effectively the exclusive right to use a distinctive mark to distinguish his product or product line from those of others.

There are four categories of marks that can be registered. These are trademarks, service marks, collective marks and certification marks. Marks are registered in accordance with an international classification system. The Trademark Act of 1946 provides for two registers of trademarks in this country: (1) The Principal Register consists of marks which distinguish the goods or services of the registrant from those of others. (2) The Supplemental Register consists of marks that are capable of distinguishing the registrant's goods or services, that have been in lawful use in commerce for at least a year and which are not registrable on the Principal Register.

The selection of a trademark for registration is a very serious business, deserving of great care and deliberation. Not all would-be trademarks can be registered. It cannot be deceptive nor falsely suggest a connection with persons or institutions, beliefs or national symbols. It cannot be immoral or scandalous. It cannot so resemble a mark registered in the Patent and Trademark Office or a mark or tradename previously used in the United States by another as would be likely to cause confusion when applied to the particular goods, or mistake or deception. It is this latter aspect of confusing similarity to a prior trademark that can cause difficulty to the well-intentioned applicant for registration.

To facilitate the search for *prior* marks in order to avoid duplication, a record of prior registered and applied-for marks is maintained in the Search Room of Trademark Operations. These compilations are indexed in various ways to facilitate such a search, but it is up to the applicant to assure that the mark is unique. As a matter of fact, the applicant must state that he is the owner of the mark and that to the best of his knowledge no one else has the right to use such a mark or another resembling it sufficiently as to cause confusion, mistake, or deception.

A digest of *pending* applications approved for publication with reproductions of the marks, the identity of the applicants, the goods or services for which the mark is intended, serial numbers, etc., is published weekly. This publication is the Official Gazette of the Patent and Trademark Office. It contains information about patents as well as about trademarks published for opposition. If a company feels that someone's pending published trademark would be damaging if granted registration, the company can oppose that action within thirty days of publication. Such oppositions are transmitted to a Trademark Trial and Appeal Board for adjudication. If no opposition is filed and no conflict found with other pending application, a certificate of registration will be issued. But responsibility of the owner does not end there.

A mark must be used on goods or services and its identity as such must be protected. It must be affixed to each article or its container or label and used in commerce, for its purpose is to indicate the origin of the goods as mentioned previously. Five years after its registration and during the sixth year the owner must submit an affidavit or declaration that the mark is still in use or that the special circumstance as to why it is not being used does not constitute an intention to abandon the mark. Otherwise, the registration will be cancelled.

Registrations remain in force for 20 years, but they may be renewed for additional 20 year periods provided they are continued in use. This useful duration of registration plus the right to protect the mark in the Federal courts makes a trademark tremendously useful.

Whereas a trademark does not provide the effective protection a product patent does, it can identify the origin of the product long after the 17 year duration of the patent has expired. Thus, the trademark continues to identify product uniformity to the physician in the countries where it is registered.

COPYRIGHTS

A copyright is a form of protection given by law (Title 17, U.S. Code) to the authors of literary, dramatic, musical, artistic and other intellectual works. This has been revised and for the most part the revision became effective January 1, 1978, as Public Law 94-553 (90 (Stat. 2541).

As indicated in the previous paragraph, the copyright relates to the *form of expression*, not the subject of the work. Whereas one might copyright a particular drawing or description of a device in a patent application (i.e., its form of expression) that would give no protection for the invention itself; only the ultimate granting of a patent would make possible the protection of the invention.

A copyright can be granted only to an author or to another, such as his publisher, to whom he grants the right to apply for it. Whereas a patent can be granted *solely* to the inventor or inventors, this is not necessarily the case for copyrights. In the case of work that a company has employed an individual to do, the employer may claim the copyright. Copyrights are registered in the Copyright Office of the Library of Congress. (The Patent and Trademark Office is responsible for Trademarks and Patents but not for Copyrights.) Until the new copyright legislation became effective January 1, 1978, a copyright had a duration of 28 years and could be renewed for a second 28 years. According to the new law (Public Law 94-553) Federal statutory copyright in original works authored on or after January 1, 1978 will be effective from the date of creation rather than publication and will endure for a term consisting of the author's life plus fifty years. If the work is hired, the employer is deemed the author and the copyright lasts for 75 years from the year first published or one hundred years from the year it was created, whichever is shorter.

The list of works that can be copyrighted is too long to present herein, but it includes books, plays, reproductions of works of art, certain motion pictures and certain sound recordings. Some categories of work that are not subject to copyright include titles, short phrases or slogans; ideas or plans as distinguished from a description or illustration; report forms or account books; works that consist of common information that contain no original authorship such as certain charts of standard values taken from common sources.

The exclusive rights provided the owner of a copyright include: (1) the right to print, reprint and copy his work, (2) the right to sell or distribute copies thereof, (3) the right to revise or transform the work by dramatization, translation or musical arrangement for example, (4) the right to record the work, and (5) the right to perform the work publicly.

Owner of the copyright may grant permission to another to reproduce or translate or perform the work publicly, but there are limitations and restrictions that must be met if it is to be sustained. For example, it is not possible to obtain a blanket copyright for an author's work, such as may obtain for the use of a trademark. Each work of an author must be copyrighted separately if it is to be protected. There is a "compulsory license" provision which permits recordings of musical works on payment of royalties after the initial recording has been authorized by the copyright owner thereof.

Failure to deposit two best copies of the work with the Library of Congress within three months of publication may result in fines but not in the loss of copyright protection. Registration of the copyright claim in the Copyright Office is not mandatory but no action for infringement may be brought until the copyright has been registered. Moreover, these rights may be lost unless all published copies carry a copyrighted notice in the prescribed form and position on the work. Such a notice for a book should appear on the title page or the page immediately following, as illustrated in the front of this publication. It consists of the copyright designation ©, the name, and the year of publication. The new law provides certain situations where failure to affix the notice will not result in loss of the copyright.

Under the new law, a single Federal system of statutory protection for copyrightable works, published or unpublished, is provided instead of the dual system of common law copyright for unpublished works and Federal statutory copyright for published works that has obtained.

Anyone requiring detailed information regarding the preparation, filing, and extent of coverage by copyright, trademark, or patent may wish to seek expert counsel or may direct questions to the proper federal agency, such as the Register of Copyrights, Library of Congress, Washington, D. C. 20559.

COLLATERAL LITERATURE

General Information concerning Trademarks (1970): Patent Office, U. S. Department of Commerce.

General Information concerning Patents (1972): Patent Office, U. S. Department of Commerce.

General Information on Copyright (1977): Library of Congress, Copyright Office, Washington, D. C.

Schwartzman, D. (1975): The expected return from pharmaceutical research: Sources of new drugs and the profitability of R&D investment, American Enterprise Institute for Public Policy Research, Washington, D. C. (Library of Congress Cat. Card No. 75-10500).

17.
The Regulation
of New Drug
Assessment and Use

PURPOSE OF THE FOOD AND DRUG ADMINISTRATION (FDA)

Ordinarily, a Federal regulatory agency (1) determines the adequacy with which a new product has been assessed before allowing it to be marketed, (2) inspects and otherwise assures the adequacy and uniformity of production practices, and (3) establishes a structure within which differences between those regulated and the agency can be resolved. Whereas a regulatory agency such as the Food and Drug Administration (FDA) falls within the Executive Branch of Government, it is sensitive to the committee structure of the Legislative Branch of Government. It is most influenced technically by the academic scientists and physicians to whom the staff goes for consultation. Such agencies do not contribute directly to the discovery, development, or delivery of new drugs. However, how a regulatory agency interprets and discharges its responsibility to protect the public can influence profoundly the growth and development of the technology within its sphere of influence, even competitively as one compares the operation of one agency with its counterpart in another government.

Anyone reasonably successful at new drug discovery or development in the United States should expect to relate to the FDA in this country in some role (as a consultant or in support of a new drug assessment) sooner or later. Consequently, it seems purposeful to introduce at this point in a general way what FDA requires of new drug evaluation and how it works. The following discussion is based on the Code of Federal Regulations Title 21, Part 130, pertaining to food and drugs and on a quarter century or so of experience in dealing with the agency. Neither authority nor experience nor the sum of the two suffices to anticipate how a given problem will be resolved since there are several sections of the agency that relate to the assessment of new drugs, each in its own way.

DEFINITION OF A NEW DRUG

To the Food and Drug Administration a new drug is quite a different thing than as conceived by the Patent Office (Chapter 16). For the FDA, *"new drug substance"* "means any substance that when used in the manufacture, processing, or packing of a drug, causes that drug to be a new drug, but does not include intermediates used in the synthesis of such substances." The newness for drug use may arise from the fact that (1) the agent has not been used previously as a drug, or (2) that some constituent of the formulation has not been so employed, or (3) new proportions of drugs have been used in combination, or (4) a new use for an approved drug formulation has been developed, or (5) that the dosage, method, or duration of administration is new, even though that drug used in other dosage, administration, or application is not a new drug.

SPONSOR OF A NEW DRUG

The term "sponsor" means the person, company, or agency that assumes responsibility for compliance with applicable provisions of the act and regulations. The sponsor may be an individual, partnership, corporation, or Government agency and may be a manufacturer, scientific institution, or an investigator regularly and lawfully engaged in the investigation of new drugs. Other terms will be defined in text unless it seems reasonable that the reader can discern their intent.

FEDERAL FOOD, DRUG, AND COSMETIC ACT OF 1938

Only since the October 10, 1962 Drug Amendments to the Federal Food, Drug, and Cosmetic Act of 1938 has the development of new drugs been so complexly subject to governmental regulation in this country. The 1906 Food and Drug Act related more to sanitation, good manufacturing practices, etc. The 1938 Act required the Food and Drug Administration sanction that a food, drug, or cosmetic was safe. This 1938 Act was evoked by the unfortunate but limited marketing of a sulfonamide formulation that was unsafe. Sulfonamides were effective for their intended use, no question about it, but there needed to be a way to assure the safety of new drugs. In the 1940's and 1950's things went along smoothly enough after everyone got used to the provisions of the 1938 Act. To be sure, after the FDA got used to their new role under that act the medical people therein expressed their annoyance increasingly that if a new drug was safe, by law it was not for them to judge whether it was effective. Their responsibility was to judge whether the evidence to support safety was adequate. Actually, as time went on, ways were found to introduce the evaluation of efficacy into the assessment of safety so that the limitations of the 1938 Act were more apparent than real. The developing concept of a drug's *therapeutic ratio* (therapeutic ratio = useful dose/toxic dose) made it clear that a therapeutic agent that was not very useful had to be very, very safe (i.e., a high therapeutic ratio). Conversely, a considerably greater risk of toxicity (a lower therapeutic ratio) could be tolerated for a drug that was useful for some otherwise unmanageable high-mortality disease.

1962 DRUG AMENDMENT TO THE FEDERAL FOOD, DRUG, AND COSMETIC 1938 ACT AND REGULATIONS

It has been said that catastrophe begets crusade that makes possible new legislation. At least this was the way public support for the 1962 Drug Amendment to the Federal Food, Drug, and Cosmetic Act was generated. Phocomelia induced by thalidomide was the catastrophe that made possible the crusade for the legislation of 1962. That new legislation gave the FDA regulatory control over the judgmental basis for adequacy of efficacy assessment as well as safety of new drugs. In addition, the agency has come to influence the principles as well as the practice of clinical research on new drugs through a series of Regulations it has promulgated. Still more recently (November 18, 1976), "Proposed Good Laboratory Practice Regulations" were published in the Federal Register. These proposed laboratory regulations are likely to be imposed on the safety assessment of new drugs *at first*. From the language of the proposal there seems reason to anticipate that this burden will be extended to the rest of the preclinical laboratories for the assessment of new drugs. By their very nature, regulations are intended to be restrictive, not conducive, to the imaginative use of resources. (See the November 18, 1976 Federal Register for details. Proposed Regulations are for guidance and comment. They are not binding unless and until published in final form signed by the Commissioner of the Food and Drug Administration.)

In general, the 1962 Regulations prescribed that research on new drugs in man was to be conducted in *three phases*, the first and the early second phase being considered clinical pharmacology, the latter part of the second and third phase being clinical trial.

THE IND

Before beginning the clinical studies in the United States, the sponsor of a new drug needs to file with the FDA a completed, signed, "Notice of Claimed Investigational Exemption for a New Drug," which statement is the so-called IND. The information that goes into the IND includes a disclosure of the structure and synthesis of the new compound, the composition of its formulation for clinical investigation and the means for controlling all this. The laboratory biological investigations that determine its activity, its secondary pharmacodynamic attributes and the safety assessment to that point together with the chemistry constitute the technical background for the IND, unless the agent has been studied abroad in which case that information (clinical or otherwise) is also included. Today, the curriculum vitae of those who participated in the preclinical assessment must be on file with the FDA or submitted therewith, as well as that of the clinical pharmacologists and the other clinical investigators who are to participate in the study.

The clinician who is to receive the drug has to sign a Statement of Investigator Form which includes a brief statement describing the proposed study. In addition, he or she has to state that the study will be conducted as planned, that proper records will be kept, that the reports that are prescribed will be made, that with certain exceptions the study will be explained to the subjects from whom signed "Informed Consent" statements will be obtained. When required, assurance is given that the study will have been presented for review and approval to an Institutional Review Committee composed of people from various backgrounds capable of understanding what is proposed, such as clergy, lawyers, and other scientists who are not involved in the study.

The sponsor, usually the drug company but sometimes a clinical investigator from another institution such as the National Institutes of Health or a University, agrees to a specified list of things. These include periodic reports on the IND project to FDA and the investigators, the reporting of adverse reactions, the prompt reporting of alarming findings to FDA and investigators alike, the retrieval of drug from an investigator at the termination of a study. The sponsor agrees that an investigator who disregards the clinical plans for the study or the procedural aspects of record keeping or reporting or who reports falsely will be dropped from the study. Also, the sponsor agrees that the investigation is not to be prolonged unduly and that the drug will not be promoted or subjected to marketing trials during its investigation.

These rules change from time to time, almost invariably by additional restrictions intended to protect the patient but which have the effect of increasing the risk to the sponsor or investigator of violating some aspect of the regulations over which he may or may not have immediate control.

Nowadays, the sponsor must wait 30 days after filing the IND before proceeding with the Phase I investigation. Actually, it is wiser to wait until some indication is received to the effect that the IND is satisfactory before starting the studies to be sure that the assessment at least gets started reasonably smoothly.

PHASE I – CLINICAL PHARMACOLOGY

According to the U. S. Regulations, the purpose of the Phase I clinical pharmacology (Chapter 13) is to procure in humans information on patient tolerance or toxicity, metabolism, absorption, excretion, and other pharmacodynamic effects when the new agent is given by the intended mode of administration. Desirably, a dosage range that may be safe is obtained. All this information should be obtained on only a few normal (volunteer) individuals. Who is a suitable individual for these studies and what animal safety studies are required before the compound is first administered seem to become more strictly defined with each revision of the regulations so it is wise to become familiar with current restrictions before initiating a new study. The sponsor is required to be familiar with these things so the individual investigator should be able to rely on this source of information. In effect, the Phase I studies amount to an assessment of the transposition of such basic information from laboratory animals to man.

PHASE II–CLINICAL PHARMACOLOGY

Phase II covers the initial trials on a limited number of patients for specific disease control or prophylaxis purposes. Sometimes this phase is broken down into early and late Phase II. In the early Phase II emphasis remains on how the body treats the drug. It is here after some Phase I information is procured that dosage-response curves are worked out, relating dose to the desired effect. It may be necessary to alter the study design from time to time so as to obtain specific information. These revisions need only be reported in the (annual) progress reports unless they have to do with concern for the patient in which case both FDA and the clinical investigators need be notified in writing promptly.

PHASE III – CLINICAL ASSESSMENT OF UTILITY AND SAFETY

Phase III is the dollars, time, and effort consuming part of the clinical trial. Actually, today, before taking a new drug into Phase III studies, the sponsor's scientists need to review with agents of FDA the data to that point and the plans for Phase III for their concurrence that what is being planned is safe and appropriate. The regulations read that "Phase III provides the assessment of the drug's safety and effectiveness and optimum dosage schedules in the diagnosis, treatment or prophylaxis of groups of subjects involving a given disease or condition."

Drug Claim Structure

These studies must be adequate both in number and design to permit assessment of the basis for the *drug claim structure* – what it is good for. What can be said about the new drug by way of promotion directly to the physician by the representatives of the marketing area or indirectly by advertising is what is allowed by the agency in the Package Circular. This is tremendously important to the future of the product. Very likely, there will be several protocols together with appropriate clinical chemistry and hematology planned to cover adequately the scope of the claim structure that both the research and marketing personnel of the sponsoring organization think is appropriate. These are usually expensive studies that may run for a year or more. Frequently, if the drug is for chronic administration, as an antihypertensive agent, for example, it may be required that a hundred or more patients receive the drug for at least a year. It usually takes several years for a single investigator to accumulate a year's experience with a drug in 50 to 100 patients.

CLINICAL TRIAL PLANS AND PERFORMANCE

A very telling statement in the regulations reads like this,

Ordinarily, a plan for clinical trial will not be regarded as reasonable unless, among other things, it provides for more than one independent competent investigator to maintain adequate case histories of an adequate number of subjects, designed to record observations and permit evaluation of any and all discernible effects attributable to the drug in each individual treated, and comparable records on any individuals employed as controls. These records shall be individual records for each subject maintained to include adequate information pertaining to each, including age, sex, conditions treated, dosage, frequency of administration of the drug, results of all relevant clinical observations and laboratory examinations made, adequate information concerning any other treatment given and a full statement of any adverse reactions and useful results observed, together with an opinion as to whether such effects or results are attributable to the drug under investigation.*

To the uninitatied, these two marathon sentences about a plan for clinical trial just might seem to include about everything, and they must have been intended to be comprehensive. At least 2 things about the statement should occur to the thoughtful individual who has read it a second time. First, the writer seems to place much the same value on the mundane aspects of record keeping as on the opinion of the investigator, perhaps more since the former is detailed and there is no guidance as to whose opinion is solicited or how it should be presented. Secondly, to one designing such studies, the most critical aspect of the statement up to the solicitation of an opinion as to whether what happened is due to the drug is the initial qualifying phrase "among other things." Thus, it is how well these "other things" are designed and done that will determine whether the assessment of the drug is worthwhile. (Perhaps it should be explained that the statement quoted above is not amplified in the subsequent paragraphs in the regulations. These subsequent paragraphs relate to other matters.) On the other hand, a few years ago the FDA and representatives of industry and professional societies did work up a sort of guide as to the number of clinical studies, the number of patients and for how long the drug was to be administered, the clinical chemistry desired, and a number of other elements of drug assessment in various categories of disease that have been more helpful.

THE NEW DRUG APPLICATION (THE NDA)

After the sponsor decides from his studies and ongoing contact with FDA medical and scientific personnel that the preclinical and clinical data are probably adequate, it is time to put all this together in a New Drug Application. This is called the NDA for short. It is the basis for judgment by the FDA personnel as to whether the studies are adequate to support the sponsors claims for it, and whether it should be approved for marketing.

The original NDA is by far the most substantive. There are several other types of New Drug Applications, however. These include (1) an amendment to the original unapproved NDA, (2) an abbreviated application for a drug previously approved, (3) an amendment to an abbreviated unapproved application, (4) a supplement to an approved application, and (5) an amendment

*Code of Federal Regulations 21, Food and Drugs 130.3.10c, second paragraph. Subsequent reference to 12a and 12b in text are to 130.4.12a or 12b.

to the supplement to an approved application. Briefly, and in sequence, (1) one can amend an original NDA on a new drug by the addition of information before it issues. Usually, this has the effect of "starting the 180 day clock" all over again on the NDA and should be avoided if possible. (2) An abbreviated application may be submitted on a compound that is already cleared as an original new drug with all the preclinical and clinical experience that initial application requires but where circumstance, such as the termination of patent status, makes possible marketing the compound by another company. (3) These abbreviated applications can also be amended before they issue. (4) More common is the supplemental application which usually incorporates information and supportive data on a new use for the product or a new formulation of the drug or, less frequently, a substantial change in the manufacture of the compound. (5) Such a supplemental application can be amended, also.

NDA Preparation

Putting together the chemical, pharmaceutical, and preclinical biological part is a considerable effort for a number of people, scientists, and administrative staff alike. The data will have been accumulated in-house, mostly, and put together as prescribed by the FDA during the clinical trial period. Much of the safety assessment data including preparation of many, many tables can be spun out by computers.

Putting together the clinical aspects of the initial New Drug Application on a brand new drug can be an Herculean task. In the first place, the data have to be accumulated from many investigators in this and other countries. These data will have been retrieved over a period of several years during which the protocols or the data requested may have been modified perhaps several times in which case the initial computer programs become inadequate and have to be rewritten. There is apt to be an inclination to wait until several studies on a single protocol are received before assessing them. This delay can lead to a lot of trouble getting the missing information, if the reports from investigators happen to be incomplete. If clinical studies are conducted abroad, they need to be included and just sheer distance makes communications harder to handle, if there were no other problems.

The problems most frequently encountered with the clinical part of the NDA relate more to the investigations than to the drug. For instance, if a compound is given for any reason to enough patients in enough clinical studies, a number of events called adverse reactions may occur, and a number of not wholly unaccountable deaths are possible. The older the patient population the greater the unaccountable deaths in a study, as the public discovered when the 1976–1977 swine flu vaccine was given first to elderly patients.

Frequency of deaths in a study depends on the type of illness being treated, the inherent effects of the compound being studied, and the condition of the patient when therapy is begun. On the whole, the quality of clinical studies has steadily improved over the years in spite of the involvement of more investigators in the study of a single compound. This improvement is due, undoubtedly, to the overall better instruction in clinical research, and the high quality of studies to which investigators aspire, and which both sponsor and FDA require, today.

NDA Format

FDA requires that the NDA be bound in volumes 2 inches thick in various colored binders according to a prescribed sequence and format. Ultimately, these volumes are loaded into a truck or a caravan and away they go to Washington with a receipt to be signed and returned in case that is the last they are heard of for a few months.* Discreet inquiry by phone or visit months later may reveal that the NDA did get through the FDA mailroom to the people who have to study and comment thereon within a period of 180 days (approximately 6 months) from the date of receipt.

What the 180 Days for Approval Means

I don't remember an application being approved within the prescribed time since the 1950's, but there are two ways of looking at that 180 days — yours and the FDA's. To the sponsor, the clock starts when the NDA is delivered to the Food and Drug Administration. To the FDA, the duration for NDA approval begins when they *accept it as filed* — which may be after 6 years of discussions between sponsor's scientist and physicians and those of FDA. Thus, by FDA calculations, the NDA is accepted or rejected within the time the regulations require them to act (within 180 days of the time they "accept it as filed").

Basis for Rejecting

Among the do's and don'ts in the regulations, there is a statement in the NDA section, actually two statements in sequence on which acceptance of

---

*The sheer mass of material transmitted to FDA when the New Drug Application is filed may be reduced markedly if its submission on microfilm proves satisfactory. This procedure is being explored. If microfilm proves to be sufficiently convenient that the sum of the advantages and drawbacks is at least equal to its storage advantage over bound volumes, it may facilitate hence expedite handling the information submitted — a worthy objective.

the application can hang indefinitely, if for no other reason. They are as follows: 12a: "An application may be refused unless it contains full reports of adequate tests by all methods reasonably applicable to show whether or not the drug is safe and effective for use as suggested in the labeling." Concurrence as to what ultimately constitutes "adequate tests by all methods reasonably applicable" can take quite a while. For instance, a medical staff man at FDA reportedly boasted that for nearly 10 years he held up all drugs for angina pectoris or hypertension on the ground that these were symptoms or signs, not diseases.

12b reads: "An application may be refused unless it includes substantial evidence consisting of adequate and well-controlled investigations, by experts qualified by scientific training and experience to evaluate the effectiveness of the drug involved, on the basis of which it could fairly and responsibly be concluded by such experts that the drug will have the effect it purports or is represented to have under the conditions of use prescribed, recommended, or suggested in the proposed labeling." This well intentioned statement was the basis for the withdrawal from the market of some respectable pre-1962 drugs because the clinical studies which constituted the basis for their approval and marketing could not measure up to the higher standards that obtained in 1962 for "adequate and well-controlled investigations." Since 1962, that 12b. statement has meant whatever it has been interpreted to mean by the regulatory agency in any specific instance.

To recapitulate, in the U. S. Regulations, ". . . An application may be refused unless it contains full reports of adequate tests by *all* methods reasonably applicable . . ." In this quotation the word *all* (author's emphasis) has the permissive effect of contributing to *the drug lag* or the delay with which new drugs have been introduced to the U. S. market since 1962 as compared to the time for their approval and marketing in other sophisticated countries abroad. (The word *"all"* in that regulation has had the effect, and seemingly the intent, of making the prior phrase ". . . *may* be refused . . ." be interpreted as though it meant − *will* be refused.) Perhaps the deletion of the word *all* from that text would be of little consequence now. Indeed, that revision is no more likely to occur than is revoking "The Delaney Amendment," which requires the removal from the market or refusal to approve any compound found to induce tumors in any animal by any means. These are well-intentioned examples of rule-making where spilled ink cannot be removed by blotting. It is clear of late that (by its involvement in the Laetril and Saccharin controversies in contradiction to authority) the U.S.A. public is searching for perhaps another way to deal with the reality of new drug regulation in this country.

NEW DRUG REGULATIONS ABROAD

The regulatory agencies in the various nations differ considerably in purpose, function, and political vulnerability. Time was when a United States based multinational company insisted, unjustifiably but pridefully perhaps, on obtaining approval to market a new drug in the U.S.A. first. Mostly, this nationalistic attitude is no longer the case. It seems unreasonable to withhold a drug from the physician in a land where its assessment has been approved and where the regulatory agency is respected by its people, such as in England, Sweden, Holland, Australia, etc. Expressed differently, the intent of the discovery and development of a new drug has to be the improvement of patient care. The assessment and evaluation of utility and safety need be designed, executed and processed with 'the view that the patient is being deprived of that "product" until it is judged inadequate or is marketed.

COLLATERAL LITERATURE

Academy Forum (1971): How safe is safe? The design of policy on drugs and food additives, National Academy of Sciences, Washington, D. C.

Blake, J. B., Ed. (1970): Safeguarding the public: HIstorical aspects of medical drug control, The Johns Hopkins Press, Baltimore.

Code of Federal Regulations, Title 21 Food and Drugs, Parts 130 to 140 (Parts 130 New Drugs, Subparts A-Procedural and Interpretative Regulations) published by the Office of the Federal Register.

Cooper, J. D. (1971): Decision-making on the efficacy and safety of drugs, Interdisciplinary Communication Associates, Inc., Washington, D. C.

Food and Drug Administration, Dept. Health, Education and Welfare (1976): (Propose) Good laboratory practice for nonclinical laboratory studies. Establishment of Regulations, Federal Register, Nov. 18.

Lasagna, L. (1976): Drug discovery and introduction: regulation and over regulation, *Clin. Pharmacol. Therap. 20:* 507–511.

SECTION III
DELIVERY

18.
Delivery

ABOUT THAT BETTER MOUSE TRAP

Everyone, certainly every ambitious young person, knows that "if you build a better mouse trap the world will beat a path to your door." I suppose few know the source of the abbreviated quotation. It is one of those half truths handed down from father to son. (I'm not sure mothers and daughters talk about mice this way.) No one told me until much later that someone has to tell the world effectively about that better mouse trap before it starts to demand the new product. Not until I was associated with industry did I come to realize that it might be better to have invented the first mouse trap rather than the better one; or that it might be more profitable to develop another way to get rid of mice (and to tell the world about it) than to fiddle around trying to make a better trap. What is still more devastating is that two individuals can market equally good products, one to become wealthy, the other to go broke. The chapters on discovery and delivery are about as far apart in this book as is the inherent understanding of the ways of the marketing expert by the scientist, and vice versa. It is hoped that this and the next chapter will give the scientist and the layman a reasonable insight into what goes into making the useful drug a successful product. It doesn't just happen that way. Morover, it will be a sorry day for medicine should the scientist and the marketing expert decide to exchange jobs.

A bothersome statement attributed to Peter Drucker, formerly Professor of Management at New York University and now at Claremont College, is that the only purpose of a business is to create a customer; that the tools used by business to create a customer are innovation and marketing. Whereas innovation is a purpose of many institutions, marketing is unique to business. Expressed differently, even optimistically, if you are in marketing you are in business.

WHEN MARKETING INTERESTS BEGIN

After the discovery, and then development, comes the delivery of a new drug to help physicians treat illness more effectively than previously. The whole complex process of marketing constitutes the delivery of the new drug. What the patient sees is the product, actually the dosage form. The process of getting it to him will have started even before the drug was discovered, very likely, if it was the product of a company's research division. If the discovery was made in some other institution and brought to that company for development and delivery, the marketing people will begin to have their input into the overall product planning even as early as the decision to work on the agent, i.e., to develop it.

PHASES OF MARKETING

There are three major phases of marketing: (1) the interrelationship with research — providing the research division with market analyses of the extent to which present therapy fulfills the physician's needs, etc.; (2) the planning of what needs to be done before marketing (what claim structure they would like to have, what production capacity may be needed, what they need to do to support the product at an anticipated sales level); (3) implementing the marketing plan — actually taking the product into the market place.

Generally, the research management of a company seeks to optimize the productivity of its scientists by discovering and developing drugs that benefit the most people. This is not so profound a statement. The individual scientist dedicated to the development of new therapy likewise needs to be discriminating in the use of his resources of time, effort, material, too. Marketing (the sales division of a company) can supply some assistance to research and development in defining and identifying those areas in which drugs, better drugs, are needed. The medically trained research personnel should know from a technical standpoint where therapy is inadequate, the magnitude of a medical problem in terms of numbers of people afflicted and its seriousness. Research should not rely on marketing for this technical information if they expect to make "breakthroughs," unusual advances.

TECHNIQUES OF MARKET ANALYSIS

What the marketing area can provide for research is the magnitude of specific markets, the sales of specific products, and the prescribing habits of physicians. To acquire these data, they subscribe to marketing research services that give such information for all prescription products in drug stores. The marketing research services do this by sampling a fairly large number of drug stores and hospital pharmacies. The data are likely to be reliable within a few percent on major items and less so on lower volume drugs. The data have to be reliable, if these marketing survey organizations are to stay in business, for a sales division can check the subscription service's figures on its own products against their own accounting. Products are grouped by categories such as psychotherapeutics, diuretics, etc., so that the size of the total market segment as well as sales of individual products are readily available.

Likewise, information is available on the prescribing habits of physicians. This is particularly important, for such information on new products anticipates the availability of actual sales figures by several months. The National Drug and Therapeutic Index is a sampling of at least a thousand physicians (rotated every few months) who fill out record forms on the patients they have seen, diagnosis, treatment prescribed and results they are trying to achieve by such therapy. In addition to data on products, such information includes an accounting of diagnoses being made, what kind of patients the doctor sees in his practice.

Most large organizations have their own marketing research department, the staff of which handles special assignments themselves. In some instances they employ outside help when that is needed. Sometimes the only way to get an answer to a specific question on which systematic records are not kept anywhere is to go to the public with questionnaires. For example, one might have to employ such a procedure to find out how many bone fractures occurred per year, what sort, how were they managed, etc.

A marketing organization is likely to have hundreds of professional representatives, previously called detail men, who are in daily contact with practicing physicians and who report back to headquarters on what the doctors need and want in their practice. The rural physician may not have at his command some of the sophisticated resources of the academic physician. What they need and want will vary with how they practice.

By blending this kind of practical information garnered by the marketing group with the technical knowledge of the research scientists and physicians more realistic objectives and priorities are possible, especially during the clinical trials of new drugs. This is the basis for their *product analysis report.*

WHAT MARKETING PROVIDES RESEARCH

As was emphasized in the chapter on chemical development, once a potential new drug gets into the developmental phases of chronic toxicity, process development, formulations, and clinical trials, costs soar into the millions of dollars. At this time, the compound is not only being assessed for safety and utility, it is being done with the intent of marketing the new drug. The interaction between the marketing and research staffs regarding the new drug should be sustained and intimate.

Before development gets very far, marketing should submit to research a report that attempts to set forth what they think they need in the new product if it is to be a success. To develop this critique, this product analysis, marketing will have made use of the resources for analysis of needs that have been mentioned in the foregoing paragraphs. They define product specifications in terms of what they think the practicing physician wants. If they can have, say, six unique claims, and the best product in that field has two, the sales forecast might be euphoric. If the product has one or two distinguishing features, the sales forecast would be reduced to something more sober. Chances are, if it has no particularly distinguishing features, they won't want it; forget it. For any or all of various reasons, they may go ahead and market the product, but if the product is not unique the sales will be disappointing and the cost of marketing high in relation to the sales.

Marketing also specifies the dosage forms that group thinks will be necessary to deliver the product effectively. For example, without a pediatric dosage form, the introduction of a new systemic antibiotic would be seriously handicapped.

This market report might well contain a preliminary marketing strategy statement as to how they propose to meet their sales forecast, and they set forth what kind of clinical support they think would be needed to convince the practicing physician that the product might be useful to him. Even for the experienced research man who knows the compound well and who knows how marketing generates such a document, that report is best read the first time at the end of the day (Friday) in the privacy of his office after everyone else has gone home. This expediency affords time to recover from his initial reaction (despair) sufficiently that by the time research and marketing meet to discuss the report that meeting is more likely to be conducted constructively.

Fifteen or twenty years ago, this close relationship between research and marketing was not so likely to exist. Each was more inclined to the attitude that the other should mind its own business. Each should, by all means. But the technical development and the development of marketing plans for the potential product do need to go hand in hand. This cooperative attitude is needed if the important new drug is to be made available effectively to the greatest number of patients for whom it is intended and in the shortest period of time. The better this is effected as a conjoint effort the more likely the outcome is to approximate the individual hopes of all concerned.

Some who read this will remember the anguish to the patient, the patient's family, and all concerned when at first there simply was not enough streptomycin to treat all the tuberculosis patients for whom the new antibiotic was indicated. When cortisone was first available, the disparity between indications for its use and the rate at which it could be supplied was even greater. To be sure, the technical problems in developing suitable production processes and facilities to meet the demand for these products were unusually severe. This was because of the still limited knowledge of large scale fermentation production of antibiotics at that time and the even less experience with steroid chemistry applicable to the problems that needed to be solved — the technical demands that needed to be met.

It takes time in addition to the fantastic intellectual (and physical) resources of good development chemists, and money in seemingly unlimited amounts to meet the needs for developing important new products. Thus, the very best marketing forecasts possible, together with the aid of precise early information from clinical research, may be needed some 2 years or so in advance of the release of a new kind of product. It could cost twenty or thirty million dollars — maybe more — to buy the equipment and to build the factories to supply the needs of patients, and of marketing.

WHEN MARKETING CAN BE A HAZARD TO RESEARCH

On the other hand, marketing is much less valuable, even a hazard, unless this is recognized, when research is directed toward totally new goals. This factual basis for anticipating new product acceptance and the need for new therapy derives from how well the needs of physicians and patients are thought to be met by available therapy. This historic basis may be utterly inadequate for judging the acceptance of a really new and uniquely effective therapy. For instance, at the time research decided to make several grams of cortisone to see what it was good for, the only likely indication was Addison's Disease; fortunately, a rather rare endocrine disease of the adrenal cortex. Market analysis would have reported, probably did, that physicians saw very few Addisonian patients, that the diagnosis often was hard to make. Those who needed therapy were managed fairly well with deoxycorticosterone (DOCA), the sales of which were too small to be interesting. Adrenal cortical extracts were on the market, but they probably received no more attention in such a report than they are given here. Anyone who has had a course in medical physiology would know the facts and could anticipate such a report.

So, if the rapport and respect between marketing and research are what they should be, the conclusion to that marketing report might read, "Sorry research, we can't help you — you're on your own." If instead, the recommendation read, "We don't see a market for your steroid — how about putting that effort on antibiotics," it would be true, forthright, and would represent the best interest of the company as they saw it. Something like this latter sales recommendation might have already been instigated if there were not a conviction on the part of some outstanding scientist, supported by research management, that making enough cortisone for clinical exploration might be worthwhile.

Another example: as I remember, the sales of all prescription diurectics the year before chlorothiazide was marketed was about eight million dollars. Medically, the need for the diuretic (saluretic) for which research was searching was obvious but not to market analysis, which relates more precisely to things as they are, not as they might be. Once the compound (Diuril) entered clinical trial, physician reaction to it became a better basis for projection of marketing needs. In its first full year on the U. S. market chlorothiazide sales were exceeded by only a single drug among all drugs of any kind. Interactions within the company were such that the demand for the product was well met both here and abroad.

THE IMPORTANCE OF TRADEMARKS AND GENERIC NAMES

The trademark for a new product is apt to be something the marketing area is expected to propose. Research, usually the chemists, suggests the non-proprietary or generic name based on some more or less evident relationship to its chemical structure. Chemists, of course, have an even greater aptitude or inclination for long cumbersome names for compounds than physicians do for diseases. The trademark has to be easily remembered, pronounced, and written. Usually, they are short — so as to be convenient to write hurriedly on a prescription pad. Usually, no one who has anything to do with discovering or developing the new drug likes either the generic or the proprietary name, the trademark. Both have to be approved as not being in conflict with any other mark. Tradenames are cleared through the United States Adopted Names Council (USAN). Preferably, the tradename should be suitable for use around the world so it should not have some obscene, absurd, or otherwise unpleasant or ridiculous connotation in some foreign language.

If the new drug is to be marketed within the life of its patent by a single company, then it does not matter much to that marketing division whether the physician or the hospital insists on using the generic or the tradename. Later, or whenever it is marketed by more than one source, the physician can still be reasonably sure whose product the patient gets by writing the drug tradename of that company or the generic name plus the company's name. If he does not care whose product is used by the pharmacist to fill the presscription, the generic name will suffice. Like the case for patents, there seems always to be some dispute as to whether or not a suggested trademark should be granted. Regardless of the merits of the case, either side, some 80 percent of prescriptions are written by tradenames whether or not the drug is marketed by one or more companies.

Trademarks do need a certain amount of care lest by their very acceptance they become part of the common language and so lose their single product identity. Kodak is a fabulous example of a trademark, the identity of which has been sustained with the products of a single company. Aspirin is an excellent example of a trademark that in time lost its individuality and is now employed to identify a specific product of many companies, unless the label identifies the compound with the name of a specific marketing organization. Vaseline was a trademark that has become part of the common language.

19.
Delivery (continued)

BACK TO THAT THING ABOUT MOUSE TRAPS

Back to the introductory sentence of the preceding chapter: it was Ralph Waldo Emerson who was credited with the quotation that "If a man can write a better book, preach a better sermon or make a better mouse trap, though he builds his house in the woods, the world will make a beaten path to his door." Emerson was a great American philosopher and poet, but judging by the quotation, he must have had someone else market his books for him. It simply is not true that once you have made a better product all you have to do is sit back and wait for people to take it away from you.

First of all, people have to know you have a better product; most have to be convinced. Even a good product will not reach its full potential without the best efforts of a good marketing organization. They have to convey this information to the doctor the way the doctor wants it, when and how it is wanted.

PHYSICIANS ARE EXCEPTIONAL PEOPLE

Physicians are exceptional people. They are particularly difficult to get to; they are awfully busy. Practicing physicians are apt to be strong minded and self confident. They are not easily convinced, especially if they have not heard about a new drug through some respected professional source. They want facts, figures, the authoritative sources of the information. They are best convinced by their own experience with the drug if it comes within their practice. Alternatively, the professional representatives are one of the most effective means of communicating product information to the physician. Even so, the professional representatives are criticized for persuading doctors to use products when they should not and to use them to excess. They are taught how to relate appropriately to the doctor within the increasing restrictions imposed on them by the regulatory agencies.

IMPORTANCE OF "FAIR BALANCE" IN PROMOTION

The type of advertising one sees on television for over-the-counter drugs is not appropriate when dealing with the physician. Whereas much of what the public sees of such advertising is emotionally oriented, information supplied to the physician should be fairly balanced between the drug's attractive features and its faults. The regulatory agencies insist on this. The major companies insist that their promotion be responsibly presented. The doctor is more apt to respond with interest to a well rounded presentation of what he might expect of the new product, both good and bad. He needs to know the "benefit to risk ratio" in general terms when he prescribes a drug for a patient.

There is so much to promotion, it is so varied, that the best way to assure the quality of the information the physician receives is to build a proper attitude toward this relationship into the entire staff that develops communications with physicians. Good quality advertising has to be built into the promotion of a product, it cannot be handled by inspection entirely, even though this matter of controls on advertising will be mentioned again. This means that those who write advertising copy and those who relate directly to the doctor or pharmacist need to know a great deal about the product and about marketing.

MARKETING STRATEGY DOCUMENT

When the new drug clinical investigations get well into Phase III, a *marketing strategy* document will have been worked out for the new drug. This spells out every marketing approach to the product. It is a blueprint of all such activities. It discusses the market in which the drug will be used, the disease, and kind of physician who will use it. How the drug is to be promoted is discussed in the marketing strategy statement as well as the various dosage forms, which physicians are to be contacted and when. It details how much effort is to go into promotion, the various means of promotion to be used, what aspects of the product will be featured, and what the pricing policy will be.

ABOUT PRICING

There are essentially three ways in which something, the product, can be priced. One is called "cost plus." This is when whatever profit to be made is added to the cost of the product to the manufacturer. A second way is to price the product "to the market." Usually, there are already products on the market for the same indications, in which case the price may be adjusted to be competitive. The third is "incremental pricing." Sometimes, it pays to help reduce overhead (general business expense) if there is capacity to produce a certain amount of material on bid for some agency at little more than cost. It stands to reason that this incremental pricing cannot be done profitably on all your products any of the time or on any of the products all the time. None of these ways applies to the occasional product which is needed as a life-saving measure but which simply cannot be priced against cost and still kept within reach of the patient who needs the drug. In this instance the price set may be trivial.

Some of the other factors in pricing relate to different classes of accounts. If the company distributes its products to wholesalers who in turn redistribute them to hospitals, etc., the price to such agents may be slightly lower, because of that service, than when sold directly to the retail pharmacist or hospital. Pricing to the distributor, wholesaler, or retailer, is not customarily influenced by regional distribution in this business, but one must remember that there will be at least one or more additions to that price for the profit of the distributor, the drugstore, for example, before the price the patient pays for his prescription is determined.

AMOUNT OF PROMOTION NEEDED

The amount of promotion needed to establish an awareness of a new drug depends on how much money is being spent by other companies on products intended for similar indications. It is like trying to be heard in the presence of noise or static, the greater the noise level the louder one must shout to attract attention. Surveys taken 3–6 months after a product is introduced may be helpful to determine how effective the promotional strategy has been in creating an awareness of the new drug. That awareness may differ considerably among specialty groups of physicians. Various specialists need be approached in different ways. Some promotional campaigns are most effectively managed on a seasonal basis; remedies for allergies in spring and fall or for arthritis mostly in the winter, for example.

PROMOTION MIX

In the overall marketing strategy, the promotion mix should have been set forth. By promotion mix is meant the budgeting of manpower, medical journal advertisements, direct mailing to physicians, samples, technical films, tapes for recordings, and symposia. As mentioned previously, sales and production estimates can be firmed up based on the Phase III clinical experience; including dosage and duration of therapy, how well the product compares with others and how effectively marketing thinks they can communicate with the physician.

Sinemet®, a new drug for the management of Parkinson's Disease, can be used to illustrate the interaction of some of the factors mentioned in promotion planning. In a previous Chapter (5), it was explained that Sinemet was a balanced formulation of two drugs, levadopa which when converted in the brain to the corresponding dopamine replaces therein that chemical deficiency of such a patient. The other compound in the mixture is carbidopa which does not get into the brain but only blocks the conversion of levodopa to dopamine outside the brain. This action increases the therapeutic efficiency of levodopa (lowers the dose) and reduces the side effects of dopamine outside the brain.

Now, market analysis will show that relatively few Parkinsonian patients get to the neurologist except by referral. Most are managed by general practitioners and internists. Promotional effort of the various kinds should be directed to these three physicians, neurologists, internists, and general practitioners. This is a disease predominantly of elderly people, so, except for an announcement to the profession as a general mailing and journal advertising, the pediatrician or obstetrician is unlikely to hear about it from the professional representative of marketing, except perhaps casually on direct inquiry by the doctor. It would be more credible and more easily understood by the doctor (who already knows about levodopa, anyway) if it is simply explained that the carbidopa in the combination potentiates the effect of levodopa, lowers the dosage needed by the patient and reduces (blocks) the side effects. To promote Sinemet as a totally new drug might be construed as misleading. To try to explain the rationale for the product in terms of competitive inhibition of enzymatic decarboxylation of levodopa, the key role of the blood brain barrier in why it works, and the importance of dopamine in central neurohumoral transmission, all in 5 minutes while the doctor is eating a sandwich and answering the phone, would be courting disaster saleswise.

Although Parkinson's Disease affects only about 0.1% of the general population, it does affect some 0.5% of patients over 50 years of age and the duration of therapy can be expected to be the rest of the patient's life. Marketing will also be able to judge what percentage of patients are likely to be treated with the product in the first, second, third year, etc., of sales. Since levodopa has been available to the physician for several years, this fact and other available (anticholinergic) products will help price the new product "to the market." All this information, together with differences in the way specialist and practitioner handle such patients, will be of aid in projecting sales, in planning initial production and in projecting what facilities and materials will be needed to meet the marketing requirements in the future.

As intimated, the pathophysiological and metabolic bases for the product are quite sophisticated. Consequently, the training program for the sales representatives needs to be carefully planned and executed. Such a subject is well adapted to teaching films and tapes for recorders and to seminars produced by authorities who have created the current knowledge about the disease and how to treat it. These teaching aids are to be seen by the physicians who treat these patients, also.

TRAINING OF MARKETING PERSONNEL

Promotion planning is to the marketing area what lesson planning is to the grade school teacher. The teacher needs to plan well what he or she expects to teach, needs to understand the background of the student (what he is likely to be interested in and can grasp). The teacher needs to know how to teach and what teaching aids are likely to be effective.

In this simple analogy of promotion planning to any other kind of teaching the marketing area may have as many as five hundred or more "teachers" who in this instance are called professional representatives and who must be taught all about the new drug. If the new drug is in a field of medicine in which the company has had no previous products, the whole marketing area must be taught the disease, the physiological basis for it, other related forms of therapy, how the physicians who handle such patients practice, and what they expect and want in a new drug. More than 50 percent of the marketing expenditures may be on behalf of these professional representatives.

The people who actually do the training of these hundreds of representatives usually are experienced representatives themselves. There may be a faculty or large training staff of these people headed by one or more physicians. The teaching material may be developed in house by the medical services department or it may be produced especially for this purpose on contract with outside groups who know how to develop such courses for training purposes.

First, the key promotional personnel may be taught by medical faculty of regional schools or they may actually be sent into a hospital to observe and learn the practical side of patient management. These people, or sometimes physicians from the research division's staff, will train the training staff. In turn, the training staff communicates all this to the field representatives. The details and procedures vary a great deal, of course. The personnel may actually be tested on what they have been taught and are expected to have learned. If they do not pass at whatever level is expected, they have to be given more training. The idea is not to try to make doctors out of them, but to train these representatives in sufficient depth that they can discuss the new product helpfully the way the doctor wants to know about it. They would not be expected to be able to discuss subjects or drugs outside the product line, but they are given refresher training from time to time on products in the line.

TEACHING AIDS FOR THE PHYSICIAN

Aids in teaching the new drug to the physician vary a great deal in purpose, form and substance. Advertising is apt to be read rapidly. It is really intended to announce, or remind the doctor about, a product. It is a sensitive, controversial form of communication. What one doctor may not notice at all may offend the next one and attract a third. Representation of fair balance between positive and negative attributes of a drug is difficult unless the whole package circular is reproduced. Customarily, package circulars are sent with direct mailings to physicians. Professional representatives are cautioned to discuss side effects and contraindications as well as indications for the drug. Nowadays, if a physician wants a sample of the new drug to see how well it works, he or she is left a card to fill out and send to the marketing area so that the material may be shipped with the package circular.

Actually, the package circular is the basic teaching aid. Claims for the product incorporated in the package circular are the *only* ones that may be included in promotional material prepared and distributed for or by the company that markets the drug. The professional representative may call the physician's attention to a publication in a medical journal that relates to a product claim, but the FDA forbids him to do so if the use for that drug set forth in that article is not in the package circular, regardless of its importance or the adequacy with which it is documented. This policy is the same for films that teach the basic aspects of a disease and how it should be managed, regardless of the authority of the individual or group of experts who are the cast of the film; as in the filming of a seminar. Of course, this same policy limited to what is in the package circular would obtain for tape recordings that may be distributed to doctors. This FDA policy does restrict in principle what can be said or written about a drug on strictly an instructional basis. Such a restriction obviously cannot relate to the publication or orderly report- ing otherwise of new information about a drug, as at scientific meetings. [Presumably, the investigator who is reporting his new information at such a meeting would have completed a Statement of Investigator form when he re- ceived the drug. The clinical work should have been done under an IND (see Chapter 17 for a discussion of the IND) and with all the usual attending re- strictions if it was conducted on human beings.]

MEDICO-LEGAL SURVEY OF PROMOTIONAL MATERIAL

Every marketing organization should have some sort of medical-legal re- view board that inspects the prototype of every piece of literature seen by the physician directly or as advertising. This is a real chore as anyone who has served on such a committee knows full well. Usually, marketing personnel, physicians from research, and the lawyers make up this group. Toward the end of a tiresome session of such a committee meeting, it might seem to an onlooker that marketing wants to overstate every claim, research wants to qualify every statement and counsel is not sure that either position is safe. Only if the whole organization is inculcated with trying to do the right thing will any system of controls work. This was impressed on me when the Inter- national Division of the company for which I worked started sending me for final approval advertising copy in such languages as Japanese, Greek, Arabic, etc. that I could not possibly read, but which presumably I had approved in English.

THE 3-A'S OF ADVERTISING

There are three A's in the approval of advertisements that help sustain per- spective and which are being passed along here, gratuitously. They are stated as questions: (1) Is the copy (and illustrative material) appropriate? (2) Is it adequate (in the sense of proper disclosure)? (3) Is it authoritative (or who says so)? In any instance, it may not be difficult for the individual to decide whether a promotional piece fulfills these three criteria. In real life, the larger the distribution of that advertisement the more certain it is to offend some one who sees it, even though it may appeal to another. Hopefully, it will be instructive or otherwise helpful to all who need to know of it.

20.
Synopsis

Interestingly, the most frequent comment among those who have read these chapters in their entirety was one voiced by my daughter, a graduate student in Physiology at the time. From her research there had begun to evolve an idea for a new drug, which is a long way from discovery much less delivery of a useful agent. To her, the process from discovery to the marketing of a new drug seemed overwhelmingly complex, time consuming, and expensive. Why would anyone try to discover a new drug, much less make a career of such work? How do you make contact with the many specialists who are needed to make a chemical a drug, one that can be brought to patients worldwide? Was there a more direct, shorter way from concept for new therapy to competiton with marketed drugs?

Why would anyone try to discover a new drug? Outside of the pharmaceutical research laboratories it is seldom that an individual or a team tries to discover a new drug. Mostly, academic scientists are content to discover some new bit of knowledge, or a better understanding of some phenomenon, or a better way of doing or measuring something. In their own way, they may be contributing to the advancement of medicine.

The examples given in Chapters 4 and 5 and still others to be recited should suffice to prove that scientists in universities and related institutions may set out to understand a disease better and in so doing discover a new drug that comes to be important in therapy. For example, when the distinguished Professor of Physiology at the Johns Hopkins School of Medicine, William H. Howell, assigned a sophomore medical student, J. McLean, to prepare thromboplastin extracts from tissues in 1916, the potent anticoagulant heparin was discovered in those crude extracts. This observation was published in 1918, but it was not until 1937 that heparin chemistry was developed to the point that the first clinical paper appeared wherein a formulation of heparin was employed to prevent thrombosis postoperatively in patients. In this country, the Upjohn Company developed the product for general use.

The University of Wisconsin's singular Karl Paul Link and his associates set out to find what it was that F. W. Schofield in Canada and L. M. Roderick in North Dakota claimed was the cause of the hemorrhagic sweet clover disease in cattle. Biochemistry is a part of the College of Agriculture at Wisconsin which has a heritage of helping the farmer in "America's Dairyland." The compound they isolated in 1934 as the cause of the disease came to be known as Dicumarol. It prevented blood clotting in cattle as the cause of the disease. In this instance, Dr. Link and The Abbott Laboratories made the compound available, and the first papers on the use of Dicumarol as an (oral) anticoagulant in patients appeared from the Mayo Clinic and the University of Wisconsin within months of the time its identity was first published by Link and his students.

The extraction of insulin from the pancreas of dogs by Frederick G. Banting and the medical student, Charles H. Best, in 1921, was one of designed discovery as developed in this text. There was a sufficient background of knowledge that their problem was thought by Banting to be one of preventing the destruction of an active substance in the pancreas during its extraction. They were successful in accomplishing the extraction of this hypoglycemic material which was active in depancreatized (diabetic) dogs. The extract proved effective when they administered it to their first juvenile diabetic subject, Leonard Thompson (age 14), January 11, 1922. The development of this product was undertaken at the Connaught Laboratories in Toronto. Production of the extract was licensed to four companies in this country of which the Eli Lilly Company did an outstanding job of developing suitable formulations.

Again, the discovery of the anticonvulsant effect of diphenylhydantoin (Dilantin) by Merritt and Putnam (Chapter 4) is an excellent example of designed discovery in an academic environment by men who not only appreciated the need for such therapy but who developed the capability to search for the compound they wanted among those supplied by Parke Davis and Co. chemists.

The first of these four examples of important drug discoveries in academic settings, the discovery of heparin by Howell, was serendipitous or so it would seem. The other three examples, those of Link, or Banting and Best, or Merritt and Putnam were designed discoveries, although the discovery by Link and his students incorporated a sensible extrapolation of an activity to utility as a drug. If there was an element of serendipity in the last three examples, it would be the useful rat poison, Warfarin, that evolved from the chemistry by Link *et al.*

Within the elements of the equation for creativity in Chapter 1, the research of Howell relied heavily on both exploration and ideation; exploration relating the impact of discernment (as to what to do) on work (what is to be done) and ideation being the impact of discernment (as to the significance of the finding) on his authoritative knowledge of blood coagulation. In this example, the intellectual use of discernment as to the significance of what was observed seems the more important. In the Banting and Best example how to go about extracting the hypoglycemic principle (insulin) and why made the difference between their success and the failure of others who were equally convinced that such a material existed. To finish the thought initiated in the second paragraph of this chapter, their discoveries were incident to the careers of these distinguished men as scientists or physicians and teachers. The discovery of new drugs was not nor did it become the purpose of their careers.

Today, there are many scientists, medical scientists, who make a career of participating in the discovery of new drugs or their development at the preclinical level. Sometimes this is by happenstance, sometimes deliberately so. Whatever the reason, once someone becomes deeply involved in the discovery and development, even the delivery of a new important drug, the fascination that attends the ongoing process and the sense of satisfaction for having done something useful for people who are ill are not easily put aside. The physician whose daily practice places him in direct contact with individual patients derives gratification from their improvement at his hands. The medical scientist who has one or more good drugs with which to identify has the sense of having helped so many more people throughout the world through others than one could attend and over a much longer time. Moreover, this sense of service by contributing to medical progress is not limited to the research physician but is shared by many people at many levels of intellectual or technical development, people who spend their useful lives in the discovery, development, and delivery of new drugs.

Chapters 2 through 5 pertaining to discovery have a common thread of continuity. It is the relationship of the development of knowledge and instrumentation to discovery. Without a body of science in chemistry, physics, and biology, discovery was by happenstance, spontaneous discovery. Many drugs or their effects undoubtedly were discovered over and over again, ultimately to be transmitted by person from generation to generation. As the bodies of knowledge in the relevant sciences and methodology became sufficiently developed, one could ask questions of a developing biology or chemistry that sometimes were sufficiently imprecise as to yield an unanticipated but useful answer. Such serendipity actually relates more to the stage of development of a particular body of knowledge than to a time in the history of medicine. When the relevance of basic functions can be identified with a disease or chemical structure, and when instrumentation is available with which to proceed precisely, designed discovery is most apt to be successful. Examples of how such knowledge of basic biology and the refinement of the relationship of chemical structure to desired biological activity have been used to discover useful therapy were presented under the headings of "Tailoring a New Drug," (see Chapters 6, 7, and 8).

The involvement of the individual in the development of a new drug he or she has discovered differs a great deal with where one happens to be in the overall structure that relates to the accumulation, distribution and use of knowledge.

If you are working on a Public Health Grant, NIH, or the like, the patent situation has changed for the better in recent years. Formerly, patents on inventions made under such grants were assigned to the public — they fell in the public domain. That was where the support came from. You may think this is the best way for everyone to profit from your gift to humanity. It does not work out very well that way. What is everyone's prerogative to share is nobody's responsibility to develop. Today, your university may be one of a number that have an institutional patent agreement with NIH whereby the university will obtain the patent, providing counsel directly or through agreement with industry. By such agreement, or by a request for waiver of rights, the university can obtain and dispose of the patent for you, as by nonexclusive or by limited exclusive license to interested organizations. Thereby, the public's interest actually is more directly and better served. What you get out of the patent arrangement depends on the details of the situation.

If you are supported by a university that has a patent policy, it will provide counsel. If it has a rather complete set up for this purpose to which you can turn, like the Wisconsin Alumni Research Foundation, just do your part, the discovery, well. They will do the rest and may give you a modest percentage of the returns. A modest percentage of a multi-million dollar product is worth the effort for most people.

If you are at a Government institution, like the National Institutes of Health, you might be better off with the credit for having discovered an important contribution to knowledge or a new use for an existing compound or drug. They are better set up to establish recognition for that sort of thing.

If you are already in the pharmaceutical industry, all the resources you are likely to need are available. All you (or your team) have to do is to discover something that is so good as to gain priority over the other interesting goings-on in the research division. You may get a dollar for your patent, a token payment. However, an important product to your credit could influence your career.

If your institution does not have a patent policy, you probably will go directly to the research management of a pharmaceutical laboratory to interest the people there in your discovery. A number of such companies have been identified with important products in this book. Even if you work out a favorable licensing agreement with one of them, your discovery will have to be good to compete for the resources of a first rate pharmaceutical laboratory. You may have to provide the enthusiasm for your discovery until it catches on, understandably. The resources are all there in such a research institute together with the management to see that they are used properly.

If you have really discovered an important drug, there are going to be lots of people to help you. Patent lawyers to tell you what needs to be done to protect your discovery (Chapter 16); development chemists who get their charge out of learning to make that new compound better than you did but in sophisticated large scale equipment and by the ton instead of in test tubes. Overcoming his technical problems are the fun aspects of the development chemists' day-to-day career (Chapter 11). Same with pharmaceutical chemists.

We would still need pharmaceutical chemists even if every compound was soluble and stable and equally available to the tissues of the body by all routes of administration, but it doesn't work that way. In real life, the formulation of a product is second in importance only to the drug, the active ingredient, itself. However, I have never known a pharmaceutical problem that was not solved or circumvented by such capable scientists if it was worth the effort (Chapter 12).

Safety assessment? Don't try to do it yourself! It is easier to cause more trouble for your new compound by not knowing what to do or how to do it in the preclinical safety assessment of a new drug than you are likely to cause for yourself elsewhere in the biological preclinical work. On the other hand, safety assessment is an exciting area to work in if you are interested and can qualify (Chapter 10).

The one thing you can do that is most likely to help smooth the road for your new compound from discovery to delivery is what you are in a position to know best. Be sure that you understand thoroughly what it does, how active it is, how it can be administered, its binding and distribution characteristics and how it is eliminated (metabolized and/or excreted). In other words, know the primary and secondary characteristics of your new compound very well (Chapter 9)! The more nearly the test procedures in laboratory animals approximate the clinical conditions of use the fewer surprises for you when the agent gets to the clinic.

Forget about how to obtain a Food and Drug Administration clearance to study the drug clinically (an IND) or how to put together a New Drug Application (Chapter 17). That is your sponsor's problem.

If you are not an M.D., you are not going to have much to say about the clinical study until they run into trouble and are ready to forget it (Chapters 13, 14, and 15). Then is when you really need to have worked up the compound in animals very carefully and thoroughly. In which case you will be the one with the facts. The chances are you can help with their problem if you are allowed close enough to it. It is like the relationship of an auto mechanic (yourself) and the man (the clinical investigator) who owns the new car with a problem. Most times, it's just that the engine has been flooded – it didn't fall out of the car – although this may not be clear when you first hear of the problem.

The bigger the clinical study the more likely the unanswerable problems and the longer and more expensive it will be to resolve them – including approval of the New Drug Application. Clinical research on breakthrough drugs, such as yours, is really apt to be research on clinical research. Anything is likely to happen. If you are young enough and really believe in your drug and have done your job, and if the sponsor of the clinical studies on your drug can afford the expense, the chances are that it will get to the market in your day. By that time you will know more about the discovery and development of a new drug than you will ever read about in books.

IN CONCLUSION

Is there any shortcut through the time and trouble of getting an interesting new chemical from your laboratory to a patient who may need it? This question was the last in the first paragraph of this chapter.

There are two ways to cut down on time and trouble. First, do whatever needs to be done right the first time. Every time you ask a stupid question of the compound or patient or one that gives an answer that is unclear as to significance at the laboratory or the clinical level the more trouble, time, and expense your sponsor will encounter with getting it approved for marketing. Second, the other way to get the drug to patients as soon as possible *after an adequate assessment of utility and safety* is to have the new drug application submitted on its merit concurrently to the drug regulatory agencies of various countries around the world the way they want it. Some act more promptly and sensibly than others and this has nothing to do with their technical competence.

There is one more thing, though, you have to learn if your new drug is going to be a marketing success (Chapters 18 and 19). The better the job you do of selling the sales division of your sponsoring company on the remarkable nature and qualities of your discovery, and the real need for it, the more effectively and more enthusiastically they will deliver your message to the physician, if they can get past the doctor's secretary.

It is a wonderful feeling to have shared an important discovery! Try it — if you are 55 or younger.

COLLATERAL LITERATURE

Banting, F. G., and Best, C. H. (1922): The internal secretion of the pancreas, *J. Lab. Clin. Med. 7:* 251–266.

Banting, F. G., Best, C. H., Collip, J. B., Campbell, W. R., and Fletcher, A. A. (1922): Pancreatic extracts in the treatment of diabetes mellitus, *Can. Med. Assoc. J. 12:* 141–146.

Banting, F. G., Best, C. H., Collip, J. B., Hepburn, J., Macleod, J. J. R., and Noble, E. C. (1922): Physiological effects of insulin, Trans. *Roy. Soc. Can. 16:* Sect. V, 1–18.

Bingham, J. B., Meyer, O. O., and Pohle, F. J. (1941): Studies on the hemorrhagic agent 3, 3'-methylene-bis-(4-hydroxycoumarin). I. Its effect on the prothrombin and coagulation time of the blood of dogs and humans, *Am. J. Med. Sci. 202:* 563–578.

Butt, H. R., Allen, E. V., and Bollman, T. L., (1941): A preparation from spoiled sweet clover [3, 3'-methylene-bis-(4-hydroxycoumarin)] which prolongs coagulation and clotting time of blood: Preliminary report of experimental and clinical studies. Proc. Mayo Clinic *16:* 388.

Comroe, J. H., and Dripps, R. D. (1977): The ten top clinical advances in cardiovascular pulmonary medicine and surgery between 1945 and 1975– Final report in two volumes, Vol. 1, Accession No. PB 265843/AS, Vol. 2, Accession No. PB265844/AS, National Technical Information Service, U. S. Dept. of Commerce, Springfield, Va. 22161.

Crawford, C. (1937): Preliminary report on post-operative treatment with heparin as a preventive of thrombosis, *Acta. chiv. scand. 79:* 407–426.

Howell, W. H., and Holt, E. (1918): Two new factors in blood coagulation: heparin and antithrombin, *Am. J. Physiol. 47:* 328–341.

Jorpes, J. E., and Bergström, S. (1937): Heparin: a mucoitin polysulfuric acid, *J. Biol. Chem. 118:* 447–457.

Lasagna, L. (1962): The Doctor's Dilemmas, Harper and Bros., New York.

Link, K. P. (1943–44): The anticoagulant from spoiled sweet clover, *Harvey Lecture, 39:* 162–216, 1943–1944.

Middleton, W. S. (1972): Values in modern medicine, U. of Wisconsin Press, Madison, Wis.

Schofield, F. W. (1924): Damaged sweet clover: the cause of a new disease in cattle simulating hemorrhagic septicemia and blackleg, *J. Am. Vet. Med. Assoc. 64:* 553–575.

Index